The territorial imperative

The Territorial Imperative explores an area of growing interest in comparative political economy – the interaction of politics and economics at the mesolevel of the polity. Noting the ubiquity of regional economic disparities within advanced industrial democracies, Jeffrey Anderson undertakes a sophisticated analysis of the complex political conflicts such disparities generate. In this study of political responses to regional crisis, the principal theoretical focus centers on the impact of constitutional orders as bona fide political institutions. On the basis of a carefully constructed comparison of four declining industrial regions within a broader cross-national comparison of unitary Britain and federal Germany, Anderson concludes that constitutional orders as institutions do in fact matter. The territorial distribution of power, encapsulated in the federal-unitary distinction, is shown to exercise a strong political logic of influence on the distribution of interests and resources among subnational and national actors and on the strategies of cooperation and conflict available to them. In the course of the study, Anderson brings together theories of intergovernmental relations, center-periphery, corporatism, pluralism, and the state. His book provides new insights into more than just mesolevel politics; indeed, the explicit focus on the political economy of regions calls into question aspects of the conventional wisdom on British and German politics, which is based for the most part on national-level studies. Viewed in the context of widespread optimism surrounding the future of regions in a post-1992 Europe, Anderson's findings also underscore the need for caution when assessing the horizons of action for subnational interests in advanced industrial democracies. Offering an innovative theoretical approach grounded in comparative empirical research, *The Territorial Imperative* will be welcomed by political economists, scholars and students of comparative politics, sociology, and public policy, political geographers, and economists and historians interested in Western Europe.

The territorial imperative

The territorial imperative

Pluralism, Corporatism, and Economic Crisis

JEFFREY J. ANDERSON

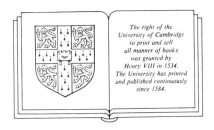

CAMBRIDGE UNIVERSITY PRESS

Cambridge

New York   Port Chester   Melbourne   Sydney

Published by the Press Syndicate of the University of Cambridge
The Pitt Building, Trumpington Street, Cambridge CB2 1RP
40 West 20th Street, New York, NY 10011, USA
10 Stamford Road, Oakleigh, Melbourne 3166, Australia

First published 1992

Printed in Canada

Library of Congress Cataloging-in-Publication Data
Anderson, Jeffrey J.
    The territorial imperative : pluralism, corporatism, and ecomic
crisis / Jeffrey J. Anderson.
        p.   cm.
    Outgrowth of a thesis undertaken at Yale University between 1984
and 1988.
    Includes bibliographical references (p.   ) and index.
    ISBN 0-521-41378-8 (hardcover)
    1. Regionalism—Great Britain.   2. Great Britain—Economic
conditions—1945-   —Regional disparities.   3. Great Britain—
Politics and government—1945-   4. Pluralism (Social sciences)—
Great Britain.   5. Regionalism Germany (West) 6. Germany (West)—
Economic conditions—Regional disparities.   7. Federal government—
Germany (West).   8. Germany (West)—Politics and government.
9. Pluralism—Germany (West).   I. Title.
JN297.R44A53 1992
320.941–dc20   91-33739
                                                                          CIP

British CIP has been applied for

ISBN 0-521-41378-8

For my parents, Lois and Bob

Contents

List of figures

List of tables

Preface

Politics is rooted in territory. State-building, war-making, pork-barreling, gerrymandering – the examples are legion. Much the same can be said about markets, which allocate resources not just to firms, sectors, factors of production, and individuals, but also to subdivisions of the national space. Indeed, the spatial dimension of the political economy is so prevalent that it is easily, if not frequently, overlooked. I wrote *The Territorial Imperative* as a modest attempt at a partial corrective. Thanks to scholarly contributions of the past two decades, we now know a great deal about the responses of states, political parties, and peak associations to economic crisis. Yet we know little about analogous phenomena at the subnational level. The present volume explores what I have chosen to call "the territorial imperative": the political foundations of the complex, interactive responses by national and subnational actors to the problems thrown up by regions in economic crisis.

This book grew out of a thesis undertaken at Yale University between 1984 and 1988. A dissertation is supposed to provide a formative experience for the aspiring scholar, and this one was no exception. For me, however, the dividends went beyond the purely intellectual. I count myself as fortunate to have had the opportunity to live in four diverse regions that lie far off the beaten paths of tourists and academics. There is far more to the periphery than the absence of the center.

Several organizations provided vital support during the field research stage of this study: the Council for European Studies at Columbia University; the Yale University Council for International and Area Studies; the Fulbright Commission; the Deutsche Akademische Austauschdienst (DAAD); and the Friedrich Ebert Stiftung. Sadly, it remains extraordinarily difficult for graduate students to piece together support for truly comparative research projects requiring extensive travel, and I would like to thank these organizations for their willingness to be flexible and to accommodate my itinerant needs. Postdissertation, the University Research Committee of Emory University provided a generous summer grant in 1989, which enabled me to conduct additional follow-up interviews. At Brown University, the Institute for International Studies and the Taubman Center for Public Policy awarded a travel grant to me in December 1990 to collect up-to-date information on the evolving regional situation in the newly united Germany.

Naturally, this book could not have been written without the contributions of a host of individuals. At Yale, I constantly drew on the advice of David Cameron, who first suggested the idea of a four-way regional comparison. Most of all, I would like to thank my thesis adviser, Joseph LaPalombara, whose steadfast support and intellectual guidance helped me through both the good and the bad patches. His insistence on a 300-page dissertation ("not one page longer!"), though it made for many a long night of editing, greatly eased the transition from thesis to book and is a standard I have taken gratefully to heart. In Great Britain, I could not have managed without Hugh Berrington at the University of Newcastle upon Tyne, whose input always drew me back to the politics of the matter. Fred Robinson at the Center for Urban and Regional Development Studies at Newcastle helped me navigate the ins and outs of the North East. Michael Keating and Richard Rose in Scotland provided me with an initiation to territorial politics in September 1985 that benefited me throughout my stay. Barbara Smith was also of great assistance in the West Midlands. And, of course, I would like to thank the (anonymous) civil servants in Newcastle upon Tyne and Birmingham, who literally opened their vaults to me. While skirting the shoals of the Official Secrets Act in matters of regional assistance cannot in truth compare with the exploits of Peter Wright or Clive Ponting, it is tricky business nonetheless, and I appreciate their candor and help. In the Federal Republic of Germany, Dr. Volkhard Riechmann took me under his wing and introduced me to contacts in both North Rhine–Westphalia and the Saarland. I value his help and his friendship greatly. The staff at the state archives in Düsseldorf and Saarbrücken went out of their way to assist my search for material, and I thank them as well. During the writing stage, I profited from the comments of Rick Doner. I would like to take this opportunity to acknowledge a considerable intellectual debt to Gary Marks and to the other (anonymous) Cambridge University Press reviewer for pushing me to develop the book's potential fully. And finally, I would like to thank my editor, Emily Loose, for her guidance and initiative.

On the personal side, this miniature odyssey owes a great deal to the unceasing support of my parents, to whom this book is dedicated. I express my unending love and thanks to my wife, Celeste Wallander, who lived this project as much as I did. I would also like to mention our baby son Nathaniel, who came along about the time this book was completed. He had absolutely nothing to do with the project, but I'd still like to thank him for brightening up our lives.

J. J. A.

1 Introduction

Milan and the Mezzogiorno, Paris and Pontivy, London and Liverpool: Throughout the postwar era of relative affluence, most West European states have encompassed two nations, one prosperous, the other poor. Resilient territorial economic divides hardened while political processes across the continent grew decidedly national in scale with the rise of the interventionist state, the appearance of catchall political parties competing in a nationwide electoral marketplace, the emergence of powerful functional interest groups, and the decline of parliaments. And they persisted in the face of a selective retreat by central governments from broad areas of economic and social policy-making in the 1980s.

Declining regional economies generate highly complex political conflicts involving myriad actors across multiple levels of the polity. At the subnational level, political and economic actors in both the public and private sectors must determine whether to articulate territorial economic demands, to mobilize indigenous political and economic resources, and to develop strategies for adjusting to changing market conditions and for securing aid from central government. At the national level, policymakers in various parts of the state bureaucracy confront the political and economic strains generated by uneven economic development, and face a choice of their own: whether and how to respond to demands for assistance. Connecting the center and the provinces are institutions, like central government field administration, political parties, and vertical interest group associations, that structure the resolution of regional economic conflicts. The present volume explores these various manifestations of the territorial imperative.

Both theoretical and substantive considerations recommend a study of the politics of regional decline. The comparative analysis of political responses to economic crisis has gained a secure foothold in political science. Understandably, scholarly attention has concentrated on national actors, principally state institutions and producer group associations.[1] Yet macroeconomic growth and contraction have spatially

---

[1] P. Katzenstein, ed., *Between Power and Plenty* (Madison: The University of Wisconsin Press, 1978); P. Gourevitch, *Politics in Hard Times* (Ithaca: Cornell University Press, 1986); K. Dyson and S. Wilks, eds., *Industrial Crisis* (New York: St. Martin's Press, 1983); P. Katzenstein, *Small States in World Markets* (Ithaca: Cornell University Press, 1985); P. Gourevitch et al., *Unions and Economic Crisis* (London: George Allen & Unwin, 1984); P. Lange, G. Ross,

1

2   The territorial imperative

differentiated impacts, so it behooves one to examine the responses of
the many actors that reside below the central arenas of politics. Just as
national patterns of crisis response flow from the interests, resources,
and capabilities of state, labor, and capital, it stands to reason that
subnational patterns, varying not only cross-nationally but also intra-
nationally, are waiting to be discovered and explained. As such, this
volume addresses a neglected dimension of the political economy of
advanced industrial nations.

This is not to suggest that the scholarly field is completely bereft of
such concerns. In the same way that inquiries into the origins and dynamics of national party systems revealed the need to study local party
politics,[2] so studies in comparative political economy have ushered in a
discernible scholarly shift to the mesolevel. Researchers, many working
within the corporatist tradition, have begun to explore systematically
the interactions among national and local state agencies and sectoral
business interests.[3] Others have drawn attention to the role of regional
governments in the development of economic adjustment strategies.[4]
Indeed, considerable optimism surrounds the mesolevel of politics; one
set of authors identifies it as quite possibly "a zone of considerable
experimentation where margins of manoeuvre and alliance possibilities
are greater."[5] This growing body of literature notwithstanding, we continue to find ourselves on terra incognita. We know little of the potential
for the expression and pursuit of *territorial* economic interests in advanced democracies or of the specific circumstances under which sub-

and M. Vannicelli, *Unions, Change, and Crisis* (London: George Allen &
Unwin, 1982).

[2] S. Lipset and S. Rokkan, "Cleavage Structures, Party Systems, and Voter
Alignments: An Introduction," in *Party Systems and Voter Alignments*, ed. S.
Lipset and S. Rokkan (New York: The Free Press, 1967), 53–6.

[3] The inaugural contribution is G. Hernes and A. Selvik, "Local Corporatism," in
Organizing Interests in Western Europe, ed. S. Berger (Cambridge: Cambridge
University Press, 1981), 103–19. See also R. King, "Corporatism and the Local
Economy," in *The Political Economy of Corporatism*, ed. Wyn Grant (London:
Macmillan Publishers Ltd., 1985), 202–28; A. Cawson, "Corporatism and Local
Politics," in *Corporatism and Welfare*, ed. A. Cawson (London: Heinemann,
1982), 126–47; R. Flynn, "Co-optation and Strategic Planning in the Local
State," in *Capital and Politics*, ed. R. King (London: Routledge & Kegan Paul,
1983), 85–106; P. Schmitter and W. Streeck, "The Organization of Business Interests," Discussion Paper IIM/LMP 81–13 (Berlin: Wissenschaftszentrum Berlin, 1981); A. Cawson, ed., *Organized Interests and the State* (Beverly Hills: Sage
Publications, 1985); and S. Wilks and M. Wright, *Comparative Government–Industry Relations* (Oxford: Clarendon Press, 1987).

[4] C. Allen, "Corporatism and Regional Economic Policies in the Federal Republic of Germany: The 'Meso' Politics of Industrial Adjustment," *Publius* 19
(Fall 1989): 147–64.

[5] P. Schmitter and L. Lanzalalco, "Regions and the Organization of Business
Interests," in *Regionalism, Business Interests, and Public Policy*, ed. W. Coleman and H. Jacek (London: Sage Publications, 1989), 227.

national actors – chronically underresourced in comparison to national actors – engage in politics about territory across territory. We are unaware of the consequences, if any, of the apparent lack of fit between interests based on territory and a political process tuned overwhelmingly to national politics. We possess little information on the distributive and redistributive conflicts that arise when market and territory collide, and the way in which such conflicts spill over into the political arena.

The paucity of hard evidence and testable theory relating to mesopolitics should be regarded as a considerable opportunity. Indeed, we can employ the regional level as a laboratory to refine our understanding of institutions and their independent impact on political phenomena. During the past decade, a number of seminal contributions to "the new institutionalism" has appeared.[6] Thanks to this literature, we have a growing appreciation of the way in which institutions, usually defined as organizations, shape interests, distribute resources, and generate incentive structures in such a way as to place a distinctive imprint on political behavior. A comparative analysis of the politics of regional decline locates a promising setting in which to extend this compelling research agenda. Not only is the regional level populated with organizations involved in constant interactions with each other and with central government, but in a fundamental sense, the regional level itself is embedded in a broader set of institutions: the constitutional rules that distribute political power across the national territory. By carefully constructing a cross-national comparison that taps this spatial-institutional dimension, we can isolate the impact of institutions that regulate the territorial exercise of political power on the interests, resources, and strategies of actors. The present study pushes the envelope of the new institutionalism by addressing the political salience of constitutional orders.

The relevance of a study of the politics of regional decline is further enhanced by ongoing developments in the European Community, specifically the implementation of its Single European Act and the more ambitious plans for economic and monetary union. Since 1985, member governments have entered into a series of linked agreements that require of them substantial concessions of sovereignty across several policy areas, including the setting of value-added tax rates, the control of national borders, and possibly even key fiscal and monetary instruments.

---

[6] The most notable is P. Hall, *Governing the Economy* (New York: Oxford University Press, 1986). On the general subject of institutions, see the two recent contributions by J. March and J. Olsen: "The New Institutionalism: Organizational Factors in Political Life," *American Political Science Review* 78 (September 1984): 734–49, and *Rediscovering Institutions* (New York: The Free Press, 1989).

During this same period, the European Commission has developed a capacity to bypass national governments and interact directly with subnational actors. These dramatic developments have been paralleled by an explosion of political activity at the subnational level. Brussels is now the target of concerted efforts by localities and regions to redress their own social and economic development needs. Since 1989, representatives of regional governments from eight member countries have convened several Europe of Regions conferences to formulate demands for direct participation in the decision-making and legislative processes at the European level. Scholars too have begun to speculate about the consequences of direct EC exchanges with regions, provinces, and other subnational units. Proponents of a Europe of Regions suggest that the interests of the European periphery, heretofore stifled by national governments, will see the light of day in a strengthened Community and subsequently usher in positive domestic and international transformations, although these are rarely spelled out in detail.[7] To assess accurately the potential for a regional renaissance in the Community, not to mention its limits, we need to know a great deal more about the interests, resources, and capabilities of the principal actors who populate the subnational level.

Problem logic, political logic, and the territorial imperative

The departure point for this study is the overarching theoretical concern of the crisis response literature with the relative impact of problem logic and political logic.[8] Do political systems handle similar problems similarly–that is, do they respond to the objective dictates of the problem itself? Or do they, out of cross-national variations in political institutions, produce different responses to similar challenges? The politics of regional decline raises similar questions. From country to country, regional economic decline affects comparable actors in broadly comparable ways. At the regional level, these include local authorities, local and regional trade unions, business firms and associations, party politicians (national, local, and, should they exist, regional), and the broader regional electorates. At the national level, the relevant actors are political parties, the peak associations of business and labor, government ministries (particularly those directly involved with macro- and microeconomic policymaking), and their field administrative machinery. Some or all of these

---

[7] I present a more sober assessment of the Europe of Regions scenario in my article "Skeptical Reflections on a 'Europe of Regions,' " *Journal of Public Policy* 10(October–December 1990): 417–47.

[8] The two logics are discussed in P. Katzenstein, *Policy and Politics in West Germany* (Philadelphia: Temple University Press, 1987), 7.

actors battle over and ultimately devise solutions to the economic problems of a particular geographical area. The goal is to explain which ones become active, in what manner, and to what effect.

This volume investigates two broad hypotheses about regional decline and the imperatives of crisis response. The first posits that similar regionally circumscribed industrial structures are prone to similar dynamics of economic decline, which in turn give rise to similar political responses. The ripple effects of firm closures, rising unemployment, outmigration, and decay of infrastructure will elicit similar responses from local and regional actors, including common economic and political objectives and common strategies for their realization. Accordingly, any observed differences in regional responses across nations are attributable primarily to variations in the structural characteristics of the regional economy and the resulting problems these generate. Politics is not necessarily irrelevant; it merely explains a trivial portion of the observed variation. In short, regional economic crisis produces a uniform problem logic to which national, regional, and local actors respond. The evidence at hand suggests that the influence of problem logic is strong. For example, Bahry identifies recurrent patterns of inter- and intraregional distributional conflicts engendered by territorial economic disparities, regime type notwithstanding.[9]

The second hypothesis anticipates that, although crisis conditions are certainly germane, insofar as economic circumstances always constrain political choice, political variables will leave a tangible imprint on the responses. Any number of elements can contribute to the politicization of territorial economic issues. Party political organizations with links to national associations are typically predicated upon geographical units of representation, while political institutions and ongoing public policies define the national space and condition authority relations within it. As such, it is necessary to distinguish between two species of political logic: a partisan-electoral logic, and a governmental logic. This step is warranted if the question "does politics matter?" is to move beyond the purely disingenuous. Previous work in comparative political economy has demonstrated time and again that politics does in fact make a difference. We need to unpack the question if the more difficult questions – when, how, and with what degree of regularity does politics matter? – are to be addressed.

A partisan logic would find subnational groups and national policymakers responding to regional crises on the basis of an electoral calculus, with interests, demands, and strategies shaped by their desire to form and maintain majoritarian coalitions. A governmental logic,

---

[9] D. Bahry, *Outside Moscow* (New York: Columbia University Press, 1987), 19.

by contrast, would flow from the political-institutional characteristics of the region, specifically its administrative attributes and its constitutional position in the broader polity, as well as from existing public policies that affect the region. These will expand or limit the resources and options available to national, regional, and local actors, shaping in the process their responses to economic decline. To the extent that either or both types of political logic influence crisis responses, any deterministic connection between economic structural variables and outcomes is untenable.

Complementary theoretical approaches and the need for synthesis

The preceding observations suggest that the object of study is not the state or interest groups or political parties or public policy, but rather the patterns and the content of relationships among actors, both public and private, within and between the national and subnational levels. Therefore, a conceptual framework capable of exploring the politics of regional decline must be sensitive to the territorial dimension of state-society interactions. There are several existing bodies of theory that would appear to lend themselves to a study of this nature: intergovernmental relations, models of center-periphery relations, group theories of politics, and state-centric approaches. Although each offers valuable insights into the problem at hand, each is unsuited in unmodified form to the analytical task at hand. In the following pages, I discuss each approach and its comparative advantage with respect to the others, and present the outlines of a synthesis that is elaborated in full in the next chapter.

Intergovernmental relations

Models of intergovernmental relations focus on the interactions between political institutions at the center and governmental organizations beneath or beyond the center. The early literature exaggerated the significance of formal hierarchical relations between central and local governments, but recent contributions have elevated considerably the conceptual sophistication of this approach.[10] These improved models

---

[10] For example, see R. Samuels, *The Politics of Regional Policy in Japan* (Princeton: Princeton University Press, 1983). He pursues his research objective, to explore "the ways in which localities get together to do things or to otherwise have influence," with a sophisticated typology of local government strategies (p. xxi). Another noted scholar working in the tradition is R. A. W. Rhodes, whose power-dependence framework of intergovernmental relations provides a central element of the synthesis discussed below. See his *Control and Power in Central-Local Relations* (Westmead: Gower Publishing Co., Ltd., 1981), *The*

recognize the interdependence of central and local governments, a condition which often leads to significant departures from the legalistic blueprints of central-local relations. They point to the frequency with which localities and regional governments behave like interest groups and not as mere agents of central government.[11] Their concern with the parameters of local power and initiative is particularly apt, as is their acknowledgment of the complex vertical and horizontal interactions, characterized by negotiation and bargaining, in which local governments engage. Models of intergovernmental relations also devote a great deal of attention to the institutional context of these interactions. Studies of federalism point to the importance of the distribution of power between the units of government in structuring interactions, and of the impact of changes in the rules of the game. With respect to the politics of regional decline, however, the principal drawback of this literature is its understandably narrow focus on inter*governmental* relations. Quite simply, these models are incapable by definition of handling the complex relationships between public *and* private actors that are characteristic of regional crisis responses.

Center-periphery frameworks

The politics of regional decline also lends itself to models of center-periphery relations. Images of center and periphery are widespread in the discipline, surfacing most frequently in studies of ethnic nationalism.[12] Although some scholars go so far as to speak in terms of the center-periphery "paradigm," most in fact employ the spatial distinction as little more than a metaphor about power in modern societies.[13] These models are generally underspecified and overly deterministic, viewing the dependent periphery in a manner reminiscent of the early literature on intergovernmental relations. On occasion, though, center and periphery have been brought together in a theoretically sophisticated manner to analyze political processes at a middle-range level of analysis.

National World of Local Government (London: George Allen & Unwin, 1986), and *Beyond Westminster and Whitehall* (London: Unwin Hyman Ltd., 1988). See also P. Gourevitch, *Paris and the Provinces* (Berkeley: University of California Press, 1980).

[11] Samuels, *Regional Policy in Japan*, 242; Rhodes, *The National World*, 11; T. Anton, *American Federalism and Public Policy* (Philadelphia: Temple University Press, 1989), 33.

[12] M. Hechter, *Internal Colonialism* (Berkeley: University of California Press, 1975); S. Rokkan and D. Urwin, *Economy, Territory, Identity* (London: Sage Publications, 1983).

[13] Y. Mény, ed., *Center–Periphery Relations in Western Europe* (London: George Allen & Unwin, 1985).

One such study is Sidney Tarrow's *Between Center and Periphery*.[14] The power of this model lies ultimately in its balanced focus on peripheral and central elites. Tarrow constructs a web of context and causality to explain why central elites do what they do, and how peripheral elites, working within a severely constrained environment, do what they can. Local elites seek to position themselves as policy brokers between center and periphery by forming strategic alliances with central officials and local interests in order to modify or even rebuff central policy directives affecting their localities. These alliances vary according to institutional and political structures; in France, the bureaucracy provides the main conduit of access for local elites, while in Italy the political parties present the most readily available opportunities for the exercise of reciprocal influence. Tarrow's analytical framework turns on the confluence of two strands of analysis. One addresses the political rationale behind the center's distributive formula for the periphery, which provides an indication of the benefit streams as well as the intended recipients in the periphery. Depending on the coalitional needs of the center, the periphery – or certain elements therein – can achieve a positional advantage that enables it to press its own needs upon the state. The second strand of analysis looks to the institutional linkages between center and periphery – specifically, their capacity to deliver the center's largesse as intended and their openness to penetration and influence by peripheral interests. Depending on how the two strands combine, the periphery may receive political compensation for its troubles, or may get nothing but more trouble.

As a serviceable framework for the political analysis of regional crisis, however, this model is both overly expansive and overly confining. Tarrow seeks to explain all political interactions between center and periphery by focusing strictly on intergovernmental relations, which, as we have seen, excludes many potentially relevant actors from the analysis. This problem is compounded by attendant difficulties in operationalization. "Center" and "periphery" are defined impressionistically, except insofar as they correspond to central and local governments. Furthermore, the model is tailored to the French and Italian cases, in that the notion of elite coalition requirements posits a dominant conservative ruling coalition attempting to integrate center and periphery in the face of urban-rural cleavages of varying strengths. As such, the model does not travel well to countries where the urban-rural cleavage is much less salient and where periodic turnover between parties of the left and right has occurred. In light of these limitations, Tarrow's model

---

[14] S. Tarrow, *Between Center and Periphery* (New Haven: Yale University Press, 1977).

serves as a guide, but not a blueprint, for the analysis presented in this volume.

Interest group and state-centric approaches

Many elements of the politics of regional decline recall theories of interest groups and interest representation, notably pluralism and corporatism.[15] As noted before, regions contain numerous actors with variable interests in the health of the regional economy. The issue arises as to whether groups are sufficiently affected by economic decline to generate a political interest, let alone a distinctly *territorial* interest, in reversing it. Moreover, the options available to activated groups are also of theoretical significance. Groups may pursue their claims individually, or adopt collective approaches that bridge localities and organizational boundaries. Finally, since groups do not operate in an institutional or political vacuum, the resources available to these groups, their organizational attributes, and the formal and informal interrelationships existing between and among them are of central concern. Corporatist and pluralist conceptions of politics appear to be relevant given their very different conceptions of

- the likelihood of group formation and action
- the membership base of groups
- the interests represented
- the distribution of power and influence within groups, particularly between members and leaders
- the resource base of groups
- the centrality of organizational maintenance to group goals and behavior
- the basis of intergroup relationships
- the relationship between groups and governmental agencies, and
- the broader political consequences of interest group activity.

A related theoretical concern applies to the structure and activities of the state.[16] Regional actors operate within an institutional and policy context defined by the state. Central government is the most visible allocator of benefits and costs to its regions, and it therefore sets a compelling agenda for regional actors. In short, as regional actors seek to access state institutions and influence their outputs, they are in turn influenced and structured by these institutions and outputs. This liter-

---

[15] A full range of citations on this literature is presented in Chapter 2.
[16] The term "state" carries a great deal of unnecessary baggage with it, the legacy of the atheoretical formalism of prewar practitioners of comparative politics and the hypertheoretical salvos of orthodox Marxist analysts. Here, the term will be employed as a convenient shorthand for government or governmental actors, but in no way does it suggest a monolithic entity charged with carrying out the unvarnished interests of any one particular class or sectional interest.

ature claims that government officials must be viewed as, at a minimum, potentially autonomous, and thus capable of exercising an independent impact on the preferences, objectives, and strategies of societal actors. Autonomy results from the role of the state in generating and sustaining various modes of order, which endows state officials with the ability to advance a partial or inclusive notion of state interest vis-à-vis societal groups, foreign states, or even fellow public officials.[17] The degree of autonomy from societal interests enjoyed by state officials and their capacity to control political outcomes represent key empirical indicators of the state's relationship to nonstate actors.

Although of obvious relevance to the subject at hand, group and state-centric approaches also fall short of the mark for the simple reason that they fail to deal explicitly with the issue of territory. Although pluralism and corporatism are diametrically opposed on a number of significant questions, both view political phenomena as shaped primarily by the interests and resources of societal actors organized around functional categories. Indeed, these approaches share a tendency to downplay the salience of territorial interests and conflicts in advanced industrial de-mocracies.[18] Both are ambiguous, for example, with respect to the interest-grouplike behavior of regional and local subgovernments – a noteworthy strength of the intergovernmental relations literature. More-over, pluralism and corporatism are internally inconsistent about the role of the state in structuring group relationships at the national level, and offer little if anything regarding the state's role across territory.[19] Amid the ongoing discussion of strong and weak states as well as of state capacity, there is precious little concerning the spatial dimension of state power and behavior. This is all the more surprising in view of the explicit territorial focus of the state-*building* literature, which one might consider the lineal predecessor of the statist revival in the disci-

---

[17] S. Krasner, *Defending the National Interest* (Princeton: Princeton University Press, 1978); S. Krasner, "Review Article: Approaches to the State," *Comparative Politics* 16 (January 1984): 223–46: E. Nordlinger, *On the Autonomy of the Democratic State* (Cambridge, Mass.: Harvard University Press, 1981); and P. Evans, D. Rueschemeyer, and T. Skocpol, *Bringing the State Back In* (Cambridge: Cambridge University Press, 1985). See also G. Almond et al., "Symposium: The Return to the State," *American Political Science Review* 82 (September 1988): 853–901.

[18] P. Schmitter, "Still the Century of Corporatism?" in *Trends Toward Corporatist Intermediation*, ed. P. Schmitter and G. Lehmbruch (Beverly Hills: Sage Publications, 1979), 15.

[19] On this issue, see inter alia S. Berger, "Introduction," in *Organizing Interests*, ed. S. Berger, 1–23; G. Almond, "Review Article: Corporatism, Pluralism, and Professional Memory," *World Politics* 35 (January 1983): 245–60; R. Martin, "Pluralism and the New Corporatism," *Political Studies* 31 (March 1983): 86–102; and G. Jordan, "Pluralistic Corporatism and Corporate Pluralism," *Scandinavian Political Studies* 7 (September 1984): 137–53.

pline.[20] Although the more sophisticated studies counsel against the temptation to treat the state as a monolithic entity, few explore the implications of the territorial differentiation of the state, preferring to concentrate on functional divisions within the national policy-making bureaucracy.[21]

Power dependence as a synthesis

The most profitable recourse is to view these four theoretical approaches as complementary rather than competing. Each has the potential to illuminate different aspects of politics in crisis regions. The goal is to construct an analytical framework that utilizes their respective individual strengths. As set out in detail in the following chapter, I choose to examine national and subnational actors not in the totality of their relationships, but in a confined policy or problem space. The approach I adopt takes the form of progressively smaller concentric circles. At the most general level are the national and subnational actors with a direct or indirect interest in the effects of regional economic decline. A subset of these actors will have a direct or indirect interest in decline within a specific region; in other words, a territorial criterion links the occupants of this circle. A further subset of the territorial subset will act on those interests in the form of distinctive horizontal (intra- and possibly interregional) and vertical (regional–national) relations organized around political initiatives for the region. The concentration on organizations involved in observable relationships in a concrete problem area will avoid the worst of the conceptual imprecision characteristic of metatheorizing about center and periphery or the state and interest groups.

The horizontal and vertical interactions among subnational and national actors in this policy area are cast in terms of the "power-dependence" framework developed by R. A. W. Rhodes.[22] Local and regional governments, subnational business associations and trade unions, and central policy-making institutions are cast as purposive actors, which must expend resources to realize their objectives. No organizational actor is completely self-sufficient, however; each depends to some degree on other organizations for resources. Out of this pervasive and asymmetrical interdependence arises the motive force for

[20] P. Anderson, *Lineages of the Absolutist State* (London: Verso, 1974); C. Tilly, ed., *The Formation of National States in Western Europe* (Princeton: Princeton University Press, 1975).

[21] One study that touches on these issues is E. Nordlinger, "Taking the State Seriously," in *Understanding Political Development*, ed. M. Weiner and S. Huntington (Boston: Little, Brown, and Co., 1987), 353–90.

[22] Rhodes, *Control and Power; The National World;* and *Beyond Westminster and Whitehall.*

cooperation and conflict. The goals of an organization influence which resources it requires, and the organization pursues strategies to regulate the process of resource exchange with other organizations. Based on the interorganizational distribution of resources and the intersection of objectives pursued by local, regional, and national actors, distinctive patterns of interaction arise within the regions: pluralist, corporate pluralist, and sectoral corporatist. The principal research goal is to identify the relative impact of problem and political logic on the emergence of these patterns, and to trace the consequences of these patterns for subnational actors and national policymakers. Central to this research goal is the selection of cases for comparison.

Research design and the selection of cases

To establish the relative weights of the two logics, one must have variation along two dimensions: the nature of the regional problem and the political-institutional attributes of the region. This is difficult to obtain within a single country. While regional economies and regional problems certainly differ across the national space, the regions themselves usually are embedded in a uniform institutional environment defined by the nation-state. That is, the institutional linkages between regions and central government and the political status of the regions tend to be fairly constant within a given political system.[23] These attributes vary cross-nationally, of course, and thus a comparative research design represents the most feasible means of overcoming the constraint imposed by single country studies. The result is a double-paired comparison.

Germany and Great Britain provide the national settings for the study. They are selected on the basis of "most similar systems," a research design that seeks to maximize the number of common characteristics, or background variables, while minimizing the unshared characteristics between cases.[24] If constructed carefully, a most-similar-systems com-

---

[23] Exceptions to this statement abound, of course. In Britain, Scotland and Wales enjoy a special status in the House of Commons (higher per capita representation relative to English regions) and direct representation in the Cabinet (the Scottish and Welsh Offices). Certain Italian or Spanish regions are granted analogous privileges. However, the privileged position of these regions within the national space tends to coincide with their ethnic distinction. It is important to stress that this particular research design explores the options available to subnational interests that do *not* possess ethnic resources for mobilization and response. For an interesting account of Scotland that addresses many issues covered in this volume, see S. Booth and C. Moore, *Managing Competition* (Oxford: Clarendon Press, 1989).

[24] A. Przeworski and H. Teune, *The Logic of Comparative Social Inquiry* (New York: Wiley, 1970), 32.

parison allows the researcher to isolate the impact of the unshared characteristics on the dependent variable while controlling the background variables. This approach has been justly criticized as somewhat inefficient in providing knowledge that can be generalized, particularly since the researcher is often hard pressed to minimize the differences beyond the point where an overdetermination of the dependent variable can be ruled out as unlikely. Yet these limitations are not of sufficient consequence to warrant its abandonment in comparative political inquiry. Especially where the researcher confronts complex political phenomena that do not lend themselves readily to quantification, the most-similar-systems approach – provided its construction is driven by genuine theoretical considerations and its design is well-crafted – is an appropriate means of generating midrange causal statements.

The background variables shared by Germany and Great Britain make up a familiar list. To name just a few, both are advanced capitalist democracies, with parliamentary systems characterized by two major political parties and significant third-party activity. Each boasts well-organized, powerful producer groups operating at the national level.[25] Each has a national bureaucracy staffed by a professional class of civil servants. Assuming that one is confident that these common characteristics are truly common, then one can be reasonably sure that any observed cross-national variations in the politics of regional decline are due to the effects of unshared characteristics.

The principal unshared attribute resides in the territorial distribution of power. Germany is a "spatial-federal" system, in which the Länder (states) retain, in addition to a significant measure of political autonomy vis-à-vis central government, a key role in implementing national policies owing to the federal government's lack of a field administrative apparatus.[26] Britain, on the other hand, is one of the most highly centralized of the major industrialized democracies, a unitary polity in which formal regional input into political and administrative decision making is vanishingly small. As a keen observer of the British case notes, "The political life of the regions wastes away while uniformity is imposed by an increasingly congested Westminster and Whitehall."[27] This elementary

[25] This is not to minimize the magnitude of the organizational differences between, for example, the Trades Union Congress, which represents over 100 craft, industrial, and general labor affiliates, and the Deutscher Gewerkschaftsbund (DGB), a peak organization representing a mere seventeen industrial unions. See Chapter 2.
[26] A. Gunlicks, *Local Government in the German Federal System* (Durham: Duke University Press, 1986), 117. For a brief but thorough overview of German federalism, see P. Blair, *Federalism and Judicial Review in West Germany* (Oxford: Clarendon Press, 1981), 1–6.
[27] B. Smith, *Decentralization* (London: George Allen & Unwin, 1985), 4. It is important here to qualify the characterization of Britain as a unitary state.

federal-unitary distinction introduces key variation in the institutional status of the regions within. British regions are administrative entities defined by central government ministries for the purposes of policy implementation and field administration. They have no democratically elected regional councils or any other representative institutions.[28] The German Länder, on the other hand, are fully equipped states in the federal sense, possessing the complete range of political institutions including state parliaments, executives, and bureaucracies.

Why should variation in the territorial structure of the state be particularly important to politics in crisis regions? If we return to the role of institutions, the answer is clear. As systems of rules and structures of meaning, institutions define the framework within which political competition takes place, thereby channeling political activity into certain kinds of conflicts and away from others. Yet political institutions are not simply arenas within which actors with predefined preferences and resources clash or cooperate. In fact, institutions define the identities, preferences, and values of individuals, groups, and societies. New institutionalists have tended to examine these intriguing issues by studying organizations: that is, bureaucracies, trade unions, business associations, political parties, and so forth. However, relatively little attention has been devoted to the study of the constitutional order as an institution capable of affecting the distribution of political values, rules, and resources. This is understandable, since scholars have been keen to avoid a return to the arid, legalistic concerns of the turn-of-the-century literature on constitutions.[29] Yet the potential significance of constitutional orders as bona fide institutions in the modern sense can hardly be disputed. Constitutions limit government by regulating legislative-executive relations and by setting out the limits of the state's jurisdiction

Rokkan and Urwin employ the term "union state" to denote a polity that "does not enjoy direct political control everywhere." Rokkan and Urwin, *Economy, Territory, Identity*, 181. Pointing to the ad hoc arrangements existing between the center and various parts of the periphery (i.e., Scotland, Wales, and Northern Ireland), the authors argue that the British state achieves "a middle ground between a unitary structure and federalism." Idem, 187. Without challenging this thesis, it is my position that within England, the British state is patterned very much on the lines of a unitary structure. Since the British regions selected for analysis reside in England (see below), the use of the label "unitary" is justified. Although these regional cases will be referred to as British regions throughout the study, they are in fact English regions.

[28] Complicating the issue is the fact that British government ministries have never employed a uniform set of regional boundaries. B. Hogwood and P. D. Lindley, "Variations in regional boundaries," in *Regional Government in England*, ed. B. Hogwood and M. Keating (Oxford: Clarendon Press, 1982), 21–49. The present study will employ the UK standard regions, which have generally been used by the government for regional economic policy-making.

[29] For example, see Hall, *Governing the Economy*, 20.

with respect to the individual. They also circumscribe government by distributing power territorially. As March and Olsen suggest, "A change in [the constitutional order] may alter the values of the state, the purpose and meaning of state actions, the rationale and legitimacy of institutional boundaries, the regulation of conflict, and the conditions under which different interests may be pursued."[30]

Constitutions are thus significant institutions in their own right. Where the distribution of territorial power is concerned, a common distinction has been drawn between federal and unitary systems.[31] Although the concept of federalism is surrounded by a definitional morass, it is generally agreed that the singular property of a federal system is the constitutional incorporation of the regions into the center's decision-making procedures.[32] In a similar vein, "the crucial, and *politically* significant characteristic of a federation is that it is more difficult than in a unitary state for the center to encroach upon the powers and status of regional governments."[33] Thus, although there are many institutional manifestations of federalism – the German variant differs substantially from the American model, for example – federal systems form a coherent category with respect to unitary systems because of this basic property.

Even the traditional literature on federalism, which connects only sporadically with the new institutionalism, suggests that this elemental distinction between federal Germany and unitary Britain is of probable significance for the politics of regional decline. Students of federalism rarely fail to point out the association between the volume and efficacy of interest group activity and the multiple access points to decision-making arenas in a federal polity.[34] Others have noted the complex yet discernible impact of federalism on the organizational structures of interest groups and on party systems.[35] Still others point to the volume and complexity of interactions between governments in a federal polity and the resulting impact of institutionalized intergovernmental bargain-

---

[30] March and Olsen, *Rediscovering Institutions*, 111. In a similar vein, Rhodes refers to the constitution as "a source of the rules of the game," and points out the pressing need to study the effects of changes in this all-important source. Rhodes, *Control and Power*, 80.

[31] K. C. Wheare, *Modern Constitutions* (London: Oxford University Press, 1964).

[32] P. King, *Federalism and Federation* (London: Croom Helm Publishers, 1982), 146.

[33] Smith, *Decentralization*, 15; italics in original.

[34] This is also known as the "multiple crack" hypothesis. W. Coleman and W. Grant, "Regional Differentiation of Business Interest Associations," *Canadian Journal of Political Science* 18(March 1985): 3. See also Anton, *American Federalism*, 79, and D. Cameron, "The Expansion of the Public Economy," *American Political Science Review* 72 (December 1978): 1253.

[35] Coleman and Grant, "Regional Differentiation"; Schmitter and Lanzalalco, "Regions and the Organization," 210; I. Katznelson, "Working Class Formation and the State," in *Bringing the State Back In*, ed. Evans et al. 273–4.

ing on the policy outputs of the national government.[36] Eisinger, in his study of regional economic policy-making in American states, suggests that federalism underpins the fierce competition among state and local governments for private investment, and speculates that similar competitive pressures are absent in unitary polities.[37] The comparison of Britain and Germany provides a means of isolating the impact of the territorial constitutional order on regional responses to economic decline. Indeed, Germany's status as a "markedly centralized federal system,"[38] in which shared powers – as opposed to parallel and independent ones – dominate the relations between the federal and state governments, lends the comparison certain aspects of a critical case study. To the extent that significant differences between British and German subnational responses can be traced to this ostensibly less distinct federal-unitary distinction, the case for constitutional orders as institutions with impact is strengthened.

To facilitate the test of the problem logic hypothesis, I select two regions from each country for detailed analysis – the North East and the West Midlands in Britain, and the Saarland and North Rhine–Westphalia (NRW) in Germany (see Figures 1.1 and 1.2).[39] These two regional sets introduce parallel variation in the type of industrial base and the timing of the region's decline. The North East and the Saarland represent a distinctive type of problem region – monostructural, with traditional heavy industrial activity and long-standing economic adjustment problems. The West Midlands and NRW, on the other hand, are comparatively diversified regional economies based on manufacturing. Their economic problems are of a more recent vintage, and coincided with (as opposed to preceded) national economic crises. In addition, each regional case study incorporates a temporal comparative dimension to assist in the identification of continuity and change in the pattern of national-subnational interactions over time. The period of study for each

---

[36] Rhodes, *Control and Power*, 75–6; F. Scharpf, "The Joint Decision Trap," Discussion Paper IIM/LMP 85–1 (Berlin: Wissenschaftszentrum Berlin, 1985).

[37] P. Eisinger, *The Rise of the Entrepreneurial State* (Madison: The University of Wisconsin Press, 1988), 55. This study disproves Eisinger's assertion. Inter- and intraregional competition is a ubiquitous feature of politics in crisis regions. The federal-unitary distinction makes its impact felt in the way in which this competition is channeled and in the consequences for subnational groups.

[38] Blair, *Federalism and Judicial Review*, 1.

[39] For the purposes of this book, the regional level is defined as the middle tier of government or administration, standing between local governments and central government. This politicoadministrative definition is distinguished from economic, functional, and planning definitions of regions. See H. Richardson, *Regional Economics* (Urbana: University of Illinois Press, 1979), 17–25.

Figure 1.1. *Standard Regions in the United Kingdom: The gray area in the North East is the county of Cumbria, an on-again off-again part of the region (see Chapter 4, fn. 1 for a brief history of this area's itinerant designation).*

Figure 1.2. *Länder in the Federal Republic of Germany: The erstwhile German Democratic Republic is shaded in light gray. The five new Länder (plus East Berlin), which combined with the 11 original West German Länder in 1990 to form a united Germany, played no part in the politics of regional decline examined in this study. The subregion identified within North Rhine–Westphalia is the Ruhr Valley.*

region is variable, beginning with the onset of regional crisis and ending in 1986.[40]

These dimensions are of probable importance to the politics of regional decline for several reasons. First, research on sectoral economic crises suggests that a given industrial structure generates distinctive adjustment challenges for political actors.[41] It seems reasonable to expect this tendency to reproduce itself at the regional level. As for the dimension of timing, the reasoning is similar to that outlined by Olson in his most recent elaboration on the logic of collective action. Whether it involves two actors or several, collective action is both difficult and costly to organize and to sustain. In the context of regional economic crisis, the response of national and subnational actors will not necessarily be automatic, since the definition of interests and the mobilization of resources require time. Thus, the pattern of responses is likely to be influenced by the longevity of the crisis, a dimension expressly built into the case comparisons.[42]

It is appropriate at the present juncture to counter a possible objection to this comparative research design. By setting British administrative regions alongside German states, isn't one comparing apples and oranges? It will come as no surprise, one might argue, that German Länder are more powerful subnational entities than their English counterparts. Yet the issue is not whether German states are better equipped to respond to decline than British regions, although this is not unimportant in the final analysis. Rather, I set out to explore whether the interactions of public and private actors in German federal states are subject to similar constraints and incentives as their English counterparts in a comparable area of policy activity. How and why actors do something is oftentimes as important as what they do.[43]

[40] Developments since 1986, including the impact of German unification, are taken up in the concluding chapter.

[41] K. Dyson, "The Cultural, Ideological, and Structural Context," in *Industrial Crisis*, ed. Dyson and Wilks, 47.

[42] Readers will no doubt recognize this argument as an adaptation of Implication 2 in *The Rise and Decline of Nations* (New Haven: Yale University Press, 1982), 38–41. The resemblance is skin-deep, however. In no way do I intend to suggest that the consequences of Implication 2 are reproduced in miniature in the regional cases. Olson's somewhat extravagant claims for his logic, of which Implication 2 is a key part, have been effectively rebutted by D. Cameron in "Distributional Coalitions and Other Sources of Economic Stagnation," *International Organization* 42(Autumn 1988): 561–603.

[43] In a similar vein, the reader should not conclude from my decision to employ a modified version of Rhodes's power-dependence framework that this study is principally about power. Naturally, the analysis and findings cannot help but touch on this crucial yet often murky concept inasmuch as they evaluate the reciprocal influence of national and subnational actors. Nevertheless, my main theoretical concern is with the impact of resource *dependence* on actor strategies

Summary

This combination of national and regional cases allows for a solid test of the problem logic and political logic hypotheses. Political-institutional context can be held constant by comparing intranational responses, while problem context can be held constant by comparing cross-national patterns. To the extent that the significant differences manifest themselves on a intranational basis, one could with reason point to a common problem logic that underpins the territorial imperative. In other words, if responses in the North East have more in common with Saar responses than with those in its British neighbor, then the weight of explanation will rest with the dynamics of the problem, not the polity. If, on the other hand, cross-national variations are more telling, the opposite conclusion is justified. In this manner, the array of national and regional cases speaks directly to the issue of problem versus political logic.

The organization of this volume is as follows. Chapter 2 sets out a framework of analysis based on group-state relations to explore the patterns of regional responses to economic decline. Specifically, I seek to explain the presence and consequences of pluralist, corporate pluralist, and corporatist relations between groups and the state at the regional level. The framework is then applied in Chapters 3, 4, and 5, which present the national and regional case comparisons. Chapter 6 ties together the threads of analysis into a comparative synthesis, which probes the debate of problem logic versus political logic.

The findings demonstrate that responses to regional crisis are political, indeed inherently so. Politics about territory is fought out across territory in both countries. Although evidence for both problem logic and political logic surfaces repeatedly, the latter is preponderant. Indeed, an identifiable political logic, principally of the governmental variety, interprets the problem logic generated by regional economic crisis, giving rise to distinctive versions of the territorial imperative in Britain and Germany. Constitutional differences influence which subnational actors develop actionable interests with regard to decline, what strategies they adopt, the degree to which the region, as opposed to the locality, becomes the relevant unit of political action for subnational actors, the opportunities for central control and subnational autonomy, and the efficacy of subnational responses. That is, the constitutional order is shown to exercise a strong influence on the territorial distribution of interests and resources, and on the strategies of cooperation and conflict available to actors at all levels of the polity. The explicit focus on the political

and on the patterns of interaction among actors. I am grateful to Matthew Woods for bringing to my attention the potential for confusion over this point.

economy of regions also calls into question certain elements of the conventional wisdom on British and German politics, and underscores the need for caution when assessing the true potential of mesopolitics in advanced industrial democracies.

2 Power-dependence and regional economic crisis

Theories of intergovernmental relations, center-periphery relations, interest groups, and the state illuminate distinctive aspects of the politics regional decline, yet each by itself is incapable of accommodating the complex multiactor and multilevel interactions that characterize this problem area. An adaptation of the power–dependence framework pulls these approaches together in a manner that highlights their complementarity. After introducing the basic elements of the original model, I propose a modified version and then employ it to explain the emergence of pluralist, corporate pluralist, or corporatist patterns of interaction between state officials and subnational actors, and to interpret the probable political consequences that flow from these patterns.

The power-dependence framework

As developed by Rhodes over several volumes, the original framework consists of five propositions:

1. Any organization is *dependent* upon other organizations for resources.
2. In order to achieve their goals, the *organizations* have to exchange resources.
3. Although decision making within the organization is constrained by other organizations, the *dominant coalition* retains some discretion. The *appreciative system* of the dominant coalition influences which relationships are seen as a problem and which resources will be sought.
4. The dominant coalition employs *strategies* within known *rules of the game* to regulate the *process of exchange*.
5. Variations in the degree of *discretion* are a product of the goals and the relative power potential of the interacting organizations. This relative power potential is a product of the resources of each organization, of the rules of the game, and of the process of exchange between organizations.[1]

This model of interorganizational relations centers on the interplay between two levels of analysis. At the microlevel, purposive organizations exist in a condition of perpetual albeit variable resource de-

---

[1] Rhodes, *Control and Power*, 98–99. Italics in original.

pendence upon other organizations.[2] Organizations manage their dependence by exchanging several different types of resources: (1) authority, or the legal right to perform certain functions; (2) monetary or financial wherewithal; (3) political legitimacy, which confers access and standing to organizations; (4) information or data-based assets; and (5) organizational means, such as people, skills, and administrative capabilities. The process of exchange resembles a bargaining game "in which [actors] manoeuvre for advantage, deploying the resources they control to maximize their influence over outcomes, and trying to avoid (where they can) becoming dependent on . . . other [players]."[3] By maximizing the amount of discretion available to them, organizations seek to achieve their substantive objectives. This microbehavior in turn gives rise to recurrent mesolevel patterns of interaction between subnational and national actors, typically clustered around the functional divisions of government. These policy networks rest upon distinctive structures of dependency, which exert a strong influence on the behavior of actors within the communities.

This approach contains several valuable insights. In the first place, although relations among organizations are predicated upon bargaining, resource exchange is not a mechanistic process in which units of common value are traded according to the canons of utility maximization. Rather, the exchange process unfolds as an inherently political activity. An organization's interests and objectives, which are the product of intraorganizational decision making and extraorganizational influence or constraints, determine which resources are valued or required if the organization is to achieve its objectives. The relative values of resources, in other words, are subjective, and they change as an organization's goals evolve. Thus, careful attention must be paid to the process of goal formation within organizations as well as to change and continuity in the content of those goals.

Second, an organization's resources confer upon it merely the potential to realize its objectives. The successful deployment of resources is dependent upon the rules of the game. Although the precise nature of these rules remains vague in successive formulations of the power-dependence model, a troubling fact in view of their consequential role, it is generally understood that the rules of the game refer not only to

[2] Rhodes employs the concepts of "micro" and "meso" in a manner that differs somewhat from my usage in Chapter 1. In particular, "micro" does not correspond to the local level of analysis, as distinct from the middle level (meso) and national level (macro). Rather, it refers to the motivational component that influences the actions of individual organizations or, more accurately, of the individuals who form the dominant coalition within each organization. These organizations can inhabit the local, regional, or national level of the polity.
[3] Rhodes, *The National World*, 18.

the legal-constitutional procedures that regulate the internal relations of the state and its relation to society, but also to the informal conventions that govern the exercise of discretionary behavior by organizations, such as the right of consultation.[4] Such rules are of critical importance, since they may favor certain organizations over others or encourage certain values and interests over others. The present concern with constitutional orders as institutions resonates with the power–dependence framework's focus on the rules of the game. In a similar vein, the successful deployment of resources is also contingent upon an organization's choice of strategies. Organizations pursue strategies to regulate the process of exchange with other organizations. An organization's choice of strategies is constrained by a number of factors, including the organization's resource assets, limitations on the substitutability of resources, the goals of the organization, and the nature of the problem involved. Strategies ultimately determine an organization's stance, whether cooperative or conflictual, vis-à-vis other organizations.

Third, the framework in no way presumes a uniform distribution of resources among actors. The pervasiveness of interdependence among organizations coexists with persistent resource asymmetries in interorganizational relationships. Although this applies to actors at all levels of the polity, it is especially relevant to the relationship between central government and subnational actors. Governmental actors, precisely because they are a part of the state, usually (but not always) enjoy substantial advantages over subnational actors both public and private across many of the resource categories identified in the power-dependence model, including authority, money, and political legitimacy. Thus, the capacity of state actors to place their imprint on the process of exchange with subnational actors is considerable, thanks to the frequency with which these officials possess monopoly control over key resources. Moreover, state actors can under certain circumstances alter the rules of the game unilaterally; this capacity must also be seen as variable and contingent.

Finally, the framework forges an explicit link between the micro- and mesolevels of analysis, an insight which strengthens the contention that networks of national and subnational actors will exhibit patterns of interaction distinguished by their degree of regularity, stability, and competitiveness. Differences among patterns are founded primarily upon variations in the distribution of resources among actors, but are also subject to differences in the rules of the game and in the interests of the actors involved. As such, the power-dependence approach provides a nuanced instrument for comparing constellations of organizations

---

[4] Rhodes, *Control and Power*, 105.

across national boundaries, and for connecting differences in the structure of dependencies to differences in the behavior of the actors.

Critique and modification of the original framework
Rhodes's original model suffers from several defects which must be noted and addressed if power-dependence is to be used to study subnational responses to regional decline in Britain and Germany. One of the more obvious shortcomings stems from its restrictive focus on the interactions among national and local governments. This is easily corrected, however, since the ideas behind power-dependence can be extended without too much difficulty to include nongovernmental actors. More worrisome are limitations associated with the "micro" elements of the power-dependence framework. The focus on resources as sources of potential power or influence begs certain key questions. The framework has little to say about the broader politicoeconomic context in which interorganizational relations unfold. This broader context, as Rhodes himself admits, is of critical importance, since the sources of the rules of the game and of the distribution of resources reside here.[5] Furthermore, while organizations are described as discretion-maximizers, the framework offers few clues as to the precise nature and origins of organizational goals. Yet goals play a pivotal role in determining which resources – and by implication which organizations – will be sought out. Thus, the microelements of power-dependence do not constitute a self-contained, deductive model of interorganizational relations. Rather, they form an interpretive framework of political behavior, and will be used as such in the following chapters. This is no mean thing. After all, if the patterned interactions observed in the regions can be traced back consistently to organizational resource dependencies, then we will have gone a long way toward confirming a common motive – subject to political definitions of interest and the broader context of rules – underlying the actions of state and nonstate actors.

The mesolevel components of the original power-dependence model suggest a promising line of inquiry but nevertheless fall short of allowing systematic comparisons of recurrent patterns of interaction among national and subnational actors. Here, recent contributions to the literature on group politics and group–state relations, which have refocused analytic attention on the subsystem level, allow us to recast the recurrent patterns of interaction identified by the power-dependence model in terms of a pluralist-corporatist continuum.[6]

---

[5] Ibid., 127.

[6] The subject of pluralist-corporatist continua is addressed in Martin, "The New Corporatism"; C. Crouch, "Pluralism and the New Corporatism: A Rejoinder,"

The premise of any continuum is that the differences between the poles are ones of degree, not kind, which implies that there are a finite number of recognizable, measurable characteristics that vary as one traverses the length of the continuum. Thus, a conceptually sound continuum must rest upon a firm consensus about the nature of the phenomenon in question. Where pluralism and corporatism are concerned, however, such an assumption is likely to lead into a thicket of controversy. Indeed, theoretical and empirical consistency grace neither the pluralist nor corporatist literatures, although the latter is somewhat more homogeneous since its major impetus originated in the desire to correct the real (and invented)[7] weaknesses of the pluralist paradigm. The apparent internal consistencies of corporatism and pluralism owe a great deal to the efforts of corporatist scholars to demarcate clear lines of battle. Corporatism depicts a political world in which pluralism – or at least the unreconstructed version promulgated by Latham[8] – is stood on its head. Where pluralists see numerous, variegated, independent groups, corporatists identify a limited number of controlling (vis-à-vis members) and constrained (vis-à-vis the state) associations. For pluralists, the interest group system is characterized by competition and fluidity; for corporatists, the watchwords are hierarchy, monopoly, and structure. In place of the neutral nightwatchman state described by pluralism, corporatist scholars insert an activist, engaged governmental sector.[9]

In fact, both literatures display wide variations in their treatment of key issues. Disputes within the pluralist tradition center on a host of

---

Political Studies 31(September 1983): 452–60; Jordan, "Pluralistic Corporatism"; Almond, "Review Article"; and J. Chubb, *Interest Groups and the Bureaucracy* (Stanford: Stanford University Press, 1983). For the record, Rhodes treats his framework, pluralism, and corporatism as "alternative metaphors." This is due in large part to his use of these "metaphors" as system-level concepts. Rhodes, *The National World,* Chapter 2.

[7] For example, see Almond, "Review Article"; R. Dahl, "Polyarchy, Pluralism, and Scale," *Scandinavian Political Studies* 7(December 1984): 225–40; A. G. Jordan and J. J. Richardson, *Government and Pressure Groups in Britain* (Oxford: Clarendon Press, 1987). These authors reject the version of pluralism presented in the corporatist literature, which they concede is empirically suspect. They argue that critics of pluralism are guilty of "professional amnesia," since much of the earlier pluralist literature incorporates the very elements it would later stand accused of ignoring. Almond, "Review Article," 252.

[8] E. Latham, *The Group Basis of Politics* (Ithaca: Cornell University Press, 1952). Bentley and Truman have often been lumped into this category, although unjustifiably so. A. Bentley, *The Process of Government* (Bloomington, Ind.: Principia Press, 1908); D. Truman, *The Governmental Process* (New York: Alfred A. Knopf, 1951).

[9] The mirror-image characteristics of pluralism and corporatism can be traced to Schmitter's oft-quoted definitions. Schmitter, "Still the Century of Corporatism?" 13–15.

vital issues, including the likelihood of group formation, the distribution of resources and, by implication, political power and influence among groups, the relationship of groups to the state, the role of the state in a pluralist system, and the political consequences of pluralist patterns of interaction.[10] Among corporatist scholars, there have been similar weighty disagreements. An early rift developed over whether corporatism referred to the political system itself or to a concrete set of institutions located within the broader political system.[11] A similar issue, relating to scope, involved the types of groups to which corporatist arrangements applied. Was corporatism restricted to the major producer groups in society, principally capital and labor, or did it apply to a broader range of associations?[12] These disagreements have been resolved in favor of a view of corporatism as a middle-level institutional arrangement that focuses primarily, but not necessarily exclusively, on the state and the peak organizations of business and labor. Perhaps the most serious unresolved debate within the corporatist literature relates to the role of the state. In some treatments of corporatism, the state is depicted as a controller, while in others it is described as subject to consistent manipulation by private groups. Others see the state as a co-equal bargainer; still others decline to go into the role of the state in any detail at all.[13] As for the consequences of corporatism, supporters are not of one mind or even three. For every pronouncement about the

---

[10] Many scholars working within the pluralist tradition anticipated the criticisms of corporatist scholars by several decades; see S. Beer, *Modern British Politics* (London: W. W. Norton & Co., 1965); J. LaPalombara, *Interest Groups in Italian Politics* (Princeton: Princeton University Press, 1964); G. McConnell, *Private Power and American Democracy* (New York: Alfred A. Knopf, 1966); T. Lowi, *The End of Liberalism* (New York: W. W. Norton, 1969).

[11] Schmitter, who distinguishes between "state" and "societal" corporatism, is best known for the former viewpoint. Schmitter, "Still the Century of Corporatism?" In recent years, he has moved away from this position. On the other side, Panitch staked out a claim as an early champion of the middle-level approach to corporatism. L. Panitch, "Recent Theorizations on Corporatism," *British Journal of Sociology* 31 (June 1980): 159–87.

[12] Schmitter opted for an expansive scope; see "Reflections on Where the Theory of Neo-Corporatism Has Gone and Where the Praxis of Neo-Corporatism May Be Going," in *Patterns of Corporatist Policy-making*, ed. G. Lehmbruch and P. Schmitter (Beverly Hills: Sage Publications, 1982), 259–79. Others, including Panitch and Lehmbruch, argued that corporatism applied strictly to national-level arrangements linking the state with the peak associations of labor and capital. G. Lehmbruch, "Liberal Corporatism and Party Government," in *Trends Toward Corporatist Intermediation*, ed. Schmitter and Lehmbruch, 147–84.

[13] See for example B. Nedelman and K. Meier, "Theories of Contemporary Corporatism," *Comparative Political Studies* 10 (April 1977): 39–60; Lehmbruch, "Liberal Corporatism." For a full critique of corporatist writings on the subject of the state, see Martin, "The New Corporatism," and Jordan, "Pluralistic Corporatism."

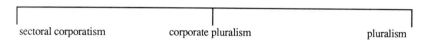

sectoral corporatism   corporate pluralism   pluralism

Figure 2.1. *A continuum of group-state relations*

salutary effects of corporatist arrangements on economic performance, regime stability, or interventionist capacity, there is a riposte that points to the negative implications for democracy, governmental capacity, economic performance, or trade union interests.[14]

Nevertheless, working definitions of pluralism and corporatism can be culled from the literature by concentrating on the areas of greatest internal consistency, and these reinforce the soundness of a continuum of group-state relations (see Figure 2.1).[15] The principal dimensions along which these patterns of interaction vary are (1) the number and variety of groups, (2) the internal hierarchy of groups and their monopoly of representation, (3) the regularity of intergroup and group-state relations, and (4) the extent to which groups participate in the implementation of policy. At one extreme, sectoral corporatist patterns are characterized by organizations of limited number and type, which exercise extensive control over membership and over the general interest area in which they operate, which engage in formal, routinized, cooperative arrangements both with other groups in the system and with government agencies, and which participate in the implementation of public policy.[16] At the other pole, pluralist patterns are characterized by a multitude of organizations and organizational types possessing low levels of internal hierarchy and monopoly of interest representation, which engage in informal, fluid, competitive relations with other groups and with state agencies, and whose role in the policy process is characterized purely in terms of pressure. In the middle, under the rubric of corporate pluralism, are the hybrids.

[14] For two particularly good empirical treatments, see M. Schmidt, "Does Corporatism Matter?" *Patterns of Corporatist Policy-making*, ed. Lehmbruch and Schmitter, 237–58; and D. Cameron, "Social Democracy, Corporatism, Labor Quiescence, and the Representation of Economic Interests in Advanced Capitalist Society," in *Order and Conflict in Contemporary Capitalism*, ed. J. Goldthorpe (Oxford: Oxford University Press, 1984), 143–78. For an early formulation regarding corporatism and trade union interests, see L. Panitch, "The Development of Corporatism in Liberal Democracies," in *Trends Toward Corporatist Intermediation*, ed. Schmitter and Lehmbruch, 119–46.

[15] I employ the term "group" here and in the following pages as a convenient way of referring to the broader category of subnational actors, some of which are not interest groups in the rigorous sense (e.g., local authorities).

[16] The term "sectoral corporatism" is borrowed from G. Lehmbruch, "Concertation and the Structure of Corporatist Networks," in *Order and Conflict*, ed. Goldthorpe, 62. For the sake of brevity, patterns of this type will be referred to as corporatist.

Thus, as one proceeds from the pluralist to the corporatist pole, the properties of the associational system begin to change: The number and variety of groups decrease; the monopoly of groups within their interest areas increases, as does their internal hierarchy; the fluidity and competitiveness of intergroup and group-state relations give way to structure and cooperation; and group participation in policy implementation increases. Changes in these various dimensions do not necessarily keep rigid pace with one another. In other words, corporate pluralism comprises several mixes of the various attributes outlined before. The distinguishing quality of corporate pluralism with respect to pluralism is the moderation of competition and the element of "structure" in intergroup and group-state relations; with respect to sectoral corporatism, the hybrid is distinctive for the larger number and variety of groups, the lack of monopoly of representation within an interest sector, and the limited nature of participation in policy implementation. Since all of these characteristics are internally related, we would in any event expect to observe broadly parallel shifts in the attributes of the interest system over the span of the continuum.

Note the various attributes that are excluded from this continuum. Nothing is said about the precise role of the state, the content of group-state interactions, or the "outputs" of different patterns in terms of democracy, stability, overload, inequality, or inefficiency. This is not because these issues are unimportant – far from it. Instead, they are excluded for three reasons. First, some effort must be made to forge a consensus out of the disparate writings on pluralism and corporatism. The various dimensions depicted in the continuum are the subjects of general consensus within each of the respective literatures; those left off are not. Second, the attributes incorporated in the continuum are empirically verifiable. Indeed, one of the great weaknesses of these literatures is the dearth of tangible, empirical referents for the concepts bandied about. By focusing on number, variety, monopoly, and so on, the researcher has a better chance of correctly identifying the associational patterns under observation. Third, and most important, the excluded attributes simply do not belong in the definition. Some, such as the role of the state, can influence the type of interaction pattern that eventually emerges; in other words, they are possible independent variables. Others, like outputs, emerge as a result of certain patterns of interaction. The goal of research should be to develop hypotheses about the probable effects of pluralist, corporatist, and corporate pluralist patterns, rather than to assign these effects a priori to the definition. This is particularly important in the context of exploring systematically the relatively unsurveyed territory of corporate pluralism.

The pluralist-corporatist continuum meshes nicely with the power-dependence framework's focus on resource dependence. The distribution of resources among and between subnational and national actors will have a strong impact on the pattern of interaction that emerges. For example, a broad scattering of resources at the subnational level will create an environment exhibiting many aspects of pluralism, including a large number and variety of organized interests with low levels of monopoly and internal hierarchy. Conversely, regional concentrations of resources can generate many of the building blocks of corporatism, specifically a limited number of organizations with high levels of internal hierarchy and monopoly of representation. The vertical distribution of resources between national governments and subnational interests also bears a theoretical relationship to the continuum. To the extent that state agencies lack control over key resources like information or organizational attributes, they will not be positioned, through the actual or implied use of inducements and sanctions, to promote a stable process of exchange among actors. This can result in the intergroup competitiveness characteristic of pluralist patterns. Resource-rich state agencies, on the other hand, possess the means to enforce stable bargaining arrangements, which is conducive to cooperation among subnational actors. The framework's focus on different kinds of resources also dovetails with one of the clear distinctions between the pluralist and corporatist poles – namely, that the state exchanges authority resources – a role in policy implementation – at one end but not the other. In general, one should be sensitive to other variations in the types of resources that are exchanged as one moves from pluralism through corporate pluralism to sectoral corporatism.

The natural affinity between the power–dependence framework and the continuum should not lead us to ignore another aspect of the mechanistic fallacy of resource exchange. Resources will in all likelihood play a significant role in shaping the relationships between public and private actors across the territorial divide, yet they are not all-determining. In particular, the goals of organizations and the rules of the game will have a powerful impact on whether actors seek to manage their resource dependence through competition or cooperation. Regardless of the objective level of resource dependence between two organizations, resource bargaining is unlikely to result if their goals are incompatible. Similarly, the rules of the game shape the political agenda and access for actors, which will open or close avenues of cooperation in a manner quite distinct from the question of resources. Thus, in our study of politics in crisis regions, the focus cannot be on resources alone. These take on importance only in an explicitly political context.

Despite this caveat, the synthesis of power-dependence and group-state theories brings with it a number of theoretical advantages. In the first place, it treats the issue of resource distribution and acquisition as an empirical question, thereby avoiding a principal shortcoming of pluralist and corporatist approaches.[17] Moreover, the synthesis underlines the fact that bargaining among actors is not the exclusive preserve of corporatist arrangements, a point made with considerable force by Martin,[18] *and* it provides a means of distinguishing pluralist bargaining from its corporatist counterpart. Finally, by acknowledging the importance of resources, goals, and rules, it provides a means of explaining changes in the pattern of interaction over time. In short, as resource dependencies change, or as objectives and rules of the game shift, so too will the mesolevel interactions among actors. The interesting questions remain, of course: What causes these changes, and what are their consequences?

The political anatomy of regional decline and the modified framework

The politics of regional decline is conceptualized here as a complex problem of resource dependence underpinned by divergences of interest, all of which exist within a broader set of institutions. At the regional level, state and local government officials will have direct, immediate interests in the performance of the regional economy. A depressed economy creates acute electoral pressures for decisive action. Local public officials face additional problems of a budgetary or financial nature. Tax revenues will dry up as firms close down and the labor force migrates elsewhere in search of employment. Local public outlays increase in the form of transfer payments to the unemployed and new programs to attract investment. Though similar electoral and financial pressures will not lead automatically to a common interest among the public authorities within a given region, these interests are perceived, either separately or jointly, in distinctly territorial terms.

Another set of regional actors with immediate interests in the performance of the regional economy are national and regional parliamentary representatives, as well as the subnational party organizations operating in the region. Sour regional economies can make even the

---

[17] Pluralists generally argue that group access to resources is unproblematic, and that power derived from resources is noncumulative; this view is usually attributed to Truman, *The Governmental Process*, and R. Dahl, *Who Governs?* (New Haven: Yale University Press, 1961). Dahl has modified this position substantially over the years, it should be noted. See his *Dilemmas of Pluralist Democracy* (New Haven: Yale University Press, 1982). The corporatist corrective – namely, that resource acquisition is indeed problematic – is undercut by a tendency to establish a priori an invariant hierarchy of group power based on the control of resources, with capital and labor at the top (and in that order). Berger, "Introduction," 13.

[18] Martin, "The New Corporatism," 96.

safest of seats seem vulnerable. Still, for any elected representative or party functionary, constituency demands must be balanced against the national claims of party politics. Furthermore, representatives from a given region are likely to confront the same problems of aggregation that plague local authorities. These problems can be exacerbated by differences in party allegiances and strengths in the region, all of which may render the development of a cohesive regional block of MPs unlikely.

The impact of regional crisis on subnational producer groups is much more problematical. Trade union officials, for example, face membership demands to protect wages and jobs as regional markets contract and plants close. During sustained periods of unemployment and outmigration, unions suffer a loss of membership, which diminishes their influence and ultimately threatens their organizational survival. Nevertheless, trade unions are essentially industrial entities, finding their base of representation, organization, and interest tied not to area but to enterprises – individual firms, industries, or economic sectors. In light of this, trade union officials and members may not perceive the effects of regional decline in *territorial* terms and seek solutions on that basis. Similar arguments apply to regional business interests. Firms confront crumbling markets for local suppliers and consumers. A stagnating regional economy also threatens the long-term investment plans of firms. Still, these are problems primarily for local firms unable to seek out greener, more profitable pastures for reasons of size, talent, or market niche. In contrast, multinationals, large firms with access to external markets, and branch plants may opt to relocate, to ride out the storm, or to shut down operations. For them, the location of production is not tied intimately to profits or even economic viability.

How might these various groups, either individually or jointly, respond to the pressures generated by regional economic crisis? What is the link between interest and action? There appear to be several options available to regional actors. They can seek economic salvation within the region itself by formulating regional promotion programs to attract domestic and international investors, or by providing comprehensive investment counseling for outside firms wishing to resettle in the region and even seed capital for new economic development. Regional groups can also focus on the political acquisition of resources from the center through either parliamentary or bureaucratic channels. Typically, they seek changes in the distributive and redistributive policies of central government as these affect the region; targeted programs include general macroeconomic policies, industrial policies, urban policy, and, above all, regional economic policy. Groups may also seek to change the existing statutory division of powers between national and subnational levels of public authority, and press for greater regional political autonomy alongside the more conventional objectives directed at ongoing government programs. Regional actors will most likely adopt mixed strategies that seek to complement a regional focus with adequate doses of central government assistance.

The anatomy of decline at the regional level demonstrates that some actors have a more immediate stake in the health of the regional economy than others, and not all possess equivalent capabilities to address the problems generated by decline. Much the same can be said for national government agencies. Regional economic disparities generate a host of political and administrative problems for national policymakers, the importance of which depends on their location within the state apparatus. That is, elected and appointed government officials face the competing demands of regions and the competing demands of intraregional actors, yet will interpret them differently. For national policymakers charged with the task of formulating programs to ameliorate regional industrial crisis, dilemmas abound. Is the regional problem of sufficient gravity to warrant a national response? If so, which regions to favor, which ones to neglect? Which actors within a region to target with benefits? Should the criteria of assistance be based on economic need or on partisan importance? For other government officials, regional problems can represent nothing more than an additional claim on scarce state resources. To the extent that the government possesses a territorially differentiated field administration, the interests of "The State" with respect to regional crisis can fragment still further.[19]

Thus, regional economic decline poses a complex, differentiated challenge to organizational actors at both the national and regional levels.[20] The modified power-dependence framework is of direct relevance, since each actor must manage a changed resource dependence flowing from the interaction of economic crisis with their specific objectives and resource requirements as constrained by overarching rules of the game. Complex patterns, whether pluralist, corporate pluralist, or corporatist, result from the confluence of the actions and intentions of private organizations and public agencies at the national and subnational levels of the polity. It is important to stress that neither center nor region can be treated as monoliths. Conflict lines based on institutional and political

---

[19] The ambiguous position of field administrative officials with respect to other parts of the state and to their societal setting is the subject of a long, well-established literature dating back at least to the work of Max Weber. See inter alia P. Selznick, *TVA and the Grassroots* (Berkeley: University of California Press, 1949); Tarrow, *Between Center and Periphery*, and J. Worms, "Le Préfet et ses notables," *Sociologie du Travail* 3 (July–September 1966): 249–75.

[20] On the task of actor designation, see F. Frey, "The Problem of Actor Designation in Political Analysis," *Comparative Politics* 17 (January 1985): 127–52.

divisions create the potential for competition, and under certain circumstances cooperation, among actors both within and across national and regional levels. The specific profile of the territorial imperative is a product of the intersection of regional and national actors' objectives and resource requirements.

The analytical framework applied: autarchy versus collaboration

To analyze political responses to economic crisis, the observer must construct a typology of alternatives or strategies, and a framework to interpret the selection of alternatives.[21] With the modified power-dependence model, the basic elements of the interpretive framework are in place. What remains to be outlined is a parsimonious way to conceptualize the alternatives available to subnational and national actors confronted with the decline of a regional economy. I cast these alternatives in terms of whether these actors, as they respond to economic crisis conditions, seek to manage their resource dependence through autarchic or collaborative approaches.

In coping with the problems thrown up by regional crisis, central government actors may adopt *inclusive* approaches to subnational actors in their policy sector, and seek to establish some degree of routinized relations with them. Or, national officials may seek to insulate the policy-making process from subnational claimants, adopting an *exclusionary* approach. In the regions, actors can purse *noncooperative* strategies with respect to other subnational actors – a parochial attitude of "every locality for itself." Conversely, *cooperative* behavior on the part of indigenous actors may occur. As the following sections will underscore, the selection of a strategy by an actor is rarely the product of factors indigenous to one particular level. In other words, whether a subnational actor views its regional environment in cooperative or noncooperative terms will depend not just on intraregional factors but also on what central government agencies are doing.

The resulting mixes of national and subnational strategies produce differing probabilities associated with the emergence of the patterns of interaction outlined in the previous section. Figure 2.2 depicts four possible outcomes. When the actions of central and peripheral actors are mutually reinforcing, the patterns ought to approach the poles of the continuum outlined in Figure 2.1. That is, if government officials pursue inclusive strategies vis-à-vis their regional environment, and subnational interests pursue cooperative activities, corporatist patterns are

---

[21] See Gourevitch, *Politics in Hard Times*, Chapter 1.

	Central actors	
	Inclusive	Exclusionary
Cooperative	sectoral corporatism	corporate pluralism
Non-cooperative	corporate pluralism	pluralism

Local/regional actors

Figure 2.2. *Strategy mixes and predicted patterns of interaction*

likely to appear. Similarly, if central actors adopt an exclusionary posture toward groups that are themselves practicing noncooperative activities within their regions, pluralism is a highly probable outcome. When central and regional approaches work at cross-purposes, corporate pluralist patterns are likely to emerge. Figure 2.2 suggests possible nuances in the category of corporate pluralism. The pattern of interaction produced by an inclusive central approach and a noncooperative regional approach may differ substantially from that generated by the opposite mix. In the absence of a lead from central government, for example, subnational actors may find it impossible to overcome those hurdles to cooperation outlined earlier, and the resulting attributes of the interaction pattern – number, variety, hierarchy, etc. – will depart significantly from those instances where central policymakers provide direction and control.

This applied framework of analysis suggests three related questions. First, do the predicted associations between strategy mixes and patterns of interaction depicted in Figure 2.2 actually obtain? Second, what influences the adoption of certain strategies by national and subnational actors? And, third, what consequences flow from these patterns of interaction? Before proceeding with the case comparisons, which address these questions, some preliminary ruminations on the latter two are in order.

The determinants of subnational strategies
A regional or local actor may encounter difficulties as it attempts to manage resource dependence on its own. Its political clout at the center is often insufficient to attract the sustained attention of governmental

policymakers, and its efforts to attract mobile investment may founder on cutthroat competition from other local and regional actors. In such circumstances, intraregional cooperation, or at a minimum the elimination of overt, zero-sum competition, can serve strategic functions. Through joint efforts, actors can pyramid resources like information and organizational attributes, which in turn can generate a greater capacity to pursue objectives by, for example, making possible the identification of policy alternatives or increasing the efficiency of responses by distributing tasks and duties. The symbolic value of cooperative action is also potentially important, particularly where central government is concerned.[22]

Yet the prospects for collaborative action among subnational actors appear remote, since the long-range benefits gained from a reversal of regional decline resemble public goods.[23] If new firms, public works, and additional job opportunities can be secured for the region through either the economic or the political market, the benefits generated – a "recuperating" or "healthy" regional economy – are in theory equally available to all in the region. From the standpoint of local and regional actors initially contemplating cooperation, collective action is thus subject to several familiar constraints. Organizing efforts may have difficulty succeeding in the absence of resource-rich actors with substantial interests in the benefits of collective action. Should such major actors be present and the collective-action problem overcome, the objectives of joint activities may be severely biased in their favor, leading to divergences between collective goals and the actual median preferences of members. Group coordination and cooperation, once established, may suffer from the free-rider problem, resulting in a suboptimal provision of the public good.

Collective action problems tell only the first half of the story. Once regional collaboration is up and running, new and very different strains are likely to emerge. Ongoing efforts to cope with regional economic problems involve the pursuit of means selected from a standard pool of possibilities: the improvement of local and regional infrastructure, particularly transport, communications, and industrial sites; the attraction of new industry and employment opportunities; and the upgrading and retraining of the regional labor force. These objectives can in fact gen-

---

[22] See T. Moe, *The Organization of Interests* (Chicago: The University of Chicago Press, 1980), 62, for an excellent treatment of these issues.

[23] "Any good can be viewed as a collective good for some set of individuals if, once it is supplied by one or more individuals in the set, it is automatically available for consumption by *all* individuals in the set." Ibid., 22. Italics in original. For the major theoretical contribution to the political economy of public goods, see M. Olson, *The Logic of Collective Action* (Cambridge, Mass.: Harvard University Press, 1971), 14–16.

erate regionwide benefits through growth and employment multipliers. However, the very process by which such objectives are realized is discrete, exclusionary, and highly divisible. New plants cannot be divided up and parceled out among the various interests and localities within a region. Footloose enterprises, and the jobs, tax revenues, and multiplier effects they create, must situate themselves in a specific location at the end of the day. The same applies to infrastructure development projects. The locational specificity of new development raises the specter of intraregional distributional conflicts, which may ultimately impede efforts to sustain cooperative relations. For example, members dissatisfied with their perceived share of the benefits may withhold or withdraw support in favor of unilateral action. Those who continue to support a collective approach may find their capacity to coordinate and prioritize among competing policy alternatives sharply diminished, since choices that favor one locality – and hence a subset of groups – over others within the region are politically costly.[24]

Thus, cooperative action among regional actors is by no means assured. Regions are populated by several varieties of actors, only some of which have explicit territorial ties to the region. Quite apart from the problem of generating a common regional interest among these actors, the creation of cooperative arrangements is subject to a variety of strains and obstacles. As such, the potential for pluralism at the regional level is high. What factors within the region encourage local and regional groups to respond cooperatively? Or, to recast the question in terms of the preceding discussion, what factors raise or lower the various barriers to cooperative action outlined before?

If institutional slack is available to local authorities, trade unions, and other relevant regional actors, a coordinated response to decline becomes more probable because the costs to regional actors will not be prohibitive. Institutional actors like local governments "typically command substantial and diverse resources and within limits a meaningful fraction may be allocated to policy-relevant tasks if and when these are perceived as useful to the maintenance and enhancement of the enterprise."[25] Of course, the regional distribution of institutional resources

---

[24] As a case in point, the development objectives of subnational actors often entail a set of spatial priorities for the intraregional allocation of benefits and development potential. All localities and subregions may be accorded equal footing. Conversely, the worst-off areas may be targeted for special attention. Actors may go so far as to draw up a system of spatial triage, in which only those areas with the greatest economic potential are allowed to receive, or to compete for, new investment. Due to the strains placed on interactor cooperation, spatial triage may be impossible to implement, however necessary it might be from an economic or political standpoint.

[25] R. Salisbury, "Interest Representation," *American Political Science Review* 78(March 1984): 68. He argues that institutions have greater access to resources

is not constant across cases; it varies according to the political and economic structure of the region in question. To the extent that certain actors possess clear-cut advantages in material and political resources, expertise, and information, they may be able to assume a leadership role in defining the regional problem, proposing solutions, and organizing the response – that is, in curbing the emergence of noncooperative strategies. Whether the principal actor is a regional government or a business association may determine ultimately whether competitive pluralism can be overcome. Consequently, the researcher must establish the resource hierarchy of actors in the region, which will provide an indication of the ability of any one actor or subset of actors to influence regional patterns of interaction.[26]

British and German regions differ across any number of dimensions that could influence the regional resource hierarchy. One notable distinction involves the structure of intergovernmental relations. Whether decision-making powers are devolved to subnational representative authorities or delegated to field administrative personnel of the central government can affect the distribution of resources in the region and the rules of the game according to which patterned interactions unfold. If state and local governments are used by central government primarily as administrative agents implementing central directives, and this relationship is established by statutory or constitutional law, then opportunities at the base to forge cooperative relationships will depend largely on the attitude of central officials. Conversely, if subnational governments enjoy broad, independent authority to undertake actions in their particular bailiwick, the impetus for cooperative arrangements with other actors in the region shifts to local and state government officials.

According to the principle of *ultra vires*, British local authorities "have no general competence to act for the benefit of the populations within their jurisdictions."[27] In the absence of a specific grant of competence from Parliament, local authorities are proscribed from undertaking actions requiring the expenditure of public funds. This is not to suggest that local authorities are toothless in the area of economic policy-making; indeed, numerous legislative acts have expanded their powers

and are more insulated from membership concerns, factors which may facilitate purposive entry into the political arena.

[26] The hierarchy is, of course, as much subject to external influence – central government policies that confer status and privileges on certain groups, for example – as it is to internal (i.e., regional) factors. This will be analyzed below. Of course, to specify the regional hierarchy in a given region is no mean feat. The best one can achieve is an ordinal ranking of actors, based on an interpretive analysis of their actions with respect to the policy problem and to one another.

[27] N. Johnson and A. Cochrane, *Economic Policy-making by Local Authorities in Britain and Western Germany* (London: George Allen & Unwin, 1981), 12.

in this field over the years. Still, the default value for British local government is zero. In contrast, the German Länder have considerable administrative resources at their disposal, as well as independent powers to tax and spend. Both the Länder and local authorities (*Gemeinden*) enjoy a constitutional right to engage in economic policy-making on behalf of their areas in the absence of federal law.[28] Although these impulses have been constrained by the emergence of joint policy-making frameworks involving federal and state governments, there is clearly greater room for independent initiative at the base than in Britain.[29]

Based on these constitutional differences, one would expect German subnational public authorities to play a much more active role in structuring the relations among actors in the region than their British counterparts. In particular, the activities of the Land (state) government with respect to its own organizational environment will be pivotal in shaping both horizontal and vertical interactions. At the national level, German policymakers are likely to face a much greater coordination deficit than policymakers in the British unitary system, since they operate within a federal system that presents them with a multitude of semiautonomous subnational governments. Ultimately, this will affect their ability to structure and manage interregional demands.[30]

Similarly, the relations between subnational party associations and their national organizations can have a significant impact on the hierarchy of actors within the region and by implication any resulting interaction patterns. If local and regional party organizations serve as administrative extensions of the national office, which transmit the national party program to the electorate and "get out the vote," then they may hold little attraction for subnational actors interested in using party organizations to inject economic demands into decision-making arenas at the national level.[31] The resulting top-down party structure can limit the extent to which elected representatives and local party organizations become involved in intraregional group interactions. The situation ought

---

[28] K. P. Wild, "Stellung und Aufgaben der Länder," in *Handbuch der regionalen Wirtschaftsförderung*, ed. H. H. Eberstein, (Köln: Verlag Dr. Otto Schmidt KG, 1978), 1.

[29] The term *Politikverflechtung* is used to describe the practice of joint policy-making. See F. Scharpf, B. Reissert, and F. Schnabel, *Politikverflechtung* (Kronberg/Ts.: Scriptor Verlag GmbH, 1976).

[30] For a similar argument, see L. J. Sharpe, "Central Coordination and the Policy Network," *Political Studies* 33(September 1985): 361–81.

[31] Similar arguments are made in the context of urban development programs in J. Webman, *Reviving the Industrial City* (New Brunswick: Rutgers University Press, 1982). As we shall see, blockages of this nature in party linkages to the center may create strong incentives for regional groups to seek a relationship with the bureaucracy for lack of a better alternative.

to be very different where party organizations at the subnational level
retain a degree of autonomy.

Regional party organizations in Britain conform to the top-down
model, serving in the main as agents of the center.[32] In the Federal
Republic of Germany, by way of contrast, the middle tier of government
provides for a significant measure of party autonomy at the subnational
level. Although state party organizations are closely tuned to the pulse
of national issues and elections, they possess substantial reserves of
organizational and political independence, due to the simple fact that
power can be won or lost at the Land level as well as in Bonn.[33]

Other local and regional actors are subject to similar constraints,
which can limit the ready availability of resources and therefore their
role in the region. For example, the relationships between subnational
trade union and business organizations and their respective peak associations take on particular significance. To the extent that business and
labor interests are organized hierarchically, and participate in concert
with state officials in national decision-making structures, a subnational
focus for these functional interest representatives may be proscribed,
or at least severely constrained. Peak associations would have an interest
in shielding the complex bargains forged in national tripartite negotiating
sessions from defection or noncompliance by members at the subnational
level. Thus, the strength of national level corporatism may sharply constrain cooperative action at the subnational level. Since neither Germany
nor Britain has been characterized by particularly strong or enduring
corporatist arrangements at the national level – the obvious cross-
national differences notwithstanding – this relationship is unlikely to materialize.

On the other hand, the internal hierarchy of labor and business does
differ across the two national cases, and this will affect the level of
resources and autonomy available to local and regional branches in each
country. In Britain, producer group linkages between national and subnational levels involve a limited number of participants: the Trades
Union Congress (TUC), representing organized labor; and the Confederation of British Industry (CBI), which speaks for business interests.
The TUC, among the weaker of the European trade union federations,
has eight regional councils in England and one each in Wales, Scotland,
and Northern Ireland. The system of regional councils was relatively

---

[32] D. Wilson, *Power and Party Bureaucracy in Britain* (London: Saxon House,
Lexington Books, 1975); Webman, *Reviving the Industrial City*, 140.
[33] G. Fabritius, *Politik und Wahlen* (Meisenheim am Glan: Verlag Anton Hain,
1978), 74; and J. Risse, "Parteiorganisation im Bundesstaat," *Der Staat*
2(1982), 239–57. State politics and state elections in the Federal Republic are
permeated with national issues and personalities; see G. Lehmbruch, *Parteienwettbewerb im Bundesstaat* (Stuttgart: Verlag W. Kohlhammer, 1976), 95.

understated until 1979, when the TUC General Council decided to bolster its regional apparatus as part of a wide-ranging reform effort "to mobilize the strength of the trade union Movement as a whole in implementing agreed strategies."[34] Each regional council received a full-time administrative staff, headed by a regional secretary, and was encouraged to play a greater role in its region. The Confederation of British Industry (CBI) is the main representative of business at the regional level in Britain. The CBI has ten regional offices in England and one each in Wales, Scotland, and Northern Ireland. Characterized as "listening posts for Centre Point [Headquarters in London],"[35] the CBI's regional structure has "varied throughout the years, usually as a function of the availability of cash."[36] The regional offices retain a significant measure of autonomy from London headquarters for position taking, initiatives, and networking with other local and regional groups. Repeated attempts since 1967 to strengthen the regional machinery notwithstanding, "the territorially based system of business representation is generally less significant than the sectorally based system."[37]

In Germany, the Deutscher Gewerkschaftsbund (DGB) and its state branches represent the interests of organized labor. The territorial structure of the DGB extends to the level of the county; above this level, nine Landesbezirke (regional districts) correspond to state boundaries, with certain exceptions.[38] The regional districts provide a range of services for members and represent the interests of organized labor to state governments. Three separate associations represent business interests in the Federal Republic of Germany, only one of which assumes responsibility for the local and regional interests of firms: the Deutscher Industrie- und Handelstag (DIHT) and its eighty-one constituent Industrie- und Handelskammern (IHKs), or Chambers of Industry and Commerce.[39] As quasipublic bodies with tasks and responsibilities de-

---

[34] Trades Union Congress, *The Organization, Structure, and Services of the TUC* (London: Congress House, 1981), 3.

[35] Official with the Northern Office of the CBI, Newcastle upon Tyne, 9 December 1985. Interview with the author. A complete list of interviews appears in the bibliography.

[36] Official with the CBI; London, 13 July 1984. Interview with the author.

[37] W. Grant, *Business and Politics in Britain* (London: Macmillan Education Ltd., 1987), 164. It should be noted that local chambers of commerce have also taken on active roles in the local economy; their importance varies from place to place.

[38] See A. Markovits, *The Politics of the West German Trade Unions* (Cambridge: Cambridge University Press, 1986), 18–23. NRW accounts for almost one third of all DGB members. As we shall see in Chapter 5, the main protagonist for the interests of organized labor in the Saarland is not the DGB, but the Board of Labor (Arbeitskammer des Saarlandes).

[39] The other two associations are the Federation of German Industry (BDI), which represents the interests of business not directly associated with collective bar-

fined by federal and state laws, the IHKs are responsible for "safe-guarding the interests of member firms, promoting the local economy, and having equal regard for the economic interests of individual sectors or firms."[40] They administer vocational and apprenticeship training pro-grams, issue certificates of origin and other licenses to business concerns, and preside over the operation of business arbitration courts. In return for statutory regulation, the federal government grants the chambers a captive membership – all firms liable for business taxes are legally ob-ligated to join their local chamber as dues-paying members. In short, the IHKs enjoy a legal status that distinguishes them from garden variety voluntary interest groups, as well as most sectoral business interest as-sociations. The IHKs also operate with absolute autonomy from the national umbrella association. The DIHT is a purely voluntary orga-nization established by the chambers to represent them at the national level. It exercises no authority over individual IHKs, and adopts as a matter of practice noncontroversial, lowest-common-denominator po-sitions to avoid conflict with the members.[41] In sum, functional interest groups in Britain and Germany are not equally placed to influence group-state interactions in the region.

Alongside the factors that influence the hierarchy of subnational ac-tors, the economic characteristics of the region can also have an impact on collaborative or competitive organizational behavior. The timing and pace of economic decline, dimensions of variation that cut across the British and German regional cases, are significant. An early, rapid col-lapse of the regional economy can create widespread, acute resource dependencies and overwhelm the divergences of interest among regional and local actors that usually hinder collaborative action. The result is a coalition of desperation not likely to emerge under less pressing circum-stances. The particular mix of industries in the region is also relevant. Since not all economic sectors within a problem region will experience the same stresses induced by decline, organizations dependent upon different sectors may come to divergent evaluations of the general re-gional situation. This can inhibit the development of regional solidari-ties. The impact of other economic factors is much more difficult to predict in advance. A noteworthy example is the regional structure of ownership and control. A high concentration of nationalized industries or branch plants in a region may frustrate cooperative interactions in the absence of a lead from government managers or parent companies.

gaining, and Confederation of German Employers' Associations (BDA), which represents employers' interests in collective bargaining.
[40] J. Weber, *Die Interessengruppen im politischen System der Bundesrepublik Deutschland* (Stuttgart: Verlag W. Kohlhammer GmbH, 1977), 101.
[41] Senior official in the DIHT, Bonn, 4 December 1986. Interview with the author.

Table 2.1. *The regional dimension of British general elections, 1931–86*

Election	United Kingdom			North East			West Midlands		
	C	L	Other	C	L	Other	C	L	Other
1931	55.2	30.6	14.2	44.4	40.2	15.4	*	*	*
1935	47.8	38.0	14.2	36.5	46.0	17.5	*	*	*
1945	36.2	48.0	15.8	29.1	55.6	15.4	*	*	*
1950	43.4	46.1	10.5	37.2	54.6	8.1	42.8	51.2	6.0
1951	48.0	48.8	3.2	42.0	56.8	1.1	46.8	52.5	0.7
1955	49.7	46.4	3.9	43.9	55.1	1.0	49.2	49.4	1.4
1959	49.4	43.8	6.8	43.8	54.1	2.1	50.7	45.9	3.4
1964	43.4	44.1	12.5	39.4	55.4	5.2	46.8	45.2	8.1
1966	41.9	48.0	10.1	37.2	58.4	4.3	44.7	50.7	4.6
1970	46.4	43.1	10.5	41.3	54.7	4.0	50.5	44.9	4.5
1974 (Feb.)	37.9	37.2	24.9	35.0	51.0	14.0	40.7	43.9	15.4
1974 (Oct.)	35.8	39.2	25.0	29.9	52.2	17.9	37.1	44.6	18.4
1979	43.9	36.9	19.2	36.0	50.2	13.9	46.7	40.9	12.4
1983	42.4	27.6	30.0	34.6	40.2	25.1	45.0	31.2	23.8

Notes: C = Conservative Party; L = Labour Party. Figures are percentages of votes cast. Percentages within categories may not total 100 due to rounding. Data are not presented for the West Midlands between 1931 and 1945 since they are not germane to the period of study.
Source: F. W. S. Craig, *British Parliamentary Election Results* (Chichester: Parliamentary Research Services, various editions), and D. Butler and G. Butler, *British Political Facts 1900–1985* (London: Macmillan Press, 1986), 225. Author's calculations and presentation.

The depth of regional party political cleavages represents another factor that can influence the emergence of cooperative strategies among subnational interests. Irrespective of resource requirements, the propensity for cooperation among these actors will vary with the partisan cast of their objectives.[42] Tables 2.1 and 2.2 depict the different balances of party strengths within the two sets of regional cases. The North East of England has been a bastion of Labour support since 1935, while in the West Midlands, a much more level playing field exists for the two major political parties. The German regions suggest mirror images of single-party dominance. Until 1985, the Saarland was the fiefdom of the Christian Democrats, while North Rhine–Westphalia has been the preserve of the Social Democrats since 1966. These interregional differences allow one to test whether the one-party hegemony of the North East and the two German Länder is more conducive to stable, cooperative

[42] The level of regional party competitiveness can also determine whether productive relationships with the national party apparatuses can be established. Such vertical alliances through party channels resemble the parentela relationship described in LaPalombara, *Interest Groups and Italian Politics.*

44   The territorial imperative

Table 2.2. *Landtag election results in the Saarland and NRW, 1958–86*

North Rhine–Westphalia					Saarland				
Election	SPD	CDU	FDP	Others	Election	SPD	CDU	FDP	Others
1958	39.2	**50.5**	7.1	3.2	1960	30.0	**36.6**	**13.8**	19.6
1962	43.3	**46.4**	**6.9**	3.4	1965	40.7	**42.7**	8.3	8.3
1966[a]	49.5	**42.8**	7.4	0.3	1970	40.8	**47.8**	4.4[b]	7.0
1970	**46.1**	46.3	5.5	2.1	1975	41.8	**49.1**	7.4	1.7
1975	**45.1**	47.1	**6.7**	1.1	1980	45.4	**44.0**	**6.9**	3.7
1980	**48.1**	43.2	4.98[b]	3.7	1985	**49.2**	37.3	10.0	3.5
1985	**52.1**	36.5	6.0	5.5					

Note: Figures in boldface signify the governing parties (or party) in the aftermath of the election.
[a] The CDU–FDP coalition was replaced by a SPD–FDP coalition within a few months of the election.
[b] The party did not surpass the 5 percent threshold, and thus failed to gain access to the Landtag.
Sources: U. von Alemann, ed., *Parteien und Wahlen in Nordrhein-Westfalen* (Köln: Verlag W. Kohlhammer, 1985), G. Ritter and M. Neihuss, *Wahlen in der Bundesrepublik Deutschland* (Munich: Verlag C. H. Beck, 1987), 147.

strategies than is the evenly balanced partisan situation in the West Midlands.

To explain the strategies adopted by subnational actors, we must go beyond the region to incorporate the influence of central government, which takes several related yet conceptually distinct forms. Public policies will strongly influence interactions in the regions, since they define the realm of the possible for subnational actors. As such, the world of policy is much like the world of fashion: Those who determine the width of ties live in Paris, not the provinces. For example, the way in which central government defines the regional problem and transmits this to local and regional actors may influence profoundly the definition of the problem at the base. If this is true, then the range of options open to regional interests will be constrained. Similarly, if a monopoly of policy instrumentation exists at the national level, as in a unitary state, then regional actors may forsake coordinated objectives and strategies in favor of the competitive pursuit of central government largesse.

Additional policy-related factors at the national level can impinge on the strategies adopted by subnational actors. All central governments operate any number of regionally relevant public policies, and their degree of coordination and relative priorities can have an impact on subnational strategies, a phenomenon captured by the notion of "sectional centralism."[43] In all modern administrative systems, specific parts of the central bureaucracy are responsible for specific government activities. The resulting division of labor manifests itself in the form of distinct policies that link separate policy-making agencies at the top with their respective clienteles at the base. This raises the possibility that functional compartmentalization at the center will be mirrored faithfully in the localities and regions, generating spatial interest compartmentalization there. "The vertical fracturing of the state," explains Samuels, "results in an equally fragmented center extending to the periphery, thereby exacerbating existing competitive relationships and rendering localities incapable of coordinated, cooperative action."[44]

The emphasis here is on the word "possibility." A fragmented center may in fact result in increased opportunities for subnational actors, acting in concert, to penetrate and then influence the incoherent national policy process on a number of fronts. If this is the case, a reduction in the level of sectional centralism may render penetration by local and regional groups more difficult, or at least force the access point higher up the administrative hierarchy. Whatever the case, the extent of sectional centralism can be held in check if central policymakers effectively coordinate related policies. While severe asymmetries in the priorities accorded to various policies will have little effect on the degree of fragmentation at the center, they too can reduce the degree of fragmentation transmitted to the region by leaving only a few policies politically and/ or financially significant to local and regional actors.

Eisinger, in his study of local and state economic development programs in the United States, posits a connection between the chaotic welter of federal programs to assist regional economies and the absence of a stable, organized development constituency.[45] In both Britain and Germany, by contrast, nationally administered regional assistance programs, flanked by sometimes complementary and sometimes contradictory macroeconomic and industrial policies, have existed for several decades; this should provide ample opportunity to establish whether organized constituencies have emerged in response to these sustained regional policy initiatives.

Finally, the government officials who administer policies for the regions must be seen as potentially active shapers of their policy environment. We are by now all familiar with "the reluctant organization pursued by public officials eager to elicit organizational involvement in governmental policy-making,"[46] or even the nonexistent organization

---

[43] Samuels, *The Politics of Regional Policy*, 244–5.
[44] Ibid.
[45] Eisinger, *The Entrepreneurial State*, 122.
[46] J. P. Olsen, *Organized Democracy* (Oslo: Universitetsforlaget, 1983), 182.

called into being by central officials to serve similar purposes. That is, quite aside from the policy-based incentives facing subnational actors, officials themselves reach out to influence actor behavior directly. The impact of their overtures will depend on the resource requirements of subnational actors and the extent to which these can be satisfied through exchange relationships with government officials.

In summary, certain favorable circumstances, like the presence of locally or regionally controllable resources, the absence of divisive political cleavages, or the benign effects of government policy and administrative practice, can help override the strong underlying tendencies toward noncooperation among subnational actors. That said, we are unlikely to unlock the secrets of the territorial imperative if we remain ensconced at the subnational level. Not surprisingly, we must move up the ladder and examine the factors which motivate national policymakers to adopt inclusive or exclusionary stances toward the regions.

The determinants of national strategies

Public officials have interests and preferences tied to their specific policy responsibilities, and will seek to advance these interests as they interact with other governmental agencies and with groups.[47] The way in which national officials perceive their policy clienteles will be a function of the specific goals they hope to achieve through policy and the resources they need to see those objectives through. These perceptions lead to the pursuit of inclusive or exclusionary strategies vis-à-vis regional actors.

National policymakers may be motivated entirely by electoral goals. The basis of representation in a modern democracy is geographic. The basis of regional policy is also geographic. Put the two together, and one can easily envision a world in which parties-in-government seek to maintain their hold on power by means of the targeted allocation and reallocation of policy benefits. Simply speaking, benefits will be awarded to supportive and potentially supportive geographical areas and withheld from unsupportive areas.[48] If this is true, then the degree of "symmetry" between majority formulas at the center and those obtaining at the regional level should provide a reasonably accurate indication of the

---

[47] This position is in line with the work of Krasner, Nordlinger, and other proponents of a state-centric approach. Krasner, for example, focuses on the preferences of central decision makers, which "must be related to general societal goals, persist over time, and have a consistent ranking of importance in order to justify using the term national interest." Krasner, *Defending the National Interest*, 14–15. See also G. J. Ikenberry, "The Irony of State Strength," *International Organization 40* (Winter 1986): 105–37.

[48] Tarrow, for example, uncovers evidence of electoral payoffs to the periphery. Tarrow, *Between Center and Periphery*, 237.

Table 2.3. *The partisan distribution of seats in the House of Commons, 1931–86*

Election	United Kingdom			North East			West Midlands		
	C	L	Other	C	L	Other	C	L	Other
1931	470	52	89	23	3	7	*	*	*
1935	387	154	74	16	14	4	*	*	*
1945	197	393	50	7	27	0	*	*	*
1950	298	315	12	7	27	0	20	32	0
1951	321	295	9	9	25	0	20	32	0
1955	345	277	8	10	24	0	22	32	0
1959	365	258	7	13	21	0	29	25	0
1964	304	317	9	7	27	0	25	29	0
1966	253	364	13	8	31	0	22	32	0
1970	330	288	12	10	29	0	30	24	0
1974 (Feb.)	297	301	37	6	30	1	21	33	0
1974 (Oct.)	277	319	39	6	30	1	19	36	0
1979	339	269	27	6	30	1	29	26	0
1983	397	209	44	5	23	2	36	22	0

Notes: C = Conservative Party; L = Labour Party. Data are not presented for the West Midlands between 1931 and 1945 since they are not germane to the period of study.
Source: Craig, *British Parliamentary Election Results.* Author's calculations and presentation.

terminus of central largesse, insofar as the region represents a plum or a pit in the majoritarian strategies of central party officials.[49]

Interesting differences within and across the regional cases surface with respect to this dimension. The size of the British regional contingents in the House of Commons varies substantially (see Table 2.3). The North East has sent between thirty and thirty-nine MPs to Parliament: a percentage of the total House that ranges from 4.6 (1983) to 6.2 (1966). The West Midlands, a more populous region, is entitled to a much larger delegation, totaling between fifty-two and fifty-eight members. These figures represent a correspondingly higher percentage of Commons membership, from a low of 8.3 in 1950 to a high of 8.9 in 1983. Purely on the basis of numbers, then, the West Midlands should play a greater role in the majoritarian calculations of British governments. As for the symmetry between regional and national party strengths, the West Midlands has backed the winner nine times out of eleven, while the North East has done so just eight out of fourteen

[49] R. M. Punnett, "Regional Partisanship and the Legitimacy of British Governments 1868–1983," *Parliamentary Affairs* 37 (Spring 1984): 142.

times. This too underlines the political centrality of the Midlands. In fact, the pattern of the North East since 1945 has been to back the Labour Party through thick and thin, meaning it is in office when Labour wins and out of office when the party loses (see Table 2.1).

Whether these characteristics will induce national politicians to skew the flow of resources from the center to the provinces remains to be seen. There is plenty of circumstantial evidence to suggest that territory is not a particularly salient aspect of British party politics. Historically, both major political parties have been decidedly national parties – to paraphrase Sharpe, "centralized parties for a centralized system."[50] Moreover, since English MPs have not developed strong regional identities and belong to a parliament ill-equipped to handle English regional issues on a consistent basis, they may not pressure government for regional favors in the first place.[51] Combined, these various factors render the delivery of benefits via party channels in Britain problematic.

In the Federal Republic, the principal political connection between the federal and state levels leads through the Bundesrat. The voting composition of the upper house is comprised of voting blocks from the sitting state governments whose size is determined by population; as the largest Land in the country, NRW is represented by a five-member delegation, while the Saarland sends a delegation of three members. The direct relationship between the composition of governing parties in the states and the balance of party strengths in the Bundesrat is of critical importance to the federal government, which must obtain the upper house's approval for a growing percentage of legislation. Thus, the composition of the Bundesrat generates majoritarian calculations for the federal government that are not present in Britain. The degree of symmetry between state and federal governing majorities is depicted in Table 2.4. There are distinct periods of partisan overlap between governing coalitions in Bonn and those in Düsseldorf and Saarbrücken. In contrast to Great Britain, where one-party majority governments guarantee that regions are either in or out of office, the prevalence of coalition formulas involving the Free Democrats (FDP) ensures a continuity of partisan relations between center and periphery. During the thirty-year period depicted, NRW governments had political links to the center in all but five; for the Saarland, party connections to Bonn obtained in twenty-five of the thirty years. These clear opportunities

---

[50] L. J. Sharpe, "The Labour Party and the Geography of Inequality," in *The Politics of the Labour Party*, ed. D. Kavanagh (London: George Allen & Unwin, 1982), 150. See also J. G. Bulpitt, *Territory and Power in the United Kingdom* (Manchester: Manchester University Press, 1983).

[51] J. McDonald, "Members of Parliament," in *Regional Government in England*, ed. Hogwood and Keating, 233; R. L. Borthwick, "When the Short Cut May Be a Blind Alley," *Parliamentary Affairs* 31 (Spring 1978): 207.

Table 2.4. *Governing majorities at the federal and state levels in Germany*

Election period	Federal government	North Rhine–Westphalia	Saarland
1957–61	CDU/CSU	CDU	CDU CDU-FDP
1961–5	CDU/CSU-FDP	CDU CDU-FDP	CDU-FDP
1965–9	CDU/CSU-FDP CDU/CSU-SPD	CDU-FDP SPD-FDP	CDU-FDP
1969–72	SPD-FDP	SPD-FDP	CDU-FDP CDU
1972–6	SPD-FDP	SPD-FDP	CDU CDU-FDP
1976–80	SPD-FDP	SPD-FDP	CDU-FDP
1980–3	SPD-FDP CDU/CSU-FDP	SPD	CDU-FDP
1983–7	CDU/CSU-FDP	SPD	CDU-FDP SPD

Note: Second tier figures depict changes in the governing coalition during the national electoral period in question.

notwithstanding, whether such partisan links are sufficient to prompt Bonn governments to include or exclude these Länder on the basis of their political utility remains an open question.

Thus, in both countries the advancement of purely electoral preferences by national policymakers vis-à-vis the regions will be constrained by the nature of political and institutional linkages that connect center and provinces. From the standpoint of mesolevel patterns of interaction, an additional observation is warranted. While an unvarnished electoral calculus will determine which regions are treated inclusively and which are not, policymakers may be relatively unconcerned about *intra*regional relationships (cooperative or competitive) among interests clamoring for regional policy benefits.

While the incentives for central officials to interpret the plight of the peripheries in terms of marginal electoral utility are ubiquitous, other considerations associated with the more mundane world of policy formulation and implementation can impinge upon their strategies toward subnational actors. In short, if central officials seek to make good policy, then they may in fact develop a keen interest in the structure and content of their potential policy clienteles. While there are many possible explanations for the blurring of the policymaker/clientele distinction, in most cases, an opening up of the implementation policy process occurs because central officials consciously engineer the change.

The adoption of inclusive or exclusionary strategies will depend in large part on the relative resource endowments of central officials. Central government officials, confronting a dearth of requisite information or technical capacity to implement and monitor policy programs, often will turn to target groups to ensure that the policy is carried out effectively. Regular consultation and participation can increase the legitimacy and stability of policies, particularly those which are either controversial or lack widespread popular support. Under certain circumstances, policymakers reach out to groups in order to exercise influence over future demands placed on government.[52] That is, granting even a highly circumscribed role in the policy process to the policy clientele is a means of bringing its demands in line with existing and anticipated constraints of a financial or political nature. The choice of inclusive or exclusionary strategies does not always rest entirely with central officials, it should be stressed. Groups in possession of substantial concentrations of resources, particularly ones that permit them to block or veto governmental initiatives, can force their way into an enhanced participatory role in the making of policy. In short, inclusion is often granted to policy clienteles under duress.

As a final note, the European Community, which "commands resources, distributes benefits, allocates markets, and adjudicates between conflicting interests,"[53] is capable of affecting the resource dependence of *both* national and subnational actors and therefore their strategies. The EC operates a number of regionally relevant programs, the most significant of which is the European Regional Development Fund (ERDF). Although the ERDF has been in place since 1975, it became an influential factor for national regional programs after a reform wave inaugurated in 1979. Between 1975 and 1987, expenditure on the fund as a percentage of the total EC budget almost doubled, from 4.8 percent to 9.1 percent.[54] While far below the amount devoted to the Common

---

[52] These various rationales for incorporating interest groups into the policy-making process are the subject of a vast literature. See inter alia Beer, *Modern British Politics;* A. Shonfield, *Modern Capitalism* (Oxford: Oxford University Press, 1966); and C. Offe, "The Attribution of Public Status to Interest Groups," in *Organizing Interests,* ed. Berger, 123–58.

[53] W. Wallace, "Europe as a Confederation," *Journal of Common Market Studies* 20(September–December 1982): 61.

[54] Commission of the European Communities, *The ERDF in Numbers,* 1987 (Luxembourg: Office for Official Publications of the European Communities, 1988).

Agricultural Program, these totals represented a marked upgrading of Community regional assistance.

Of far greater significance are the increased administrative powers assigned to the European Commission.[55] Before 1979, member states received ERDF expenditure allocations wholly on the basis of fixed national quotas negotiated by their national representatives in the Council of Ministers. The commission enjoyed little control over who got what and where, and in the end, its influence resided largely in its prerogative to deny approval to project applications.[56] Since 1979, the commission has claimed discretionary control over an increasingly larger portion of fund allocations, and has sought to redirect EC regional benefits to the neediest parts of the Community.[57] It has also elevated the importance of the official "regional development programmes," which member governments must have on file in Brussels in order to submit eligible applications to the fund. Members must submit detailed profiles of problem regions, lists of project proposals from local authorities and other public bodies, and medium-term development targets. The scope for a hands-on Community role also expanded with the move away from ad hoc, project-based assistance to a so-called programme contract approach, which seeks to promote coordinated projects and schemes that are implemented over a period of several years and are designed to attain clearly specified objectives within an assisted region.[58] ERDF reforms enacted in 1984 distinguish between programmes organized by the Community and those organized by the national governments, and specify that priority is to be given whenever possible to the former. The significance of this new emphasis lies in the potential for long-term, direct relationships between the commission and groups of subnational actors, particularly local and regional governments. The commission has promoted the new programme contract approach vigorously, sending delegations out into eligible regions throughout the Community to drum up interest and requiring national

[55] For an overview of the ERDF reforms of the 1980s, see H. W. Armstrong, "The Reform of the European Community Regional Policy," *Journal of Common Market Studies* 23(June 1985): 319–44; N. Vanhove and L. Klaassen, *Regional Policy: A European Approach* (Aldershot, Hampshire: Gower Publishing Co. Ltd., 1987). Another round of reforms were enacted in 1989; see Anderson, "Skeptical Reflections."

[56] J. Mawson, M. Martins, and J. Gibney, "The Development of the European Community Regional Policy," in *Regions in the European Community*, ed. M. Keating and B. Jones (Oxford: Clarendon Press, 1985), 30.

[57] In 1984, 91.1 percent of aid went to five countries: Italy (34.7%); the United Kingdom (26.7%); France (11.5%); Greece (11.3%); and Ireland (6.9%). This practice intensified after 1984. Commission of the European Communities, *European Regional Development Fund: 10th Annual Report (1984)* (Luxembourg: Office for Official Publications of the European Communities, 1985).

[58] Armstrong, "Community Regional Policy," 336.

governments to consult with local and regional authorities in the drafting of programme applications.

Parallel to the strengthening of the ERDF, the commission has made increasingly vigorous use of its competition policy powers under Articles 92 and 93 of the Rome Treaty to police member regional programs. Member governments contemplating new aid policies or alterations of existing ones must receive advance approval from Brussels before proceeding, and the commission has the power to use the European Court of Justice to enforce its decisions. The commission has been particularly keen to limit the geographical coverage of regional policy and the level of award rates in the wealthier member countries, above all the Federal Republic. As such, the interaction of EC regional and competition policies has reduced the ability of many member states to orient their policies to *intranational* economic disparities. On the one hand, the commission is increasing the resources and authority of its own regional policy; on the other, the commission is restricting the regional policy measures that certain member states may implement. These developments underscore the likely relevance of supranational influences on the strategies that national and subnational actors adopt to manage resource dependence under conditions of regional economic crisis.

To summarize, factors present at the subnational, national, and supranational levels can influence the extent to which central government officials formulate and implement policies directed at declining industrial regions in isolation or with the participation of affected interests in the regions. Whether national strategies combine with those of subnational actors to produce the predicted patterns of interaction remains to be seen, of course.

The consequences of pluralist, corporate pluralist, and corporatist patterns of interaction

What are the anticipated consequences of the mesolevel patterns identified before? Although a full treatment of this question must await the comparative case studies that follow, we are in a position to venture a few educated guesses.[59] Subnational actors typically seek resources from the center through party-parliamentary and/or bureaucratic channels. The traditional literature tends to cast an organization's choice between channels of access as a constrained utility-maximization exercise. For example, Finer proposes a "law of inverse proportion," which predicts a negative relationship between an interest group's use of party-

---

[59] From the present vantage point, it is difficult to predict the consequences of corporate pluralism. Since the outputs of the hybrid patterns will in all likelihood approximate those of pluralism and corporatism, it is appropriate to await the results of Chapters 4 and 5.

parliamentary and bureaucratic avenues of access to central policy-making arenas.[60] In other words, groups that employ partisan links to the center to acquire largesse will find it difficult to establish productive relations with a nonpartisan bureaucracy, and vice versa. It stands to reason that the prevailing pattern of interaction among subnational and national actors will render certain avenues more profitable, or less risky, than others. Specifically, there may be a strong correlation between pluralist patterns and the search for resources through parliamentary channels, while sectoral corporatism is more likely to lead subnational actors to opt strictly for bureaucratic channels of access.

Two competing hypotheses relate to the impact of pluralism on the efficacy of subnational responses. On the one hand, a pluralist system might produce a demand overload on national policymakers that results in a watering down of the spatial bias on which an effective regional policy depends. Numerous local and regional actors, pressing their particularistic claims on the state, may prompt government officials to extend assisted status to larger and larger portions of the country. On the other hand, pluralism might create opportunities for government officials to insulate the policy process. Particularly where government officials must decide between the competing claims of problem regions, a fragmented, competitive set of local and regional interests may be easier to ignore than a coherent, unified regional front. If we can find a relationship between pluralism and regional *inefficacy* at the center, measured in terms of below average shares of regional assistance or a lack of eligibility for policy benefits, then the consequences of pluralism may in fact be negative for regional interests.

Predictions about the effects of corporatist patterns are also complex. As discussed earlier, regional actors have an interest in exploiting the information or technical needs of central policymakers; to do this, these actors will seek to curb pluralism and replace it with more coordinated forms of interaction that improve their control over scarce, valued resources. To the extent that subnational organizations acquire a measure of control, or wield veto sanctions over policy implementation, they can gain access to the decision-making process and exercise influence. If their positional advantage is substantial enough, they may even be granted a formal role in the policy formulation and implementation process. Under particularly favorable conditions of resource exchange, subnational actors may be able to diversify their goals vis-à-vis the state and to open up new channels of interest intermediation. Corporatist access to policy-making arenas, however, is not necessarily costless for these actors. In a situation marked by substantial resource asymmetries

---

[60] S. Finer, *Anonymous Empire* (London: Pall Mall Press, 1966), 43.

in favor of the state, corporatist relations with government will lead to modifications of group interests and objectives, as well as to constraints on the forms of cooperation they pursue. If we can find a region in which pluralist patterns give way to corporatism with the help of government actions, we may be able to identify subsequent changes in the interests and policy demands of the local and regional actors. One might also expect to find a relationship between corporatist patterns and the stability of interorganizational relations, similar to the findings on national level corporatism.[61] Regional corporatism may impose intolerable strains on the internal cohesion of organizations; if this is the case, then one would expect corporatist patterns to be highly unstable and short-lived.

Problem logic, political logic, and the politics of regional crisis: a reprise

The modified power-dependence framework provides a powerful way to conceptualize politics in declining regions. Regional economies can be distinguished in terms of several structural attributes, including the mix of industries and the predominant pattern of ownership. Such variations will result in different mixes of actors, especially among labor and capital, and therefore different mixes of economic interests and resource bases in the region. The attendant problems associated with regional economic decline produce resource losses for a host of actors whose existence is anchored in the region – local and state authorities lose tax revenues, trade unions lose members, political representatives lose votes. In many cases, the losses are net to the region, as jobs and workers seek out more favorable economic conditions. Nevertheless, the resulting negative shift in resource dependence from actor to actor is not necessarily comparable. In other words, decline affects different actors differently, and is therefore likely to produce different interests and different perceptions of the urgency of the response from within the region. Moreover, the existing distribution of resources in the region, which is closely related to the overarching constitutional order, may open up or preclude certain options for actors, such as independent or autarchic responses to decline. The difficulty of changing that distribution, which involves amending critical rules of the game, will vary for subnational and national actors depending on the nature of the constitutional order. For example, national officials in a federal state will not enjoy the same range of discretion in changing the rules of the game as their counterparts in a unitary state.

---

[61] See Panitch, "The Development of Corporatism."

Furthermore, by casting the strategic alternatives in terms of cooperation or noncooperation at the subnational level, the framework allows
for a more refined characterization of the scale of territorial politics
within the region. To the extent that a majority of organizational interests in the region adopt cooperative approaches, the scope of political
activity coincides with the boundaries of the region. On the other hand,
should few or no actors of consequence perceive their resource needs
in collective terms, subregionalism or localism is the likely result. A
major question is whether there is a relationship between constitutional
order – federal or unitary – and the predominant territorial scope of
political activity.[62]

The power-dependence framework also provides insights into the circumstances in which subnational responses are likely to bear the imprint
of a partisan or governmental logic. To recall the discussion in the
introductory chapter, a problem logic-based explanation would attribute
any observed differences in regional responses to variations in the structural characteristics of the regional economy and the resulting problems
these generate. As for the two variants of political logic, a partisan logic
would explain the pattern of interactions among subnational groups and
national policymakers in terms of an electoral calculus, while a governmental logic would produce responses that flow from the political-
institutional characteristics of the region, such as its administrative attributes, its constitutional position in the broader polity, and regionally
relevant public policies.

The two political logics and their interrelationships are cast into sharp
relief by the modified power-dependence framework. These logics involve the exchange of different types of resources between national and
subnational actors. A response driven by partisan logic is characterized
by the straightforward exchange of spatially circumscribed political resources, namely votes, for central policy benefits. The regular exchange
of partisan resources will most likely be carried out through party-
parliamentary channels. Responses propeled by a governmental logic
rest on the exchange of information, political legitimacy, and organizational assets for government-provided benefits and, in some cases, a
role in the implementation of policy; these types of activities are most
easily carried out via bureaucratic avenues. Subnational responses will
be particularly effective when local and regional actors possess both
kinds of resources and face a government in need of both. However,
from the standpoint of subnational actors, these resources do not necessarily coincide and are not fungible. The territorial constitutional order

[62] For a review of the American literature dealing with the impact of "the invisible
walls of state boundaries" on political behavior, see Anton, *American Federalism*, 56.

will produce a distinctive distribution of resources relevant to a governmental logic, but the allocation may bear little relation to the distribution of partisan votes across the national space. Subnational actors in possession of the former resources, but lacking the latter, will face different constraints on action than those in possession of both, neither, or the reverse mix.

With the modified power-dependence framework, we are now in a position to begin the empirical analysis of regional responses to decline in Britain and Germany. The next chapter outlines the view from the top – national regional policy and the approaches of national policymakers in each country. It is followed by successive chapters that outline and compare subnational responses in two sets of regional cases.

3   Central governments and regional policy

Although regional disparities in growth and employment are a universal feature of industrial economies, there is no generally accepted theory of regional economic development, only a collection of partial and often contradictory ideas.[1] Traditional location factors, like the presence or absence of adequate infrastructure, skilled labor reserves, and markets, can determine whether firms decide to set up shop or to continue doing business in certain regions. To the extent that location factors are cumulatively negative or positive within a geographical area, regional stagnation or growth can result. The role of inherited industrial structure is also given considerable play. Through multiplier effects, a preponderance of fast-growing (declining) sectors can propel (restrain) the regional economy's overall growth rate. Other factors of importance include the overall performance of the macroeconomy, the role of urban markets, and the effects of governmental taxation and spending programs. Empirical research has established that few of these factors are completely irrelevant. As such, they suggest an imprecise set of prescriptions for national policymakers and regional interests. Like a collection of old folk remedies, they occasionally produce results, and therefore are difficult to dismiss out of hand.

Regional economic policy is the most transparent manner by which benefits are allocated to problem regions. The traditional rationale for a nationally administered regional economic policy is to promote interregional equity by inducing capital and labor to locate in areas which would not necessarily be chosen by investment decision makers.[2] Such programs seek to alleviate regional disparities in unemployment, to prevent the breakdown of communities caused by the outmigration of the indigenous population, and to ensure relatively equal life chances across the national territory. The canons of economic efficiency are also pressed into service to justify regional policy, particularly its role in curbing inflationary pressures in prosperous parts of the country by channeling investment and demand to regions with idle production capacity and labor reserves.

---

[1] H. Richardson, *Regional Growth Theory* (London: The Macmillan Press, 1973).

[2] Richardson, *Regional Economics*, 229. The literature on regional policy is simply vast, and no attempt is made to evaluate or summarize it here. For an excellent overview and bibliography, see H. Armstrong and J. Taylor, *Regional Economics and Policy* (New York: Philip Allan Publishers, 1985).

57

Regional policy creates spatial market biases by designating areas, either coextensive with the political region or not, within which certain actors and certain activities are eligible for state assistance. There are four basic instruments of regional policy: state industry, infrastructure provision, positive incentives, and negative incentives.[3] The first is a relatively underused regional policy instrument in Europe, prevalent only in Italy and Austria. The other three instruments are widely employed across western democracies. The provision of infrastructure – new roads, rail links, communications, and additional sites for industrial development – aims to correct deficiencies in regional location factors. Most regional policy instruments take the form of direct financial incentives to induce industry and/or labor to relocate. Positive incentives consist of capital grants, soft loans, accelerated depreciation allowances, tax concessions, and labor subsidies. Negative incentives and controls are designed to enhance the effects of existing positive incentives by discouraging economic development in prosperous areas through licensing requirements and other forms of regulation.

The design of regional policy and the mix of instruments vary from country to country. There may be greater or lesser flexibility for national officials in the implementation of policy. The definition of assisted areas is in certain cases based on transparent criteria, such as unemployment or growth rates, and in others on ad hoc decision rules. Decisions about territorial coverage, target groups, benefit levels and awards may be lodged entirely within a single level of government, or they may be distributed throughout the administrative hierarchy, requiring cooperation between sets of government officials at different levels. Benefits to assist declining regions on occasion apply exclusively to private firms, but in most cases extend to local authorities and public utilities. If the intent of policy is to encourage the development of specific industries or types of infrastructure in the assisted area, only certain kinds of firms are granted eligibility.

Any of these characteristics can have a powerful impact on the strategies adopted by national and subnational actors. For example, the mix of policy instruments determines who is entitled to what and where, which can influence whether certain actors take an interest in the state of the regional economy. The area coverage of regional policy creates strong parameters for the geographical scope of group interaction in the regions. The less extensive coverage is within a region, the more difficult it may be for indigenous groups to foster regionwide cooperation. Actors within the subregions and localities not covered by regional policy will

[3] K. Allen, C. Hull, and D. Yuill, "Options in Regional Incentive Policy," in *Balanced National Growth*, ed. K. Allen (Lexington: Lexington Books, 1978), 2.

have a different set of interests in comparison with those in areas that are designated for assistance; this may create conflicts and divisions that inhibit cooperation.

The present chapter examines British and German national approaches to regional decline along five dimensions: (1) the aims of policy; (2) the instruments of policy; (3) the policy implementation system; (4) the coordination of regional policy with related government programs; and (5) the party political connection. It compares elements of policy continuity and change in each country up through 1986; although much of the ensuing discussion of German and British regional policy remains accurate to the present-day, we will treat the period of study as self-contained so as to facilitate the analysis of regional responses in later chapters. British and German regional policies, while sharing many basic similarities, differ in ways that are potentially significant for the politics of economic decline in their respective regions.

British regional economic policy

Britain, along with Italy, possesses one of the classic North–South economic divides in Europe, a situation largely attributable to the south-easterly political, cultural, and economic pull generated by London. Concerted national efforts to alleviate regional economic disparities date from the Great Depression. During the period of study in question, sixteen successive parliamentary acts and a number of administrative edicts combined to form a long policy history which reflected the seriousness and resilience of the country's regional problems (see Table 3.1).

Despite the stream of legislation, the overall policy approach, the targeted areas, and the set of instruments remained surprisingly constant and, with the exception of two distinct periods, largely impervious to party politics. Regional policy expenditure crested during the 1970s (see Figure 3.1), benefiting from a remarkable degree of consensus among political and economic circles at the national and subnational levels.

The aims of policy

Although official government pronouncements on the objectives of regional policy convey a natural dovetailing of social and economic goals, British regional policies in practice reveal an overriding concern with social objectives. The focus on unemployment "black spots" dates from the 1930s, when legislation targeted social dimensions of regional crisis like unemployment, outmigration, and the breakdown of communities. Concerned with regional equity and balance, central policymakers

Table 3.1. *The statutory basis of British regional policy*

1928	Industrial Transference Scheme
1934	Special Areas (Development and Improvement) Act
1937	Special Areas (Amendment) Act
1945	Distribution of Industry Act
1947	Town and Country Planning Act
1950	Distribution of Industry Act
1958	Distribution of Industry (Industry Finance) Act
1960	Local Employment Act
1963	Local Employment Act
1965	Highlands and Islands Development (Scotland) Act
1966	Industrial Development Act
1967	Finance Act (REP and SET)
1970	Local Employment Act
1972	Industry Act
1975	Industry Act
1982	Industrial Development Act

looked upon regional policy as "a system of 'first aid' rather than as an integral part of an economic strategy for expansion."[4]

A significant yet short-lived break with the equity approach to regional disparities occurred in the early 1960s, when British policymakers, trumpeting the virtues of planned state intervention in the economy, grafted regional policy onto national planning objectives.[5] In 1963, the Conservative government announced that henceforth, regional policy would target "growth points" or "growth zones" within the regions. This new emphasis, an explicit rejection of the black spot approach, would support national growth by rewarding economic potential. "It will not be possible," the Chancellor of the Exchequer stated in 1963, "to run this country at its full potential on a steady basis so long as full employment in Scotland and the North East and Ulster mean overfull employment and serious shortages of labor in the Midlands and the South. The need for further progress with the problems of regional unemployment is, therefore, both social and economic."[6]

Despite the apparent finality of this shift in emphasis, the growth-

[4] D. W. Parsons, *The Political Economy of British Regional Policy* (London: Croom Helm Publishers, 1986), 137. See also A. Booth, "The Second World War and the Origins of Modern Regional Policy," *Economy and Society* 11 (February 1982): 1–21.

[5] Interest in planning did not necessarily translate into aptitude. For contemporary accounts, see Beer, *Modern British Politics*, and Shonfield, *Modern Capitalism*. A more comprehensive analysis is provided in Hall, *Governing the Economy*.

[6] *Parliamentary Debates* (Commons), 5th ser., vol. 675 (1963), col. 479.

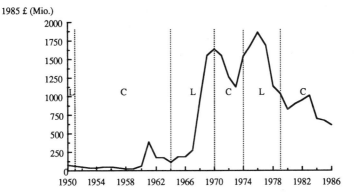

1985 £ (Mio.)

Note: L = period of Labour government; C = period of Conservative government. This figure combines a number of different time series that are not strictly comparable; it is to be used merely to indicate global changes in government expenditure. Expenditure items include regional development grants, selective financial assistance, investment grants, and advance factory building.

Sources: United Kingdom, Parliament, House of Commons Expenditure Committee (Trade and Industry Subcommittee), *Regional Development Incentives: Minutes of Evidence, Session 1972/73; HC327* (London: HMSO, 1973), 457; Northern Region Strategy Team, *Technical Report no. 2* (Newcastle-upon-Tyne: NRST, 1975), B7; Annual Reports of the 1972 Industry Act and the 1982 Industrial Development Act; Annual Accounts of the Scottish Development Agency; Annual Accounts of the Welsh Development Agency.

Figure 3.1. *British government expenditure on regional policy*

oriented regional policy did not endure. Although the 1964 Labour government continued, indeed perfected, the rhetoric of growth, it remained just that – rhetoric. In practice, the government returned to the original approach forged in the 1940s, using job opportunities as the principal yardstick by which regional policy objectives were measured. When the Thatcher Government announced in 1983 that regional policy served purely social objectives and could not be justified on economic grounds, it exorcized the last vestiges of the growth rationale.[7]

British policy instruments
The government's original regional program, the 1928 Industrial Transference Scheme (ITS), attempted to encourage labor mobility – a quin-

---

[7] See the British government's 1983 White Paper. United Kingdom, Secretary of State for Trade and Industry, *Regional Industrial Development (Cmnd 9111)* (London: HMSO, 1983), 4.

tessential "workers to the work" approach. Unemployed laborers in the "distressed areas" were provided with financial assistance to enable them to seek employment in the prosperous areas of the country, notably the Midlands and the South. The abandonment of the ITS reflected a growing awareness of the political and social disruptions that accompanied this policy. Since then, British regional policy sought consistently to bring work to the workers. The consolidation of this approach was by no means instantaneous; in fact, the Special Areas Act of 1934, Britain's first regional policy anchored in parliamentary law, manifested a continuing ambivalence toward financial incentives to private industry.[8] The legislation created a limited number of instruments designed strictly to facilitate the development of infrastructure and housing construction. Direct assistance to private firms became available one year later, when government officials were empowered to finance trading estates (industrial parks) in the special areas. In addition, the Special Areas Reconstruction Association was established to provide modest financing for eligible firms.[9] Trading estate powers were then codified and expanded in the 1937 amendment, which created additional instruments to aid private firms through tax, rent, and rate subsidies.

The trend toward enhanced government capabilities to coax footloose industry into the problem areas continued in the postwar period. The Distribution of Industry Act 1945 strengthened government's powers to build and lease advance factories, to finance trading estates, and to disburse grants and loans to local authorities (for infrastructure improvement and land reclamation) and private firms. Government purchasing preference schemes rounded out the set of instruments. Revised building grants were introduced by the 1960 Local Employment Act. In 1963, standard investment and building grants were added, as was free depreciation for firms in assisted areas. Free depreciation was replaced in 1966 by a system of 40 percent investment grants. The Labour government introduced three new employment-related assistance schemes in 1967: the Regional Employment Premium (REP), the Selective Employment Premium (SEP), and the Selective Employment Tax (SET). Investment grants were replaced by free depreciation in 1970, and the SEP and SET were withdrawn. The 1972 Industry Act eliminated free

[8] See F. Miller, "The Unemployment Policy of the National Government 1931–1936," *Historical Journal* 19 (March 1976): 453–76; A. Booth, "An Administrative Experiment in Unemployment Policy in the Thirties," *Public Administration* 56 (Summer 1978): 139–57.
[9] See C. Heim, "Limits to Intervention," *Economic History Review* 37(November 1984): 533–50.

depreciation in favor of regional development grants, and added a selective assistance scheme. The REP was abolished in 1977.[10]

Postwar regional policy also introduced a negative instrument. Government officials used controls on industrial development and location (Industrial Development Certificates: IDCs) to steer industry away from the prosperous areas to the problem areas, where such controls did not apply with equal force. Investors in the South and the Midlands had to acquire approval certificates from government officials before undertaking new developments or expanding existing premises beyond a certain size. The stringency of IDC controls varied over time. Periods of very tight control occurred in the immediate postwar period, as well as from 1965 to 1970. After 1972, IDCs gradually lost their potency, as central policymakers either refused to withhold permits or set the exemption limits so as to be of little deterrent value.[11] IDCs were officially abolished by the Thatcher Government in 1981. The variable strength of IDCs notwithstanding, the combination of positive and negative incentives linked in a zero-sum manner the fortunes of prosperous and problem regions in Britain, and thereby created the potential for sharpened interregional political conflict between the haves and the have-nots.[12]

In line with the social justification for British regional policy, unemployment rates governed the designation of assisted areas, although policymakers retained a wide measure of discretion. The closest approximation to a published statement of specific selection criteria occurred in the early 1960s, when officials announced an unemployment rate of 4.5 percent as the ceiling above which localities could be designated as assisted areas. Government officials soon retreated from this benchmark. Generally speaking, officials preferred the flexibility conferred upon them by a discretionary system, although they encountered opposition from interested parties in many of the problem regions. Whitehall generally envisioned a loosely drawn map of assisted areas to maximize the flexibility of business location decisions. Local authorities and MPs, on the other hand, were much less interested in incentive frameworks of this nature, and pushed for a tightly bound map so as to

[10] See C. Law, *British Regional Development since World War I* (Newton Abbot: David & Charles Publishers, 1980).

[11] In 1964–5, 26 percent of IDC applications were refused in the Midlands and the South, compared with just 2 percent in 1979–80. J. Mawson, "Changing Directions in Regional Policy and the Implications for Local Government," *Local Government Studies* 7(March–April 1981), 69.

[12] North East interests traditionally have belonged to the have-nots, while those in the West Midlands over time have moved from the haves to the have-nots.

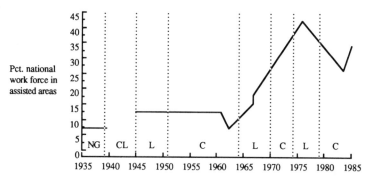

Note: NG = period of National Government; CL = period of Conservative-Labour coalition; L = period of Labour Government; C = period of Conservative government.

Sources: D. Yuill, "Regional Incentives in Britain," in *Balanced National Growth*, ed. Allen, 35–54; J. House, ed., *The UK Space* (London: Weidenfield and Nicolson, 1982); Parsons, *The Political Economy of British Regional Policy*.

Figure 3.2. *Assisted-area coverage of British regional policies, selected years.*

"deliver the goods."[13] Given the political sensitivity of area designation, decisions as to which areas were to be placed on the map, or more importantly taken off the map, were kept well away from Parliament.

British policymakers usually adopted a "broad banding" approach to area designation, in which large, contiguous areas received assisted status. Only during the period 1960 to 1966 did British governments pursue a narrow selection approach.[14] Although the boundaries of British assisted areas changed over time (see Figure 3.2), the core problem areas remained the same, centering on southwest Scotland, South Wales, the North East, and the North West. Between 1966 and 1976, several new categories of assisted areas were created, and the overall map was extended. For example, the creation of special development areas in 1967 was a response to the rundown in the coal-mining industry. The lack of transparent selection criteria eased the expansion of area coverage.

The implementation of British regional policy: bilateralism and centralization

Consistent administrative goals shaped the policy delivery system in Britain: the need for information; the limitation of clientele demands

[13] Civil servant, Regional Policy, Department of Trade and Industry, London, 21 June 1984. Interview with the author.
[14] Allen et al., "Options in Regional Incentive Policy," 13.

and intraregional competition; the prevention of cross-regional coalitions; and the desire to block any substantial deconcentration of policy-making powers to the subnational level, either to the field administration or to nongovernmental actors. The government accorded these objectives different priorities over the years, largely in response to the increased powers granted by postwar legislation. Nevertheless, they remained central to the government's view of regional policy and the provinces, and set the parameters for the division of labor between headquarters and field administration.

The delivery system of the 1930s was unique in many respects, a product of the government's lack of conviction about the need for a regional policy and the modest policy instruments at the bureaucracy's disposal. The Special Areas Act designated two unpaid commissioners to carry out policy, one for Scotland and the other for England and Wales, and established a Commissioners' Office in London. The special-areas administrative machinery, formally separate from the Whitehall bureaucracy, operated under the direction of the minister of labour. The commissioners were to supplement, not replace, the ongoing activities of Whitehall ministries; as a result, all major assistance decisions had to be approved in interdepartmental committees in London.[15] The commissioners appointed district commissioners based in each of the special areas to gather information and to mobilize local initiatives.[16] In fact, the dearth of effective instruments and data on which to base sound policy decisions led the commissioners to develop close relationships with subnational actors.

This ad hoc bureaucratic arrangement ended in 1939, when the outbreak of WWII prompted the government to place the special-areas legislation in cold storage. After 1945, an official Whitehall ministry administered regional policy: the Board of Trade (BoT) until 1969; the Ministry of Technology from 1969 to 1970; and the Department of Trade and Industry (DTI) thereafter.[17] With the passage of the Distribution of Industry Act, departmental headquarters, in possession of enhanced instruments and increased informational resources, assumed responsibilities for the major decision making associated with regional policy, such as evaluation of IDC permit requests and assistance applications above a certain order of magnitude.[18] Some discretionary powers were

---

[15] Public Record Office (PRO): LAB23/25, 19 November 1934 and 1 January 1935. The 1937 amendment did in fact confer a measure of discretionary powers on the commissioners, particularly where the trading estates were concerned.

[16] *Parl. Deb.* (H.C.), 5th ser., 293(1934): 1997.

[17] The DTI has since undergone several name changes. To avoid confusion, it will be referred to here as the DTI.

[18] Until the early 1950s, the Treasury handled matters relating to the provision of loans and grants to private firms. In the early 1960s, responsibility for the

placed in the hands of the field administration; for example, regional civil servants controlled the construction of advance factories both as to quantity and location. The 1972 Industry Act left the most visible imprint on the administrative division of labor. The act increased the availability of automatic assistance, in the form of regional development grants (RDGs), and selective aid (selective financial assistance: SFA) under Section 7 of the act. While the RDGs continued to be allocated under centralized administration procedures, the new emphasis on selective assistance required an element of decentralization in the policy delivery system. DTI regional offices administering assisted areas were allowed to award grants on their own authority under guidelines established in London.[19] DTI civil servants in the regions received additional personnel to aid in the processing of selective assistance applications.

The autonomy of the regional civil service should not be exaggerated. In 1980, the government reformed the system of advance factory building, placing most of these matters in the hands of semi-independent management teams. SFA schemes offered only limited possibilities for discretionary activity by regional civil servants. Between 1972 and 1985, selective assistance represented just 16.5 percent of total regional policy expenditure under the Industry Act. Furthermore, the DTI regional offices applied SFA provisions as evenly as possible across the country. For example, once a firm received an SFA offer, the regional office in question circulated the terms of the offer to other regional offices in the country in order to eliminate the possibility of competitive bidding.[20] These practices tended to minimize interregional variations in the criteria for project selection and overall award rates.

Within the centralized postwar delivery system, government regional offices continued to play direct roles in their regions. Many aspects of policy, including the designation of assisted areas and the siting of advance factories, necessitated links to local and regional interests. As a case in point, SFA prompted the creation of new consultative machinery

management of advance factory building was transferred from the BoT to a quasipublic corporation, English Industrial Estates Corporation, Ltd. The BoT and its successor departments continued to retain a large degree of control over policy, however. After 1980, the corporation became subject to newly established guidelines which granted the organization autonomy from continual oversight by the DTI and its regional offices. However, English Industrial Estates was to be run on a for-profit basis, which reduced the political potential of this deconcentration of powers.

[19] Regional offices could award grants up to £2.0 million on projects whose total investment did not exceed £10.0 million. Anything above those ceilings was to be referred to London.

[20] B. Hogwood, "The Regional Dimension of Industrial Policy Administration," in *Regional Government in England*, ed. Hogwood and Keating, 111–13. Civil servant, Northern Regional Office of the Department of Trade and Industry, Newcastle upon Tyne, 27 March 1986. Interview with the author.

to advise regional civil servants. Regional Industrial Development Boards (RIDBs) were established to bring together officials and local businessmen, trade unionists, and other individuals with industrial experience in the region. The boards rarely disagreed with proposals put forward by the DTI regional offices, which led to the comfortable result that "in practice their view [was] rarely set aside."[21] Furthermore, most if not all British regional policy benefits required the exercise of free will on the part of investors, who had to be made aware of available assistance. Regional government offices increased take-up by funding groups that advertised the availability of assistance and the high points of the region. Government financial support for English regional development organizations, which averaged approximately £117,000 per year during the 1970s, reached a peak of £743,000 in 1979–80 and thereafter leveled off at around £600,000.[22]

Thus, throughout the period of study, government policymakers recognized the need to gain access to local and regional information and to limit bidding for investment and mobile firms between regions and localities.[23] Nevertheless, in the postwar period the principal rationale behind inclusive strategies shifted perceptibly in line with the government's changing resource requirements. Central government grew less interested in acquiring information, and more intent upon shaping the kinds of demands put forward by subnational actors. As Chapter 4 will document, this led to a transformation of the resource exchange relationships between government and regional groups dating from the 1930s. That being said, officials remained averse to the idea of according official status and statutory powers to regional bodies. The precise form of field administrative relationships with indigenous groups was left to officials on the scene, and this element of discretion led to different patterns of interaction across the country.

Speaking in general terms, then, the system of implementation was highly centralized, concentrating decision-making powers and information resources in the Whitehall bureaucracy. A corollary of this arrangement was that the regional civil service possessed few discretionary powers and little control over resources. The resulting division of responsibility between headquarters and field administration should raise serious doubts about the likelihood of "capture" by local and regional interests during this period, if only because there was so little to capture.

[21] United Kingdom, Department of Industry, *Industry Act 1972, Annual Report* (*HC 619*) (London: HMSO, 1976), 36.

[22] N. Rigby, "Industrial Promotion or Demotion?" *Northern Economic Review* 3(May 1982): 29.

[23] Ministerial concern about an explosion of demands in the postwar period dates from as early as 1943. PRO: BT64/3440, 9 March 1944.

Furthermore, the implementation process linked the center with problem regions in a series of insulated, bilateral relationships, which placed limits on the emergence of interregional coalitions of interest. This situation stands in marked contrast to the German system.

Interpolicy coordination

Historically, British regional policy was politically and administratively weak in relation to the expenditure and priority claims of several related policies. Policy compartmentalization was high, which suggests that sectional centralism played a part in shaping the interactions between national and subnational actors.

Macroeconomic and sectoral policies. Macroeconomic priorities set the broad parameters for regional policy in Britain. The special areas legislation of the 1930s preserved the overarching commitments of the National Government to orthodox fiscal and balance of payments objectives. Examples of the conditional priority accorded to regional policy in the postwar period are numerous. Distribution of industry policy fell victim to the balance of payments crisis in 1947, when export considerations became paramount. Whoever could produce fastest and cheapest for foreign markets received the green light from government regulators, regardless of where their production facilities were situated.[24] After 1976, when the largest single cut in regional expenditure to date took place, outlays for regional policy became increasingly vulnerable to general fiscal constraints.[25] The cuts announced by the Thatcher Government were only the most recent examples. Other economic goals occasionally took precedence as well. For example, export and growth priorities for the South and Midlands drove the progressive relaxation of IDCs in the 1970s.

The general relationship of sectoral policies to regional policy is not as easy to characterize. Policy for the automobile industry in the 1970s periodically supported the objectives of regional policy, but in a manner that undercut sectoral efficiency and competitiveness, not to mention

[24] Advance factory building in the development areas was put on hold, and development controls in the South and Midlands were relaxed. The impact on the development areas was profound: The percentage of new industrial building situated in the DAs between 1945 and 1947 was 51.1 percent; the proportion slipped to 17.2 percent between 1948 and 1950. Total regional assistance had fallen by 50 percent by the end of the decade. United Kingdom, Select Committee on Estimates, *The Development Areas, 2nd Report HC 139* (London: HMSO, 1956).

[25] Regional policy expenditure went from £903 million in 1975–6 to £530 million in 1977–8 (figures in 1978–9 prices). The abolishment of REP accounted for most of the cut. W. Grant, *The Political Economy of Industrial Policy* (London: Butterworths, 1982), 59.

the long-term regional interests of groups in the principal vehicle-producing region, the West Midlands.[26] But for the most part, industrial policies to promote high technology, small firms, and individual sectors were administered with little explicit regard for regional policy concerns. Similarly, policies for the nationalized industries were devised in isolation from regional considerations. Throughout the period, government-appointed managers ran the coal and steel industries according to national interests and objectives, with profitability the principal investment criterion.[27] The consequences manifested themselves not only in the adverse regional impact of these investment strategies, but in the degree of insulation from regional policy-making that the managing boards of these industries enjoyed.

The separation of industrial from regional policy objectives was reflected in Whitehall's administrative structure. According to one official, because the DTI sponsoring departments dealt with questions of investment and worried about the viability of their industries, "they did not want the regional policy people to lean too hard on their clients."[28] As a result, there was little if any coordination within the DTI itself between the industrial sponsoring departments on the one hand and the regional policy division and regional offices on the other.

Regional planning. Britain has never enjoyed a fully coherent regional planning apparatus. Nevertheless, a legislative framework for town planning has been in place since the 1920s.[29] Carried out largely by individual local authorities, town planning comprises land use planning, zoning, the management of population growth, and other related issues. During this period, regional economic policy and town planning proceeded along separate legislative and institutional tracks despite the considerable overlap of their objectives.[30] The ministries in charge of regional

---

[26] S. Wilks, *Industrial Policy and the Motor Industry* (Manchester: Manchester University Press, 1984), 78.

[27] R. Hudson, "The Paradoxes of State Intervention," in *Public Policy Studies*, ed. R. Chapman (Edinburgh: Edinburgh University Press, 1985), 58; B. Jones and M. Keating, *Labour and the British State* (Oxford: Clarendon Press, 1985), 62. British Steel Corporation's policy, for example, has been characterized as "not particularly susceptible to decisions made on regional grounds." J. J. Richardson and G. F. Dudley, "Steel Policy in the UK," in *The Politics of Steel*, ed. Y. Mény and V. Wright (New York: Walter de Gruyter, 1987), 365.

[28] Civil servant, Regional Policy, Department of Trade and Industry, London, 21 June 1984. Interview with the author.

[29] For a highly readable account of the twists and turns of postwar town and country planning legislation, see J. B. Cullingworth, *Town and Country Planning in Britain* (London: George Allen & Unwin, 1982).

[30] The turning point came during the war, when the BoT assumed responsibility for regional economic policy, while physical planning went to the Ministry for Town and Country Planning. Parsons, *British Regional Policy*, 106.

economic policy had few links to those responsible for town planning, which were the Ministry for Housing and Local Government (MHLG) before 1970 and the Department of the Environment (DoE) thereafter.

This division had two important repercussions. In the first place, it divorced the administration of policy for the declining regions from policy directed at the prosperous areas.[31] Planning for growth in the South evinced little explicit connection to managing decline in the North. And when the two policies collided, as they did increasingly over IDCs in the 1970s, the stage was set for interministerial conflict in Whitehall and interregional conflict in Parliament and the bureaucracy. A DoE official described the situation in 1984: "Intraregional issues are largely conceived in terms of a planning framework. . . . Interregional issues, involving the distribution of resources, have always been broadly conceived in terms of a market approach, largely unregulated. In this sense, there has always been a tension between intraregional planning and interregional industrial policies, and this manifests itself in a tension between the Department of Industry and the DoE."[32] Second, because local authorities were hived off into a separate policy-making community, with different assumptions and procedures, the resulting sectional centralism created the potential for fragmentation at the regional level.

A concerted effort to inject regional economic issues into the broader framework of regional planning occurred in 1964, when the Labour government established planning machinery at the regional level to complement the national plan. Under the direction of the Department of Economic Affairs, a Regional Economic Planning Council (REPC) and Board (REPB) were set up in each of the eleven official planning regions. The councils, advisory bodies comprised of government-appointed local notables, were to assist in the formulation and implementation of official regional plans. In their endeavors, the councils received the technical assistance of the planning boards, which brought together senior government officials from regional departments whose responsibilities impinged upon economic planning for the region. Neither the boards nor the councils were allowed to encroach upon the powers and responsibilities of local authorities or those of existing government departments.

[31] One aspect of planning policy has had, on occassion, an explicit link to regional policies – namely, new towns policy, which commenced in earnest after the war. New towns, designated by central government and granted special powers of a finite duration to attract and develop new industry, were intended to relieve population pressures on congested areas like London and Birmingham, and to slow the process of depopulation in some of the depressed areas of the country. The effect was to create new, powerful local authorities in the region. See M. Aldridge, *The British New Towns* (London: Routledge & Kegan Paul, 1979), and Cullingworth, *Town and Country Planning*.

[32] Civil servant, Plans and Regional Policy, Department of the Environment, London, 9 July 1984. Interview with the author.

The story of the regional planning machinery is in general not a happy one, particularly for the councils.[33] In 1966, the government transferred responsibility for regional plans from Whitehall departments to the councils, which stripped the plans of their official status.[34] The collapse of the national plan in 1967 further weakened their already tenuous position. The Heath Government followed suit in 1970, effectively relegating the councils to adjunct participants in land-use planning exercises. As the dust settled, they were left to find their own niche within their respective regions, and it is perhaps no surprise that they "tended to become regarded as pressure groups and parochial regional advocates."[35] Many council initiatives shattered on a lack of interest or administrative coordination in London. The close embrace of civil servants and government ministers also created constraints on independent action for council members. The Thatcher government put an end to this experiment in regional consultation in 1979, when it officially abolished the councils.[36]

Two things in particular are significant about the regional planning machinery. First, it was completely divorced from the administrative and implementation structures responsible for regional economic policy. This presented planning councils in the assisted areas with considerable problems of coordination. Second, on a more sanguine note, both the councils and the boards opened up new possibilities, however constrained, for the indigenous mobilization of regional interests. In both the North East and the West Midlands, the councils would play significant roles in the efforts of local and regional groups to develop responses to decline.

The Scottish and Welsh devolution issue. Controversy over the devolution of limited legislative and executive powers to Scotland and Wales occupied British political elites during much of the 1970s. Of the five

---

[33] The literature on the demise of the regional planning machinery is vast, as are the causal analyses advanced. For an especially insightful account, see P. D. Lindley, "The Framework of Regional Planning 1964–1980," in *Regional Government in England*, ed. Hogwood and Keating, 169–90.

[34] This was the result of government dissatisfaction with the councils' agitation to grant the regional plans statutory authority and with the high profile role adopted by many councils, which were seeking to build a representational base within their regions. Ibid.

[35] Ibid., 182.

[36] There was little opposition in Whitehall to the government's decision; in fact, the speed with which it was carried out suggests that plans may have been waiting for the Conservatives when they took office. Many ministries viewed the planning council meetings as "a waste of time, and the change in government provided an opportunity for certain departments to rid themselves of a nuisance." Civil servant, Plans and Regional Policy, Department of the Environment, London, 9 July 1984. Interview with the author.

policies outlined in this section, devolution stands out: It was not so much a program as an important episode in British politics.[37] The rise of Scottish and Welsh nationalism in the late 1960s, coupled with a dwindling Labour majority after the 1974 elections, threatened the foundation of Labour's long-standing strategy to win power at the national level. Since the 1920s, Scottish Labour party organizations had agreed to back the Labour Party's commitment to wield centralized power from London in return for favorable treatment for Wales and Scotland through preferential expenditure policies. As the decade of the 1970s began, this informal compact looked increasingly endangered.

For the Labour government, concessions to Scotland and Wales became necessary in the face of the rise of the Scottish National Party. Separate economic development agencies were created in 1975–6, and proposals for devolved assemblies came very close to becoming law.[38] The thinly veiled attempts of the Labour government to buy off Scotland and Wales with modified constitutional solutions raised thorny distributive and institutional issues in England proper. Not only did English political and economic interests decry the proposed constitutional advantages about to be conferred on Scotland and Wales, but they began to look into the historical pattern of preference enjoyed by these regions.[39] Government ministers were unable to keep the agenda from widening to include issues far more radical than the normal set relating to regional policy. Actors in the English regions, above all the North East, began to consider minidevolution proposals of their own.

Urban policy. Policy for Britain's inner cities – an "intra-regional emphasis"[40] – took center stage during the late 1970s. Urban policies,

---

[37] This section draws heavily on B. Jones and M. Keating, "The British Labour Party," in *The Territorial Dimension in United Kingdom Politics*, ed. P. Madgwick and R. Rose (London: Macmillan Press Ltd., 1982), 177–201; M. Keating, "The Debate on Regional Reform," in *Regional Government in England*, ed. Hogwood and Keating, 235–53; and V. Bogdanor, "Devolution and the Constitution," *Parliamentary Affairs* 31 (Summer 1978): 252–67.

[38] Created by an Act of Parliament, the Scottish and Welsh Development Agencies are endowed with substantial powers, including direct investment in industry, the creation of new companies, and the provision of finance and advice to industries. For an excellent treatment of these and other related issues, see M. Keating and D. Bleiman, *Labour and Scottish Nationalism* (London: Macmillan Press Ltd., 1979).

[39] Scottish expenditure on most programs was running about 20 percent ahead of the British average by the mid-1970s. The intense scrutiny of Scottish and Welsh affairs brought about by the devolution episode put an end to these hidden advantages: Expenditure in England, Scotland, and Wales is now pegged at 85:10:5.

[40] M. Stewart, "The Role of Central Government in Local Economic Development," in *National Interests and Local Government*, ed. K. Young (Aldershot, Hampshire: Gower Publishing Co., Ltd., 1983), 109. Milestones include the

consolidated and expanded during the 1980s by the Conservatives, posed a major challenge to regional policy.[41] Urban Programme expenditure in 1984–5 exceeded regional policy expenditure in all of England and Wales. Furthermore, a significant portion of that expenditure went to areas outside the traditional development areas.[42] And finally, the increasing emphasis on urban policy encouraged a growing interventionism among local authorities. With the help of new powers granted by central government, local authorities addressed the economic problems facing their cities by acquiring land and premises for development, distributing loans and grants to local industry, promoting their cities at home and abroad, and providing business advisory services.

As a result, actors in the traditional development areas soon faced an ambiguous situation. In the first place, efforts to secure benefits for their regions were handicapped by overall government expenditure caps and the growing emphasis on inner-city problems irrespective of regional location. Second, the local authority approach represented both a new field of potentially autonomous activity and a source of fragmentation and instability. Local authorities, using their newfound powers and channels of access to Whitehall, often sought individual solutions over common regional ones. The fracturing of the center's policy efforts, containing new incentives for subnational actors, posed a clear threat to the development and maintenance of regional solidarities.

EC regional policy. Historically, British central officials have viewed the ERDF in terms of two overriding objectives: to maximize the amount of money obtained from the program for British recipients, and to minimize the political and administrative impact of the program on domestic policymakers and subnational actors. They were reasonably successful on both counts during this period.

After the ERDF assumed a pivotal role as the quid pro quo for British acceptance of the terms of membership in the early 1970s, national

publication in 1977 of the government's White Paper on the inner cities, and the passage in 1978 of the Inner Urban Areas Act.

[41] British governments made few concrete attempts to coordinate the two policies. Although the government's 1983 White Paper acknowledged the connection between urban and regional policies, the effort was largely window dressing. Civil servant, Plans and Regional Policy Section, Department of the Environment, London, 2 July 1984. Interview with the author. According to one official, urban policy was the regional policy of the Thatcher Government. Senior civil servant, West Midlands Office of the Department of the Environment, Birmingham, 12 February 1986. Interview with the author.

[42] In 1982–3, Greater London and the West Midlands attracted 58 percent of all Urban Development Grant expenditure; only 28 percent went to the North and North West. P.J. Damesick, "The Evolution of Spatial Economic Policy," in *Regional Problems, Problem Regions, and Public Policy in the United Kingdom*, ed. P. J. Damesick and P. A. Wood (Oxford: Clarendon Press, 1987), 50–51.

officials maintained a keen interest in the fund. Indeed, Britain did quite well for itself in the ERDF. Between 1975 and 1986, UK regions received the equivalent of £2.4 billion, or 22.8 percent of total ERDF expenditure. Britain's per capita share of Community regional policy expenditure over the same period came to 184 ECUs, fourth best in the EC league table. Of the ten most assisted regions in the EC, Britain placed four of its own: Scotland, Wales, the North East, and the North West.[43] These achievements are an indication of British bargaining leverage in Brussels and of the seriousness of the country's regional problems.

Officials pursued the goal of limiting the administrative impact of the ERDF with equal vigor. For example, the government deflected EC efforts to enforce the principle of "additionality," which stipulates that Community assistance be disbursed in addition to, not in place of, ongoing national regional policy expenditure. The domestic administrative structure set up to handle ERDF matters reflected an intense desire by Whitehall officials to guard their position as the principal allocators of economic benefits to the regions. In spite of the spate of ERDF reforms, individual applications for assistance continued to be routed through London, which minimized the number of direct interactions between subnational actors and the Brussels bureaucracy. The rationale behind these arrangements was simple; as a British civil servant stated in 1976, "Political constraint enters in here. It is an article of faith in Great Britain . . . that countries must run their own regional policy. It's a question of politics, of votes. No country will give up the right to determine subsidies to its own regions. No country is going to turn this over to an international authority."[44]

Viewing the ERDF reforms as a convenient opportunity to soften the impact of domestic expenditure cutbacks, the Thatcher Government welcomed the expansion of ERDF benefits, though it sought to limit "the scope for the Commission to interfere unduly in its less programmatic approach or its own decisions about the types, and preferred location, of the regional investments to be financed."[45] Although the development-programme requirement created new responsibilities for Whitehall civil servants, they were able to strip it of any legal or policy status. "[The development programme] is recognized essentially as a

[43] All figures taken from Commission of the European Communities, *European Regional Development Fund: 12th Annual Report (1986)* (Luxembourg: Office for Official Publications of the European Communities, 1987).

[44] Senior civil servant in Regional Industrial Development, Department of Industry, London, 12 November 1976. Interview conducted by J. LaPalombara, Yale University.

[45] H. Wallace, "Distributional Politics," in *Policy-making in the European Community*, ed. H. Wallace, W. Wallace, and C. Webb (New York: John Wiley & Sons, 1983), 96.

contrivance. . . . It is supposed to be a strategic document, but it is really rather more of a shopping list."[46]

Although Whitehall succeeded in holding Brussels at bay, the ERDF exercised a discernible though modest impact on the contours of British regional policy. EC pressures were behind the 1977 decision to abolish the Regional Employment Premium, and the 1984 decisions to modify the system of regional development grants.[47] The fifteen-year flow of regional policy benefits from Brussels also stabilized domestic programs. In the words of a senior DTI civil servant, "[ERDF expenditure] . . . enabled us to continue with, or perhaps I should say forced us to maintain, the same level of regional policy expenditure over time."[48] These pressures continued into the 1980s, when the Thatcher Government abandoned its intention to reduce drastically the area coverage of British regional policy. Extended assisted areas would ensure that Britain received the maximum benefit from the money available from the ERDF, since nonassisted areas remained ineligible for fund programs. British officials were also forced to adapt to the intensified competition for fund assistance generated by the Community's greater powers of allocation. To this end, Whitehall adopted a "mothership" role, encouraging and mobilizing local authorities to take advantage of the enhanced source of regional aid.[49] In general, DoE regional civil servants took the lead in organizing local authorities and other relevant subnational actors. Since the DoE was responsible for coordinating general infrastructure planning – the placement of access roads, the reclamation of derelict land, and so on -- the regional offices became actively involved in setting priorities and formulating assistance proposals within the regions. DoE actions were driven by a desire to compensate for the organizational and planning weaknesses of the local authorities, historically dependent public actors that endured increased financial and administrative constraints during the Thatcher years.[50] The view in the regional offices paralleled that in London: The ERDF represented a potentially lucrative source of assistance for problem regions at a time when expenditure on national regional policy was on the decline.

[46] Civil servant, Northern Regional Office of the Department of the Environment, Newcastle upon Tyne, 21 February 1986. Interview with the author.
[47] Considerations related to competition policy were paramount. Civil servant, Economics Division, Department of Trade and Industry, London, 27 June 1984. Interview with the author.
[48] Senior civil servant, Department of Trade and Industry, London, 12 July 1984. Interview with the author.
[49] M. Keating and M. Rhodes, "The Status of Regional Government," in *Regional Government in England*, ed. Hogwood and Keating, 80.
[50] R. A. W. Rhodes, "Territorial politics in the United Kingdom," *West European Politics* 10 (October 1987): 21–51.

British regional policy and partisan politics

One can observe a pronounced cyclical quality to the relationship between regional economic policy and party politics in Britain. During the
1930s and 1940s, the Labour Party distinguished itself as the sole, consistent advocate of a national regional policy that took work to the
workers. This position grew out of its electoral stake in the crisis-ridden
industrial regions of the country, and the heavy burden that transference
schemes placed on individual workers and families. Labour's alternative
to the ITS provoked strong opposition among Conservative government
ministers and backbenchers, who clung to prevailing economic ortho-
doxies. Government ministers and backbenchers proclaimed their dis-
taste for controls on industrial development, and only gradually moved
to institute the modest positive incentives for industry contained in the
special-areas legislation.[51] Nevertheless, Labour's role as champion of
the distressed areas proved nettlesome to the government; Whitehall,
wary of the political repercussions, moved with great care in considering
the fate of the special areas as the decade of the 1930s drew to a close
and the exigencies of war making became paramount.[52]

The Conservative Party eventually committed itself publicly to continuity in regional policy in 1951. The resulting bipartisan consensus,
expressed through official statements and budgetary decisions, grew
during the 1960s, and peaked in the aftermath of the 1972 Industry Act,
itself a Conservative product. During this second phase, regional policy
remained a politicized affair, but in a manner difficult to equate with
pure electoral politics.[53] To be sure, differences between the parties
existed. Labour exhibited a marked preference for direct grants and
advanced factory building, while the Conservatives favored tax credits
and other indirect subsidies. Grants or investment tax credits, capital
versus labor subsidies, positive or negative incentives for mobile industry
– these defined the terms of debate. This was not the stuff of fiery election
manifestos. That policy was not driven by purely electoral considerations
during the period of consensus derives from a simple observation: The
assisted areas continued to center on the original special areas of the
1930s, located in the North East, Cumberland, Wales, and parts of
Scotland. All of these were solidly Labour, yet regional policy was
pursued with more or less equal vigor by both parties. Politics played
a more nuanced role than the simple rewarding of supporters and the

[51] Characterized by Prime Minister Chamberlain as "experimental" and by current
scholars as "a public relations exercise," the Special Areas Acts of 1934 and
1937 represent quintessential symbolic politics. Miller, "The Unemployment
Policy"; Parsons, *British Regional Policy*.
[52] PRO: HLG30/31, 21 December 1937; LAB23/180, 4 May 1938.
[53] On occasion, regional politics furthered electoral objectives. See the discussion
in Chapter 4 of the Conservative government's plan for the North East in 1963.

punishing of opponents.[54] In general, governments of both the left and the right reacted to territorial demands for preferential treatment by expanding the area coverage of regional policy.

Regional policy provided governments-of-the-day with the opportunity to be seen to be doing something about the problem of unemployment. Indeed, governments tended to reemphasize regional policy during periods of increased unemployment, as happened in 1958–60 and again in 1970. Because of this strong bipartisan consensus and the fear of political backlash in the country, governments were loath to eliminate or deemphasize regional policy. For example, Conservative efforts to downgrade regional policy in the relatively prosperous 1950s were tempered by a desire to avoid unfavorable comparisons to the previous Labour government.[55] The Cabinet decided to implement modest expenditure cuts instead of the more contentious act of descheduling assisted areas.

This broad commitment to regional policy began to disintegrate in the mid-1970s. Several long-term factors contributed to the breakdown of consensus, including the emergence of unemployment as a national and not just regional phenomenon in the aftermath of the 1974 OPEC crisis, the severe fiscal constraints facing British policymakers, the perception of minimal achievement in the problem regions after forty years of regional policy, and the growing crisis in the inner cities. Still, the Thatcher Government delivered the final blow, when shortly after its 1979 election victory it announced large cuts in regional policy expenditure and area coverage in the coming years. Regional policy in the mid-1980s stood at its weakest point in over twenty-five years (see Figure 3.1).[56] With the disappearance of the depressed areas' monopoly on unemployment by 1979, the straightforward political dimension became increasingly visible. Evidence of this third, and highly partisan, phase in the history of regional policy comes primarily from the manner in which the government sought to downplay the problems of Labour strongholds and to shift attention to electorally marginal regions in the Midlands.[57] Despite many opportunities, the Thatcher governments resisted the temptation to rejuvenate regional policy as a means of de-

---

[54] Studies of the timing and placement of government-built advance factories during this period find no evidence whatsoever of any electoral connection. P. Slowe, *The Advance Factory in Regional Development* (Aldershot, Hampshire: Gower Publishing Co., Ltd., 1981), 19.

[55] PRO: BT177/1459, 1954; BT173/7, 26 January 1954.

[56] As a percentage of UK GDP, expenditure peaked by the end of the 1970s at approximately 0.85 percent. This figure dropped to 0.4 percent by 1982. Armstrong and Taylor, *Regional Economics and Policy,* 177.

[57] This is the tale of the North East and the West Midlands, respectively, which is detailed in the following chapter.

claring a public relations war on unemployment. Vestiges of the old consensus lingered, to be sure; her ministers in 1981–2 found it impossible to follow through on their stated intention to abolish regional policy because of, among other things, political pressure from Conservative MPs in assisted areas.[58] Nevertheless, the terms of debate changed dramatically.

The politics of regional policy at the national level appears to offer a complex palette of options for regional interests. During the first and third phases, the partisan nature of debate opened up opportunities for interactions based on a partisan-electoral logic of exchange. During the far longer second phase, the constrained nature of party conflict offered few avenues for political-territorial exchange along Scottish and Welsh lines. On the other hand, the period of policy consensus should provide a secure basis for group initiatives in the problem regions, and a roadblock to those in the prosperous areas. Any advantages that might have accrued to the traditional problem regions disappeared with the breakdown of consensus in 1979.

German regional policy

Although one can point to a long line of policies enacted during the period framed by this study (see Table 3.2), regional problems in the Federal Republic of Germany never achieved the magnitude of those in the United Kingdom. The stellar performance of the German national economy during most of the postwar period distributed its results fairly evenly over the country. Furthermore, the pattern of population and industrial settlement in the Federal Republic was characterized by the absence of a single power center, on the order of Paris or London, which united economic and political hegemony in a manner conducive to the rise of sharp disparities in growth, employment, and income.

Nevertheless, this spatial picture grew less accurate over time, as industrial crises in coal, steel, textiles, and chemicals took their toll on the localities and regions in which they were situated. Beginning in the late 1970s, political debate over regional problems was cast increasingly in the image of the North–South gradient (*Nord-Süd-Gefälle*): the aging, declining industrial areas in the northern states (Bremen, Hamburg,

---

[58] Some attribute the mini-U turn to the steady decline in the government's overall popularity during this period, and the fact that the review took place in the run-up to a general election. Official with the Birmingham Chamber of Industry and Commerce, Birmingham, 27 February 1986. Interview with the author. "The battle [for regional policy] would have been lost if Conservative policies writ large had retained their appeal." Former senior civil servant, Northern Regional Office of the Department of Trade and Industry, 26 March 1986. Interview with the author.

Table 3.2. *The statutory basis of German regional policy*

1951	Distressed Areas (*Notstandsgebiete*)
1953	Zonal Border Areas (*Zonenrandgebiete*)
1954	Regional Assistance Program (*Regionales Förderungsprogramm*)
1959	Development Program for 'Central Places' in Rural Undeveloped Areas (*Entwicklungsprogramm für Zentrale Orte in ländlichen, schwach strukturierten Gebieten*)
1968	Regional Action Programs (*Regionale Aktionsprogramme*)
1969	Joint Task for the Improvement of Regional Economic Structure (*Gemeinschaftsaufgabe "Verbesserung der regionalen Wirtschaftsstruktur"*) Investment Allowance Act (*Investitionszulagengesetz*)
1971 +	Annual Framework Plan (*Rahmenplan*) under the terms of the Joint Task
1972	Zonal Border Promotion Act (*Zonenrandförderungsgesetz*)
1982	Investment Allowance Act (*Investitionszulagengesetz*)

NRW) set against the dynamic, high-tech growth areas of the south (Bavaria, Baden-Württemberg). Although the statistical evidence for a uniform gradient was ambiguous, the term gained considerable political currency: a well-heeled version of the North–South divides of Great Britain and Italy.[59] Like Britain, a long-standing bipartisan consensus on federal regional policy began to show signs of wear in the 1980s, giving way in the process to a nascent politicization of this policy area (see Figure 3.3).

The aims of policy

Regional policy objectives in Germany flow from Article 72 of the Basic Law, which guarantees an equality of living standards throughout the country. In contrast to the British case, policy objectives did not remained fixed on a stable criterion or principle, but shifted over three distinct periods.[60] Between 1945 and 1955, regional policy displayed a mixture of social, economic, and political goals. Initially, the principal task was to aid those parts of the country adversely affected by wartime destruction and to promote the development of backward rural and peripheral areas, "thereby easing the rate of migration from those areas

[59] See R. von Voss and K. Friedrich, ed., *Das Nord-Süd-Gefälle* (Stuttgart: Verlag Bonn Aktuell GmbH, 1986).
[60] H. H. Eberstein, "Grundlagen der Regionalpolitik und ihre wesentlichen Grundsätze," in *Handbuch*, ed. Eberstein (1972), 1–46; U. Casper, "Background Notes to Regional Incentives in the Federal Republic of Germany," in *Balanced National Growth*, ed. Allan, 97–130.

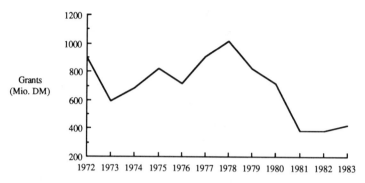

Source: Ewringmann et al., *Die Gemeinschaftsaufgabe*, 272.

Figure 3.3. *Regional policy expenditure (GRW) in the Federal Republic, 1980 prices*

to the as-yet-unreconstructed cities."[61] Objectives were primarily social in nature, focusing on the dislocation caused by unemployment and outmigration. New objectives began to emerge alongside the old in 1953, a product of the hardening division of Germany and the onset of the Cold War. "Barbed wire and minefields suspended abruptly the last economic contacts between areas on both sides of the demarcation line. Previously integrated economic areas were forcibly separated. Firms in these areas ... had to adjust to new, often distant supplier and consumer markets in the western parts of the Federal Republic."[62] Policymakers established the *Zonenrandgebiete* (zonal border areas), a forty-kilometer-wide swath of territory extending along the borders with the German Democratic Republic and Czechoslovakia. Aid for these areas reflected, among other things, a political necessity – namely, to stiffen the resolve of these front-line areas against the East. These objectives reflected a political commitment to regional assistance that extended well beyond straightforward economic considerations.

During the second phase of policy, from the late 1950s to the late 1960s, regional policy changed to accommodate a new economic environment. Questions of balanced development assumed priority in an era of unprecedented national economic growth. The deliberate shift to an economic and planning rationale for regional policy arose out of the effects of Germany's *Wirtschaftswunder* (economic miracle).[63] The man-

---

[61] B. Reissert and F. Schnabel, "Fallstudien zum Planungs- und Finanzierungs-verbund von Bund, Ländern, und Gemeinden," in *Politikverflechtung*, ed. Scharpf et al., 76.

[62] W. Albert, "Die Entwicklung der regionalen Wirtschaftspolitik in der Bun-desrepublik Deutschland," in *Handbuch*, ed. Eberstein (1971), 2.

[63] H. H. Eberstein, "Grundlagen," 13.

ufacturing areas of the country suffered from labor shortages resulting from full employment and general industrial congestion, problems which increasingly impinged on the capacity of firms to keep pace with domestic and international demand by the traditional method of expanding their scale of operations. Officials modified regional policy objectives in order to lure industries away from the congested areas to those parts of the rural periphery considered to have growth potential. Policymakers were motivated primarily by growth and efficiency considerations, although the social dimension continued to receive attention. Problems of depopulation and social decay were addressed, if not everywhere, at least where they fit in with the broader economic rationale. Between 1951 and 1967, federal regional policy expenditure totaled approximately 2 billion DM; fully three quarters of this sum funded infrastructure projects.[64]

A watershed in policy objectives occurred in 1967, inaugurating the third phase of regional policy. The nation's first severe recession caused dislocation not only in the classic problem areas but in the heretofore prosperous parts of the Republic: heavy industrialized areas like the Ruhr Valley in North Rhine–Westphalia and the Saarland.[65] Lower growth rates and high unemployment shattered the promise of eternal prosperity in these areas. As a result, regional policy began to incorporate – slowly, conflictually, yet inexorably – the economic and social claims of the industrial problem regions alongside the traditional commitment to the modernization of the rural periphery.

Policy instruments in the Federal Republic of Germany
Like Britain, Germany's regional policies were all governed by the principle of taking work to the workers. Schemes included investment grants and allowances, soft loans, depreciation allowances, and infrastructure assistance. The passage of the *Gemeinschaftsaufgabe "Verbesserung der regionalen Wirtschaftsstruktur"* (joint task for the improvement of regional economic structure) and the Investment Allowance Act in 1969 set the parameters of policy for the remainder of the period.[66] Automatic assistance was available in the form of the investment allowance, which was administered by the federal government and constituted the bulk

---

[64] Reissert and Schnabel, "Fallstudien," 76.
[65] These regions are known as *Monostrukturen* (monostructures), a reference to their lack of a diversified industrial base.
[66] The *Gemeinschaftsaufgabe* will be identified henceforth as the GRW. Additional assistance schemes included the European Recovery Program (ERP) soft loan program and a special depreciation allowance for firms in the zonal border areas.

of annual regional policy expenditure.[67] Discretionary assistance to industry, financed on the basis of equal contributions by the Bund (federal government) and Länder, consisted of the investment grant. These grants were payable on a broader range of activities than the investment allowance, including start-ups, extensions, rationalization, and/or reorganization. The award rate structure was extremely complex, varying by project type and by location of the proposed project. The GRW also provided support for local authority infrastructure development, such as access road construction, sewerage and drainage systems, and the like. Infrastructure projects to aid tourism, as well as job training facilities, were also eligible for support. In the years after 1972, the set of regional policy instruments was modified several times to include a greater emphasis on service industries and the promotion of innovation and new technologies.

Selection criteria for assisted areas prior to the GRW were a veritable hodgepodge, the product of the various types of problem area that regional policies sought to target. Of these, the political definition of the zonal border areas represented the most straightforward set of criteria. Designation criteria for the other areas were more complex. During the early 1950s, areas that surpassed certain thresholds of unemployment and labor market conditions could be named as *Notstandsgebiete* (distressed areas). With the move to a planning-based regional policy in the late 1950s, policymakers added outmigration and per capita GDP indicators to determine the selection of assisted areas, renamed *Bundesausbaugebiete* (federal growth districts). Furthermore, a system of coverage based on "central places" emerged to reflect the new concern with growth zones and development axes. Small and midsized towns (i.e., not areas), possessing a stable tax base and a core of infrastructure and industry capable of self-sustained growth, were eligible for designation as *Bundesausbauorte* (federal growth places). Thus, by the end of the 1960s, criteria for selecting assisted areas formed a mix of broad-banding and narrow-banding approaches.

The GRW framework established in 1969 sought to replace these various selection criteria with a unified system. The legislation defined three types of problem areas: the zonal border areas; areas whose level of economic development lay substantially under the federal average; and areas that were vulnerable to structural shocks because of a de-

---

[67] The investment allowance was a project-related grant, restricted largely to start-ups and extensions, and contributed a fixed percentage to eligible investment proposals. The award rate stood at 10 percent in the zonal border areas. In other assisted areas, the rate was originally set at 7.5 percent and was later increased to 8.75 percent. Casper, "Background Notes," 105. The investment allowance was abolished in 1990.

pendence on a limited range of industrial activity. The task of revising the criteria to accommodate these various problem types was both time-consuming and politically acrimonious. New designation criteria, which were distinguished by their transparency and sophistication, took effect in 1975, several years after the beginning of negotiations between federal and state officials. The system was hailed by many as refreshingly free from political manipulation, although we shall see that this evaluation is somewhat misleading.

The 1975 selection criteria took the following form. First, the building blocks of assisted areas changed: 178 contiguous regional labor markets replaced boundaries based on local authority jurisdictions.[68] Each labor market received an aggregate score based on the cumulative value of three separate indicators: (1) a labor reserve quotient, which measured the projected labor surplus in the area (assigned a weight of 1.0); (2) per capita regional income (assigned a weight of 1.0); and (3) a measure of regional infrastructure provision (assigned a weight of 0.5). Labor market regions with scores below a negotiated cut-off point were designated as assisted areas. Over the course of the next six years, two additional indicators were added to the list: a wage level indicator and one measuring regional unemployment.[69] Taken together, these indicators incorporated, however uneasily, the different types of problem areas defined by the GRW. The infrastructure and regional income indicators, for example, spoke to the traditional problems of the rural periphery, while the labor reserve quotient aimed primarily at the emergent problem areas in the industrial core of the nation.

Finally, policymakers opted to distribute aid within assisted areas on the basis of the *Schwerpunktprinzip* (focal point principle). Within each assisted area, towns and cities meeting certain minimum size conditions and designated as "labor market centers" in Land planning programs were eligible for designation. Projects receiving regional assistance were required to locate in one of the focal points (*Schwerpunkte* or *Schwerpunktorte*: SPOs).[70] Annual negotiations determined the total number of SPOs and their allocation among the Länder. SPOs were ranked hierarchically: Awards in the zonal border areas for investment grants

---

[68] By 1986 there were 179 labor market regions.

[69] The additional selection criteria, in particular the unemployment indicator, resulted from sustained political pressure from areas hard hit by unemployment. Proponents argued that the labor reserve quotient was not sensitive enough to sharp, short-term rises in unemployment.

[70] Actually, only direct assistance to industry had to take place within a SPO, with some degree of flexibility. Infrastructure investment projects could receive GRW assistance anywhere within the broader assisted area. Between 1972 and 1985, 57.1 percent of infrastructure assistance went to projects in SPOs. Bundesamt für gewerbliche Wirtschaft.

reached a maximum of 25 percent, while those in other assisted areas varied among 10, 15, and 20 percent. In sum, area designation followed a severely modified broad-banding approach, which resembled in effect a two-stage process: first, the selection of large assisted areas, comprised of regional labor markets; and, second, the selection of smaller areas or nodes in the assisted area as the final (potential) destination of regional assistance.

Such selection criteria suggest a set of universal decision rules. Nonetheless, a considerable amount of ad hockery characterized the GRW. Certain parts of the country were designated assisted areas sui generis – that is, they were not required to meet the minimum values stipulated by the indicator package, but received automatic assisted-area status. These included the zonal border areas and, until 1986, the Saarland. Furthermore, the GRW was used on occasion in a flexible manner to address short-term crises concentrated in areas that did not qualify for regional assistance. Specifically, GRW policymakers approved a total of five *Sonderprogramme* (special programs) between 1972 and 1986.[71] These programs all had strictly limited time horizons, and were financed off the GRW budget. The first, fourth, and fifth programs provided for temporary extensions of designated assisted areas. The *Sonderprogramme* represented clear departures from the image of an objective, apolitical policy. Federal officials argued that the practice was fully in tune with the spirit of the GRW, notably the objective of targeting very different kinds of problem regions within a single framework. However, officials acknowledged that these programs were often difficult to distinguish from classic "firefighting" or "black spot" approaches to regional policy.[72]

The coverage of regional policy was perennially prone to expansionary tendencies. In 1963, designated assisted areas held 19 percent of the country's population; the figures for 1968 and 1970 were 21 percent and 31 percent, respectively.[73] The total number of *Bundesausbaugebiete* in

[71] The five *Sonderprogramme* were (1) to create jobs in areas threatened by Volkswagen plant closures, 1975–7; (2) to promote infrastructure development in assisted areas, 1977–80; (3) to assist areas in the Saarland and Rhineland–Palatinate hard-hit by the collapse of the steel industry, 1978–81; (4) to create employment opportunities outside the steel industry in the steel producing areas of the country (*Stahlstandorteprogramm*), 1982–5; and (5) to create employment opportunities outside the shipbuilding and steel industries in Bremen, 1984–7. D. Ewringmann et al., *Die Gemeinschaftsaufgabe "Verbesserung der regionalen Wirtschaftsstruktur" unter veränderten Rahmenbedingungen* (Berlin: Ducker & Humbolt, 1986), 248–52.
[72] Civil servant with the Planungsausschuß, Federal Economics Ministry, Bonn, 4 December 1986. Interview with the author.
[73] K. Geppert et al., *Vergleich von Präferenzsystem und-volumen im Land Berlin und in den übrigen Bundesländern* (Berlin: Deutsches Institut für Urbanistik, 1979), 20–1.

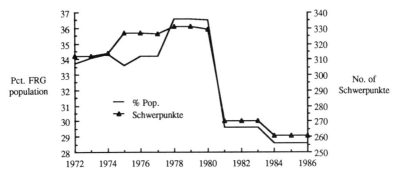

Source: GRW *Rahmenpläne*, 1972–86.

Figure 3.4. *Assisted-area coverage in the Federal Republic, 1972–87*

1968 reached 129. Similarly, between 1960 and 1968, the number of *Bundesausbauorte* increased from fifteen to eighty-one.[74] Things were no different under the GRW. Coverage inflation was most apparent in the early years of the GRW, when the federal government sought to build support among various Länder for the new policy initiative. In view of the difference between assisted areas and SPOs, however, drawing conclusions from the data is not easy (see Figure 3.4). Severe scaling back took place in the late 1970s and again in 1983, as the federal government sought to reduce expenditure as well as to improve the efficiency of the GRW by concentrating diminishing resources on fewer areas.

The implementation of regional policy: the shift to multilateralism and decentralization

Prior to the introduction of the GRW, federal regional policy was highly centralized. Bilateral negotiations between federal officials and the participating state governments took place over boundary designation and funding levels. States with assisted areas received a fixed proportion of annual federal regional expenditure – a *Landesquote* (state quota) – calculated on the basis of assisted-area population. The Land administration collected industrial and infrastructure assistance applications, determined their eligibility, and then forwarded them to Bonn for final approval. The *Landesquote* determined the overall aid ceiling.

In 1969, this centralized, bilateral administrative framework gave way to the system of regional action programs (*Regionale Aktionspro-*

---

[74] Casper, "Background Notes," 99.

gramme), which required the Länder, in consultation with the federal government, to establish quantified goals for federally assisted regional policies and a capacity to monitor the results. The action programs were then incorporated into the GRW, which became law on 1 January 1970. The GRW replaced the existing administrative machinery with the Planning Committee (*Planungsausschuβ*: PA), which brought together on a regular basis ministers and staff from the Federal Economics Ministry, the Federal Finance Ministry, and the various state economics ministries. The PA, supported by several working subcommittees, determined all aspects of regional policy: overall territorial coverage of regional policy, the criteria for area designation, funding and benefit levels, and each Land's quota of SPOs and funding.[75]

Each year, the states submitted their applications for the coming year. Drawn up according to a standard format, the applications provided a multiyear projection of assistance and of job-creation goals for the *Aktionsprogramme* contained within their boundaries, coupled with a review of past developments.[76] Furthermore, the Länder were entitled to submit specific requests for changes in the number, type, and location of their SPOs. PA participants then bargained over these applications, with decisions reached by a voting formula. The Bund carried eleven votes, while each Land retained a single vote for a total of eleven. Binding decisions had to pass by a three fourths majority, or seventeen votes. Thus, neither level of government could outvote the other in the absence of some overlap in opinion. More important, the system was designed in such a way that successful proposals would have to obtain the support of the federal government. The final PA agreement was published in the form of an annual framework plan (*Rahmenplan*). The action programs were financed on the basis of equal contributions by the federal government and the state in which those programs lay. Each Land assumed responsibility for the implementation and administration of its programs. The decision-making responsibilities of the PA did not end with the annual framework plan review. On a less regular basis, the PA also considered core structural changes to the GRW framework, including the boundaries of the *Aktionsprogramme*, the selection indicators, as well as overall funding levels and allocations. Without fail, these were contentious experiences for PA participants, occurring in 1975, 1981, and 1986.

---

[75] The typical agenda of a PA meeting was determined by the annual applications of the Länder; on occasion, one of the participants requested the convening of the PA to discuss an emergency issue, such as a proposal for a special program. Civil servant with the Planungsausschuβ, Federal Economics Ministry, Bonn, 4 December 1986. Interview with the author.

[76] There were a total of twenty one *Aktionsprogramme*.

The significance of the PA lay in its qualities as a decision-making arena. In contrast to the previous German policy arrangement and to the British system, GRW policy-making was a multilateral affair.[77] Thus, bargaining within the GRW framework was extremely complex, involving the competing *and* simultaneous claims of central government and the eleven states. For federal and state participants, the high threshold of consensus produced strong incentives to logroll. Thus, although critics of the GRW complained that it represented an unwarranted centralization of power in the Bund's hands, it is perhaps more accurate to speak of the Bund having created a common bargaining table and then reserving a seat for itself at the head.

The PA format produced a number of additional consequences. In the first place, it was strictly an intergovernmental affair, excluding parliaments and nongovernmental actors at both the national and state levels. And, despite the highly formalized nature of the process, each Land retained substantial flexibility in the implementation of its GRW programs. For example, the states were entitled to apportion their share of funds between industry and infrastructure assistance as they saw fit, which enabled them to address the particular needs of their areas without central or multilateral direction. The Länder put this flexibility to good use; for example, only 12.2 percent of NRW assistance between 1972 and 1985 went to infrastructure projects, while the figure for Bremen during the same period was 82.7 percent.[78] Furthermore, state governments with more than one *Aktionsprogramm* were entitled to shift funds between them, subject only to perfunctory PA approval. These were factors of no small consequence for the pattern of group interactions in the German regions, as we shall see. For one, the system led to a strengthening of the Land governments vis-à-vis their own constituencies.

A final comment on implementation is appropriate here. One of the major reasons for creating the GRW framework was to curb states' expenditure on regional policy programs. After fourteen years of joint policy-making, it was apparent that the GRW had restrained competitive bidding for regional investment among the Länder, but the impetus at the state level to engage in regional policy-making continued unabated. The explanation is both constitutional and political. State policymakers faced strong political pressures to create indigenous regional programs. In light of this, the federal government was reluctant to encroach upon the prerogatives of the states, and erected instead a set of voluntary restraints via the GRW. Any attempt by Bonn to move beyond this

---

[77] Reissert and Schnabel, "Fallstudien," 82.
[78] Bundesamt für gewerbliche Wirtschaft.

arrangement would have resulted in a dissolution of the federal-state consensus underlying the GRW.[79]

Interpolicy coordination

Like Britain, the federal government did not create explicit coordination mechanisms linking regional policy with related programs at the federal level. Nevertheless, regional policy as law and as stated principle was solidly anchored in relation to both general economic policy and regional planning (*Raumplanung*).[80] With the shift to an openly interventionist stance by the federal government after 1967, regional policy was integrated along with other industrial policies in the broader framework of *Strukturpolitik* (structural policy). This, along with its constitutional foundations, made regional policy less vulnerable to short-term political and fiscal pressures than is the case in Britain.

Macroeconomic and sectoral policies. Sustained national prosperity spared federal policymakers the task of choosing between macroeconomic priorities and regional policy for many years. Toward the end of the period of study, however, the budgetary commitment to regional policy weakened as the *Wirtschaftswunder* receded into memory and fiscal constraints pushed their way to the foreground. This trend gained momentum in early 1980, part and parcel of a broader effort to reduce the overall level of federal subsidy expenditure. The campaign to cut government subsidies failed at an aggregate level; in actual fact, between 1981 and 1986, federal subsidies rose by 40 percent.[81] However, in the aftermath of the *Wende* in 1983, regional policy was targeted quite vigorously for expenditure reductions. According to a state official in the Saarland, "The brakes are being applied everywhere, but with more force in some areas than in others. The interests in the PA are more manageable than in a policy area like technology assistance, where firms can threaten a loss in international competitiveness if subsidies are removed."[82]

Sectoral policies have a long history in the Federal Republic, despite the prevailing myths about the noninterventionist proclivities of the German state. At times, these policies contradicted the overarching aims of federal regional policy. For example, research and technology development, administered by the Federal Ministry for Research and Tech-

[79] Geppert et al., *Vergleich*, 25; Reissert and Schnabel, "Fallstudien," 98.
[80] As stated in "Principles of Regional Economic Policy," *Bundestagsdrucksache* V2469 (16 January 1968).
[81] European Commission, "Bulletin of the European Communities," 21 (December 1988), 68.
[82] Members of the Structure Policy-Industrial Policy Division, Saar Ministry of Economics, Saarbrücken, 11 November 1986. Interview with the author.

nology, became an increasingly important policy area in terms of both rhetoric and expenditure. The distribution of R & D outlays favored the southern parts of the country, while large areas in the north and east received very little in the way of assistance.[83] The fact that most Länder started up their own technology promotion policies, often with an explicit regional dimension, mitigated the potentially adverse distributional effects of these federal programs.

Energy policy and coal. The problems in the German coal industry had a distinct regional impact, due to a geographical concentration of extraction and production facilities in the Ruhr Valley of North Rhine–Westphalia and in the Saarland. Yet the federal government's position regarding the coal industry was always bound up closely with its assessment of the energy requirements of the national economy.[84] Throughout the 1950s, the government sought to ensure a steady supply of cheap energy for industry, particularly firms in the export sectors. Through a combination of subtle intervention and an open reliance on market forces, government encouraged firms to use cheap imported oil and, when necessary, supplies of foreign coal from the United States and eastern bloc countries.

The crisis in the coal industry met with little initial sympathy from the government. Although ministers expressed concern over the mounting job losses and the resulting social hardship, few policy responses to aid the industry were forthcoming, at least initially.[85] Massive layoffs, which peaked in 1964, combined with a depressed labor market to create a volatile social and political situation in the coal-mining regions. As a result, the federal government became increasingly involved in the industry's adjustment efforts. Between 1962 and 1966, the government introduced a host of new programs, including assistance for rationalization, price support programs for domestic coal, import controls on

[83] In 1977, only eight percent of BMFT project assistance went to applicants in the GRW assisted areas. Those eligible for assistance, namely universities, research institutes, and high tech firms, were concentrated in the more prosperous areas of the country like Bavaria and Baden-Württemberg. Ewringmann et al., *Die Gemeinschaftsaufgabe*, 192.

[84] This section is based on W. Abelshauser, *Der Ruhrkohlenbergbau seit 1945* (Munich: Verlag C.H. Beck, 1984), and P. Schaaf, *Ruhrbergbau und Sozialdemokratie* (Marburg: Verlag Arbeiterbewegung und Gesellschaftswissenschaft GmbH, 1978).

[85] As a civil servant stated in 1968, government thinking at the time revolved around macroeconomic considerations. "The difficulties in the coal industry must be thoroughly acknowledged, but they must always be seen in the context of the development of the entire economy, and here a supply of the cheapest possible energy takes on the greatest importance." Quoted in Abelshauser, *Der Ruhrkohlenbergbau*, 104.

foreign coal, a tax on heating and fuel oil, and retraining and social assistance for the unemployed.

Events culminated in 1966 with the conjuncture of two momentous events: the country's first severe economic recession, and the accession to power of the Social Democrats as junior coalition partners of the Christian Democrats. The former brought the coal crisis to a head, while the latter provided the political impetus for a federal response. The result was the 1968 Coal Law (*Kohlegesetz*), which sought to stabilize the coal industry in the Ruhr and the Saarland by creating a state-supported rationalization cartel as well as a host of economic and social measures. Unlike previous federal responses, the new programs explicitly addressed the regional dimension of the crisis in the Ruhr and the Saarland. The coal legislation provided a flanking measure (*flankierende Maßnahme*) – the investment premium – to attract new firms.[86]

Although the link between coal and territory grew less explicit during the 1970s, the federal government continued to play an active role in energy policy. In the aftermath of the 1973 OPEC crisis, the Schmidt government developed the Priority Coal Policy (*Kohle-Vorrang-Politik*) to promote the use of domestic coal.[87] The main justification of this policy was macroeconomic and related to national security. Nevertheless, since it created a stable environment for the coal industry, and since the policy was supported by complementary state programs in the major coal-producing states, it provided an important baseline for federal and state efforts to address the economic structural problems in these areas.[88] Although rationalization measures in the coal industry were not coordinated directly with regional assistance and regional programs, there was a more transparent connection between the two policy areas than existed in Great Britain.

Policies for the steel industry. Structural changes in international production and demand patterns, dating from the mid-1970s, produced the steel crisis.[89] Between 1974 and 1975, German crude steel production fell by 24 percent. The country's share of world steel production also fell dramatically. Between 1974 and 1980, the industry shed approxi-

---

[86] The investment premium was the lineal predecessor of the investment allowance, the regional policy instrument for all problem areas introduced in 1969.

[87] See Minister für Wirtschaft, Mittelstand, und Verkehr des Landes Nordrhein–Westfalen, *Energiebericht NRW* (Düsseldorf, 1982).

[88] Hence the universal condemnation in NRW and the Saarland of statements by the federal economics minister that he intended to seek cuts in the subsidies going to coal and steel concerns. *Rheinische Post*, 7 June 1985.

[89] This section is based largely on J. Esser and W. Väth, "Overcoming the Steel Crisis in the Federal Republic of Germany 1974–1983," in *The Politics of Steel*, ed. Mény and Wright, 646.

mately 60,000 jobs, the loss concentrated in the Ruhr, the Saarland, and smaller production centers in Bavaria and Bremen. Federal policies for the steel industry were not as explicitly interventionist as the crisis response for coal in the late 1960s. Precrisis policies included the rationalization measures in the coal industry, which resulted in heavily subsidized energy for the steel industry. On top of that, tax relief and investment aids were granted to steel producers on occasion to assist in the expansion and modernization of production facilities.

In coping with the steel crisis, the federal government was constrained by the steel policies set down by the European Community. Nevertheless, the federal government took repeated independent action. In 1978, the Federal Ministry for Research and Technology set up a Steel Research Program to encourage producers to expand their R & D programs. In 1981, this program was followed by the Support Program for the Steel Industry, which set aside 1.8 million DM to fund new investments and the social programs associated with labor redundancies in the industry. The federal government was closely involved with state efforts to prevent large plant closures and a permanent loss of production capabilities and job opportunities. In a manner similar to the coal crisis, the federal government also addressed the regional dimension of steel rationalization measures. On two occasions, policymakers used the GRW to create replacement jobs in areas where reductions in capacity had occurred. In 1978, a program for the Saarland–Westpfalz area received PA approval; a similar program followed for NRW in 1981. In both cases, policymakers forged an explicit link between sectoral policies, which aimed at a managed reduction in capacity, and regional policies, which sought to create new employment opportunities in the affected localities.

EC regional policy. German regional problems were more muted than Britain's, and this was reflected in German policymakers' interest in the ERDF as well as the size of the country's share. Between 1975 and 1986, Germany received only 4.1 percent of ERDF funds, and placed none of its regions on the list of the ten most assisted areas in the Community. The country took in the lowest per capita share of ERDF expenditure in the Community: thirty-one ECUs per person, in comparison with figures of 283 and 259 for Ireland and Italy, respectively.[90] The bulk of Germany's share during this period financed infrastructure projects in the zonal border areas and the 20 percent SPOs; in 1981,

[90] All figures from Commission of the European Communities, *European Regional Development Fund: 12th Annual Report (1986).*

these areas received 74.5 percent of the German allotment.[91] National discrepancies in who paid and who received colored the position adopted by the Germans in Brussels. Whereas the British generally pushed for increased ERDF funding, German officials balked at these proposals in view of their trifling expected share.[92] As de facto paymaster of the ERDF, Germans were openly skeptical of moves to create a larger regional fund at the European level.

The most telling impact of the ERDF on German regional policy centered around the reforms initiated after 1979. Although the FRG did not experience major problems meeting the EC's requirements regarding regional development programmes – the various GRW *Aktionsprogramme* were submitted unchanged to the commission – this turned out to be small consolation to federal policymakers. As one of the wealthiest members of the Community, the Federal Republic did not fare well under the new Communitywide assistance criteria promulgated by the European Commission. Moreover, Germany found itself the target of repeated efforts by the commission to regulate federal and state regional assistance programs through its competition policy powers. Not only were the Land governments required to obtain commission approval of their regional programs in advance, but Bonn officials had to submit the annual framework plans to the commission for review, and these repeatedly became the subject of formal proceedings initiated under Article 93. In keeping with the overall priority accorded to the less developed regions in the EC, the commission sought to limit the areas covered by German regional policies as well as their award rates.

Although the federal government generally complied with Brussels decisions, this did not prevent officials from expressing their strong objections to the commission's attempts to regulate domestic regional programs.[93] Bonn officials bridled at the criteria used by Brussels, which, because of their orientation to Communitywide unemployment and per capita GDP averages, made it very difficult for the Federal Republic to address intranational regional disparities. German officials argued that the enforcement of these criteria placed excessive restrictions on their right to grant regional assistance under Article 104 of the Rome Treaty and, moreover, limited their ability to fulfill a constitutional obligation under Article 72 of the Basic Law to secure an equality of living standards

---

[91] Commission of the European Communities, *European Regional Development Fund: 7th Annual Report (1981)* (Luxembourg: Office for Official Publications of the European Communities, 1982), 39.
[92] See S. Bulmer and W. Paterson, *The Federal Republic of Germany and the European Community* (London: George Allen & Unwin, 1987), Chapter 9.
[93] Regierung der Bundesrepublik Deutschland, "Memorandum zur Beihilfenkontrolle der EG-Kommission im Bereich der nationalen Regionalförderung" (Internal Document, 1986).

across the national space. "All one has to do is to travel to some of Germany's border areas . . . to realize that no matter how bad things are in Portugal, these areas have to be helped. It is the obligation of national policymakers to orient themselves to the national average, not the EC average."[94] Finally, they criticized EC interventions as disruptive of intergovernmental relations in a federal system. The constant challenges to the framework plans placed additional, unwanted burdens on PA negotiations. Several Länder, most notably NRW, fell victim to the ERDF regulations, and they attempted to use the PA as an arena in which to counter what they perceived as unwarranted challenges posed by the commission. Thus, unlike Britain, where officials welcomed the ERDF as a convenient filler for overall national expenditure cutbacks, federal officials in Germany believed that the policy was often more trouble than it was worth.[95]

Despite the apparent hardships, there was a silver lining in all of this for federal officials. Bonn officials were able to employ the commission as a welcome if unacknowledged ally in their attempts to push through expenditure cuts and reductions in area coverage through the PA. Although the commission usually demanded too much in the opinion of federal officials, blaming an insensitive and unshakable Brussels bureaucracy proved an effective way to resist Land demands for regional assistance. In short, federal officials used the lurking presence of the commission selectively to improve their bargaining position in the PA.[96]

German regional policy and partisan politics

The history of German regional policy, in a direct parallel to the British case, also followed a three-phase partisan cycle. During the years of Christian Democratic stewardship, regional policy served a relatively small, stable number of rural areas, each a bastion of conservative electoral support.[97] Sporadic attempts by the opposition Social Democrats to draw attention to the growing crisis in the coal fields were generally unsuccessful. The recession in 1967, coinciding with the upheaval in national politics, created an opening for interests in the new industrial problem areas. The Social Democratic–Liberal coalition, not surprisingly, was more attuned to the demands of these areas.[98]

However, the monostructural regions did not displace the traditional problem areas, either in 1967 or after the Christian Democrats left office

---

[94] Civil servant with the Planungsausschuβ, Federal Economics Ministry, Bonn, 4 December 1986. Interview with the author.
[95] Senior official in the DIHT, Bonn, 4 December 1986. Interview with the author.
[96] The principal response to the fund reforms occurred at the Land level, outside the formal, highly institutionalized *Gemeinschaftsaufgabe*. See Chapter 5.
[97] W. Albert, "Die Entwicklung der regionalen Wirtschaftspolitik," 7.
[98] See Abelshauser, *Der Ruhrkohlenbergbau*.

in 1969. The resolution of this partisan-territorial conflict resulted in an enlarged federal budgetary allotment to accommodate the increase in demands for assistance. To be sure, old habits died hard. Early negotiations to establish a unitary system of eligibility criteria for the GRW proceeded initially along party lines, with the SPD–Länder and the federal government intent upon pushing through a set of indicators that would favor the older industrialized regions. The intrusion of Länder politics, namely, a state election, caused the breakup of this front in the PA, and the bargaining leading up to 1975 reforms took on a decidedly more state-related hue.[99]

During this second phase of the cycle, national party politics became a more subdued aspect of German regional policy than in Britain. The reasons lay primarily in the efforts of the federal government to rein in overall state spending on regional policy. As early as 1968, it was clear to both Christian Democratic and Social Democratic policymakers that the existing national framework was ill-equipped to contain the explosion of regional and industrial policy expenditure at the state level. Competitive bidding for industry among states had grown commonplace, and the lack of fit between federal and state policy goals threatened to vitiate the federal government's program. Beyond that, federal policymakers were seemingly incapable of patrolling their own backyard: The bilateral method of coordination with Länder had led to an ineluctable expansion of area coverage. The federal government's answer – the GRW and its decision-making process centered in the PA – created strong incentives for the Länder as Länder.

Until 1985, sharp, often bitter conflicts punctuated PA proceedings, but they originated in Land-based calculations of advantage and interest. As a decision-making body, the PA brought the competing claims of states whose assisted areas were predominantly rural and underdeveloped together with states whose regional problems tended toward the industrialized, monostructural variety. Länder with high concentrations of industrial problem areas sought to minimize the weights assigned to infrastructure provision and regional income, since these handicapped their problem areas. Similarly, they pushed for a higher weighting of the labor reserve quotient and, beginning in the mid–1970s, for the introduction of an unemployment indicator. As a result, negotiated changes to the basic parameters of the policy-making framework invariably provoked the sharpest clashes: the total coverage, the selection indicators, and the allocation of expenditure. These were inherently linked, so that one could not effect changes in one area without auto-

---

[99] Reissert and Schnabel, "Fallstudien," 89.

matically inducing changes in the others. Since the Bund sought to limit overall area coverage in order to increase the efficiency of policy, the system operated under severe constraints, which produced a tendency toward stasis. "The PA is an arena with high consensus requirements," explained a Bonn civil servant. "A readiness to compromise on the part of participants is essential if things are to work."[100]

The federal government, whose role is often described as that of a referee, managed these elemental conflicts in the PA in various ways. Early on, the federal government sought to limit conflict by advancing essentially Pareto optimal decisions. The federal government's response to the coal crisis in 1966–7 – a massive infusion of regional policy funds to the coal communities in the Ruhr Valley and the Saarland – provoked protests from the advocates of the rural problem areas, who argued that the traditional system of regional incentives could not compete with the new instruments. Their complaints had a basis in fact – from 1968 to 1971, 2 billion DM flowed to the industrial problem areas, an amount equal to the total regional policy expenditure for the rural problem areas during the previous seventeen years.[101] The creation of the investment-allowance scheme, the *Aktionsprogramme*, and ultimately the GRW eased these conflicts by making everyone better off. Länder were allowed to bring their existing *Aktionsprogramme* into the GRW without major reductions in funding levels or coverage. Furthermore, Länder with minimal or nonexistent *Aktionsprogramme*, like NRW and Baden–Württemberg, received substantial increases in funding allotments, since the Bund believed that concessions were necessary to gain their support for the GRW.[102] Thereafter, to accommodate the interests of NRW and other states, the Bund increased total area coverage, the number of SPOs, and the overall expenditure levels rather than reduce the existing shares of Land participants. The federal government also promoted decisions that circumvented the basic principles of the GRW. For example, when the industrialized state governments began to press for a shift in the indicator system to their benefit, the Bund responded with compromises that violated existing criteria in order to sidestep the more contentious issue of fundamental reform of the GRW. Such compromises included the use of special programs, as well as the admission of areas and *Schwerpunkte* that did not meet the selection criteria.

Thus, during the second phase, there was a continuous conflictual dimension to German regional policy at the national level, yet it was

[100] Civil servant with the Planungsausschuβ, Federal Economics Ministry, Bonn, 4 December 1986. Interview with the author.
[101] Reissert and Schnabel, "Fallstudien," 77.
[102] Ibid., 80.

driven primarily by the interests of state governments, not parties.[103] Recounting a conflict in the PA in 1982, the minister of economics for the state of North Rhine–Westphalia remarked, "This is simply an instance of the struggle for power that goes on in a federal system of government. I do not consider this to be something out of the ordinary. On the contrary, the affair belongs to the normal course of political business. . . . I have always emphasized that the Land must express its interests."[104]

The origins of the third phase in national regional policy can be traced back to the mid-1970s, when the underlying consensual atmosphere in the PA began to dissipate, due to the worsening problems in the industrialized areas and to the Bund's push for significant reductions in the overall commitment to regional policy. The federal government's decision to reduce assisted-area coverage to thirty-four percent of the country's population, while leaving the *Sonderstatus* (special status) of the zonal border areas and the Saarland intact (together, these areas totaled approximately 14 percent), proved to be a festering source of conflict within the PA, which opened the door to reappearance of partisan conflict over regional policy.

The third phase commenced in 1986, when overt party conflict surfaced in the PA for the first time in over fifteen years. In the context of a major reform of the GRW, the Bund and six states – seventeen votes, a bare majority – approved a new assisted-areas map and indicator package over the vehement objections of five Länder. Not only was the vote notable for the high level of discord, but the line dividing the ayes from the nays ran squarely along party lines. Members of the majority, including the federal government, were all CDU or CSU-led, while those in the minority were SPD-led (NRW, Bremen, Hesse, the Saarland, and Hamburg). Participants and observers disagree as to the cause of the dispute. Some argue that the SPD – Länder, led by NRW, were attempting to embarrass the Bund with a deadlocked PA in the run-up to the 1987 general election. Others maintain that Bonn decided to orchestrate the vote to embarrass the *Ministerpräsident* (Land prime minister) of NRW, Johannes Rau, who was leading the SPD in the national election campaign. Whatever the case, opinion is unanimous that the fragile working relations and consensual habits of the PA were dealt a damaging blow. By siding with the CDU–Länder, the federal

---

[103] As Chapter 5 will show, this stands in marked contrast to the situation within the Länder, where the politics of regional decline is laced with party politics. See Chapter 5.

[104] Proceedings of the Economics Committee of the Landtag of NRW, 20 January 1982, 2.

government failed to uphold its obligations as referee and consensus-builder.[105]

Whatever the underlying motivation for conflict, the perennial struggle that took place within the PA belies the notion of transparent objectivity for which German regional policy is renowned. According to a NRW civil servant, the proceedings of the PA in actual fact were "distributional conflicts concealed by pseudo-science."[106] Debates over methodological and statistical rigor, hammered out in the PA subcommittees, were surrogates for the clash of naked territorial and increasingly partisan interests.

Summary

As Table 3.3 suggests, German and British regional policies share a number of similarities, and we would expect these common elements to generate common parameters for central and regional actors. Since national governments defined the problem in similar ways and targeted identical beneficiaries with a comparable instrumentarium, the policy clientele facing policymakers in both countries should be broadly similar. In fact, regional policy as practiced in Britain and Germany creates two distinct policy clienteles in the regions: direct beneficiaries of policies, principally firms and individual local authorities, and territorial interest coalitions. The latter category embraces two conflicting camps: current or emerging problem areas, intent on securing favorable designation, and prosperous regions, which seek to limit the scope and strength of regional policy. Thus, these common attributes of regional policy should present national policymakers with similar types of territorial demands and conflicts.

For regional groups in Germany and Britain, these common characteristics of regional policy increase the likelihood of noncooperative strategies. In the first place, the principle of bias inherent in regional

[105] Members of the Structure Policy–Industrial Policy Division, Saar Ministry of Economics, Saarbrücken, 11 November 1986. Interview with the author. Almost immediately, the Bund moved to patch up the wounds. It approved a massive special program for the coastal areas in 1987 (Bremen and Hamburg, both SPD-led, benefited directly from this), and agreed to consider a NRW proposal for an extension of the special program for the steel-producing areas. The growing intrusiveness of the European Commission in Land regional policy-making after 1986 also contributed to a reduction in the level of acrimony in the PA, as Bund and Länder joined ranks to fend off further incursions from Brussels. Civil servant, Federal Economics Ministry, Bonn, 30 November 1990; economic adviser to the Parliamentary caucus of the Social Democratic Party (SPD), Bonn, 30 November 1990. Interview with the author.

[106] Senior civil servant, NRW Ministry of Economics, Düsseldorf, 31 October 1986. Interview with the author.

Table 3.3. *British and German regional policies compared*

Regional policy	United Kingdom	Federal Republic of Germany
basic principles and policy aims	work to workers area bias social goals	work to workers area bias social and economic goals
instruments	positive and negative incentives infrastructure development	positive incentives infrastructure development
eligible applicants	business firms local authorities	business firms local authorities
assisted-area selection criteria	opaque unemployment	transparent multiple indicators
system of implementation	centralized and bilateral	pre-1969: centralized and bilateral post-1969: decentralized and multilateral
principle nexus b/w center and regions	government field administration	Bund-Land arenas in Bonn
central strategies vis-à-vis regions	mix of inclusive and exclusionary	pre-1969: mix of inclusive and exclusionary post-1969: inclusive
sectional centralism	high	medium
strength of regional policy	peak in 1975; downward thereafter	peak in 1978; downward thereafter

policy will tend to fragment the periphery, severely hampering in the process the emergence of broad territorial coalitions arrayed against the center. Furthermore, this particular constellation of policy principles, beneficiaries, and instruments can, under the right circumstances, lead to an intraregional splintering of relations among actors. To the extent that the designation of an assisted area is not coterminous with the administrative boundaries of the region (thus, by implication only a subset of regional businesses and local authorities are eligible for assistance), conflict and competition may come to dominate intraregional interactions, with pluralism the probable result. These inter- and intraregional conflicts are likely to be accentuated by the global downward trend of regional policy expenditure that began in both countries at the end of the 1970s. Responding to perceptions of continued policy failure, governments relieved themselves of the burden of responsibility with a flourish of rhetoric about the values of local democracy, initiative, and autonomy. In Britain, the emphasis turned to urban policy, while in Germany, as Chapter 5 will document, the Länder were encouraged to develop technology assistance programs. This "decentralization of penury"[107] produced smaller regional policy pies, which could be expected to prompt sharp conflicts among subnational actors.

A final shared characteristic of German and British regional policies, one which has implications for resource exchange between national and subnational actors, concerns the partisan-electoral cycle of policy-making. In both countries, an initial phase marked by party clashes over the scope of policy and, more important, the territorial terminus of policy benefits gave way to a cross-party consensus. During this second phase, regional policy-making proceeded incrementally as bureaucratic considerations, such as consistency of criteria, logrolling, and the management of clientele demands, dominated the process. Toward the end of the 1970s, the consensus in each country began to crumble, and was eventually supplanted by a third phase in which partisan calculations were once again ascendant. The existence of these cycles raises the possibility that the opportunities for central-regional interactions characterized by a partisan logic will be much higher in the first and third phases, while a governmental logic is more likely to take hold during the second phase. In other words, the more an electoral calculus governs the resource requirements of national officials, the greater the probability that favorably positioned subnational actors will respond with offers to exchange votes for benefits. As documented in Chapter 2, the four regions examined in this study vary in terms of partisan-electoral resources.

Alongside these similarities, a host of differences raises interesting questions about the ultimate impact of national level factors on patterns of interaction in the regions. The use of negative instruments in Britain, which has no counterpart in Germany, should accentuate the conflict between assisted areas and nonassisted areas. Still, the opaque selection criteria employed in Britain may render national policymakers less exposed to regional demands for changes in policy eligibility status. Such tendencies could be strengthened by the implementation system in Britain, which was highly centralized and predicated upon bilateral relationships between London and the various provinces, intermediated by field administrative agents weak in resources. In other words, the British

---

[107] Mény coins the term in *Center-Periphery Relations*, 7.

system should afford a high degree of insulation from outside demands for policymakers in Whitehall, whereas the German policy-making framework is much more accessible to territorial interests defined by the state governments. Unlike Britain, where conflicts normally arose between declining and prosperous regions, the battle lines in Germany were drawn between competing versions of the regional problem. This introduced an element of competition into the German policy-making process not witnessed in Britain; the attempts by Bonn governments to reconcile these problems were a principal feature of regional policy there, necessitating elaborate mechanisms at the federal level. Particularly in the aftermath of the 1969 reforms, Bonn (by its own design) faced an institutionalized array of both problem and prosperous regions, each able to point to a reasonably codified set of selection criteria as it defined its claims. Once again, however, the implications for national and regional actors are ambiguous. Participation for subnational actors does not necessarily translate into automatic and sustained influence, and multilateral bargaining does not mean that the federal government is completely at the mercy of the unrestrained demands of regional claimants. Indeed, the opportunities for central management and control may have been much greater in the "penetrated" German policy system than in the insulated British system.

We are now in a position to examine the changing pattern of relations between central and subcentral actors in the four regions selected for analysis. The next chapter will examine the British set of cases, followed by a chapter dealing with the German Länder.

4   The British regions

As inhabitants of a centralized unitary state, local and regional actors in Britain appear to confront a stacked deck. One might expect this to result consistently in sporadic, uncoordinated, and ultimately ineffective responses, as subnational initiatives falter due to the dearth of resources at the regional level. In actual fact, actors in the North East and the West Midlands engaged in consistent and often effective attempts at regionwide coordination. These initiatives, subject to many of the centripetal strains described in the opening chapters, were nevertheless highly dependent on central government support. In both regions, the impact of government policy and the administrative process on patterns of interaction was not unmediated. Civil servants stationed in the government's regional outposts played a vigorous, independent role in shaping group objectives and relationships. Without minimizing the significant differences between these regional cases, it is possible to identify a modal subnational response in Britain – the attempt to escape the unwelcome consequences of competitive pluralism by creating more structured relationships among local, regional, and national actors. Government willing, corporate pluralism was the result.

The North East, 1928–86

The North East is situated along the eastern coast of England between Cleveland and Berwick-upon-Tweed.[1] During the Industrial Revolution, the ready availability of coal reserves in the region attracted a range of industries, including iron and steel production, chemicals, shipbuilding, and heavy engineering, each of which depended on a cheap, steady supply of this fossil fuel. There was a price to be paid for the resulting

[1] In 1965, central government added the counties of Cumberland and Westmoreland (from 1974, combined to form Cumbria) to the original three counties comprising the North East – Northumberland, Durham, and Cleveland – and renamed it the Northern Region. Additional minor boundary adjustments took place in 1974. In 1980, Cumbria was incorporated into the North West Region, and the Northern Region became the North East once again. In order to minimize unnecessary confusion, the region in all its incarnations will be referred to as the North East throughout the study, regardless of the time frame. The following account draws heavily on the work of J. W. House, *The North East* (Newton Abbot: David & Charles Publishers, Ltd., 1969), N. McCord, *North East England* (London: B. T. Batsford Ltd., 1979), and *Public Policy Studies*, ed. Chapman.

101

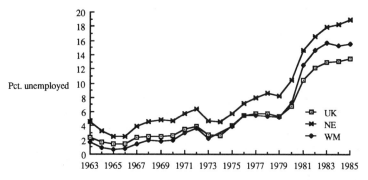

Source: Department of Employment.

Figure 4.1. *Regional unemployment relative to the British national average*

growth and prosperity: a markedly one-sided, homogeneous industrial structure, highly vulnerable to cyclical and long-run shifts in the demand for its products. With the onset of the Great Depression, the regional economy suffered "a decline into poverty . . . from the heights to the depths."[2] Indeed, one would be hard-pressed to come up with a region whose name and history are more associated with the popular image of a problem region than the North East. The collapse of the coal industry in the late 1950s and 1960s and the decline of steel and shipbuilding in the 1970s and 1980s dealt severe blows to the regional economy. Between 1958 and 1973, the region lost 117,000 jobs in the mining industry, 25,000 in shipbuilding, and 13,000 in metalworking. In the period 1979–82, regional manufacturing employment fell by 22 percent (over 90,000 jobs).[3] Postwar regional unemployment rates continued to outstrip the national average (Figure 4.1). In this context of perennial decline and crisis, North East patterns of interaction between subnational and national actors varied across four distinct periods since the early 1930s.

Pluralistic fragmentation before 1934
Until 1934, groups in the region coped with the mounting effects of the Great Depression in an uncoordinated manner. At the behest of their constituencies and local organizations, North East MPs lobbied intensely

[2] R. Chapman, "Public Policy Studies," in *Public Policy Studies*, ed. Chapman, 3.
[3] R. J. Buswell, "The Northern Region," in *Regional Problems*, ed. Damesick and Wood, 170.

but unsuccessfully in Parliament to elicit government initiatives to reduce unemployment in their constituencies, while local government officials organized deputations to bring direct pressure to bear on ministers in London.[4] Each viewed the regional situation from a geographically circumscribed vantage point. While cooperative initiatives surfaced on occasion at the local or subregional level, attempts to expand the geographical base of these initiatives foundered on strong opposition.[5] Although groups recognized that they were all in the same boat, they chose to cast separate lifelines to the mother ship Westminster and Whitehall. Cries for help might be voiced in unison on occasion, but rescue would be an individual affair.

The proliferation of organizational activity drew the worried attention of two government ministries. Officials in the Ministry of Health, responsible for local government affairs, and in the BoT shared a common interest in preventing local and regional actors from engaging in counterproductive competition for new industry and government largesse. The Ministry of Health expressed concern about spiraling increases in local government outlays for industrial promotion and speculative infrastructure development, all of which would increase the tax burden on local ratepayers. The BoT hoped to limit local and regional distortions of its ongoing national campaign to attract overseas investors to the UK. As a result, Whitehall drives to organize the region's interest groups gradually intensified. In 1931, BoT regional officials began to encourage various groups to form a single organizational umbrella that could promote the region and act as liaison with government officials.[6] However, these sporadic attempts to organize the region from above proved fruitless in the absence of a firm national policy that spoke to the problem of regional decline. Government ministries had little if anything to offer these groups in exchange for undertaking a rationalization of their interest organizations. As a result, the pattern of relations remained decidedly pluralist during this period.

---

[4] PRO: HLG30/42 and 59, BT64/11 IM3506; *Proceedings of the Newcastle-upon-Tyne City Council*, 11–12/1933.

[5] Examples of subregional group coordination include the Tyneside Industrial Development Board and Conference (TIDB, TIDC), and the Teesside Industrial Development Board. The TIDC, responsible for the greater Tyneside area surrounding Newcastle, had to contend with two sets of intraregional opponents to an extension of its territorial activities: those interests from other parts of the North East, particularly on Teesside, which were concerned about Tyneside's "imperialist" tendencies; and its own membership, particularly Newcastle upon Tyne City Council, concerned about a dilution of the conference's promotion efforts. NEDB circular, 17 July 1933.

[6] PRO: BT64/11 IM3506; 4 February 1931.

The rise and fall of strong corporate pluralism, 1934–65

Two government initiatives directed at the North East frame this period of group-state relations. The Special Areas Act of 1934 ushered in fifteen years of strong corporate pluralism in the region. A consolidation of group activities, centered around the creation of a regional development organization (RDO) and designed to tap the new source of government assistance, resonated with the political and administrative needs of government officials responsible for implementing the new policy. However, close relations between groups and government officials began to loosen soon thereafter, as Whitehall's needs shifted to the management of clientele demands. A robust form of corporate pluralism came to an end in 1963 with the government's Hailsham Initiative, which bypassed existing consultative channels in the interests of rapid policy results and thus contributed to the marked weakening of relationships among groups and government officials.

The special areas (SA) commissioner, charged with administering the 1934 legislation, faced the daunting task of producing immediate results in the depressed areas with a weak set of policy instruments and without the support of Whitehall. To square the circle, the commissioner cultivated links to the regions capable of sustaining him both in his substantive policy objectives and his running battles with other ministries. With regard to the North East, he sought to treat the region as a single entity, and the 1934 act provided him with an adequate supply of carrots and sticks to succeed where the BoT had failed only a few short years before. The SA Office extended government finance to promotional efforts and projects on the condition that local authorities, labor, and industrial interests pool their resources and act through a single representative body.[7]

The commissioner found a receptive audience in the region – groups were becoming increasingly cognizant of the benefits of regionwide cooperation, which would give them control of regional resources like planning powers, land, and political weight. Since these resources were dispersed among numerous actors, particularly local authorities, it was essential to eliminate *intra*regional conflict and competition over their use. Coordination would enable the North East to compete with other regions in the attraction of investment and government aid. A civil servant in the region echoed this line of reasoning: "Wherever the factory is placed on the North East all will benefit in varying degrees, but no advantage will be obtained if the development does not come North at all. Up here we all sink or swim together."[8] Now that access to

---

[7] PRO: MH61/14, 11 January 1935, HLG30/18, 12 July 1935; HLG30/52; 30 January 1935; BT104/1, 11.1934; BT104/1, 8 May 1935.
[8] PRO: BT64/3486, 25 April 1944.

government largesse appeared to depend on the elimination of non-cooperative strategies, several North East groups moved quickly to package themselves for the new institutional player in Whitehall.[9] They stressed their ability to collect and assemble detailed statistics on the North East, including the mix of firms, market potential, labor supply, infrastructure provision, and the distribution of employment. This information, in scarce supply in Whitehall, helped to cement relations with the Commissioner's Office.

With the formation of the North East Development Board (NEDB) in 1934, a single, regionwide organization began to represent the economic interests of the North East. Its membership base encompassed a broad spectrum of actors, including local authorities, industry, labor, parliamentary representatives, academics, and other local notables. The board's federal administrative structure was to serve as a model for future North East RDOs.[10] Local development boards fielded inquiries from potential investors, provided information to indigenous firms, and collected data on sites and markets for use in promotional campaigns. The NEDB concerned itself with regional development issues and the delicate task of interacting with government officials. By 1935, the board had established itself as the principal vehicle for regional interest articulation and as the main link between North East groups and government policymakers.

The board employed control over scarce informational resources to secure stable, productive relations with central government, and in turn used the promise of stable, productive relations with central government, as well as the threat of government sanctions, to elicit the cooperation of the often fractious local and regional groups under its aegis. The role of gatekeeper imposed several tangible constraints on the board. First, the organization had to treat its various members equally, or at least not be seen to be favoring any one territorial subset of members unduly. To accomplish this, the board chose to follow the priorities of the commissioner, and supported his focus on unemployment black spots, concentrated in South West Durham and Lower Tyneside, which had been hardest hit by the contraction of coal mining and shipbuilding. Second, the board felt compelled to conduct its activities on a strictly nonpartisan basis. By emphasizing the apolitical nature of its claims, the NEDB sought to limit membership conflicts based on

[9] PRO: BT104/1, 23 November 1934.
[10] These include the Northern Industrial Group (NIG), 1943–53; the North East Development Association (NEDA), 1944–53; the North East Industrial and Development Association (NEIDA), 1953–61; the North East Development Council (NEDC), 1961–73; the North of England Development Council (NoEDC), 1973–86; and the Northern Development Company, Ltd. (NDC), 1986 to the present.

party political differences and to secure stable links to central government independent of the vicissitudes of party politics. This proved to be a demanding aspiration in a region dominated by a Labour Party mired in opposition and desperately seeking to make political hay out of the crisis in Britain's industrial heartlands. These constraints – an inability to prioritize among subregions and a nonpartisan demeanor – were to characterize efforts to coordinate interests in the North East well into the 1980s.

Cracks in the strong mutual support relationship between the commissioner and North East actors began to appear after passage of the Special Areas (Amendment) Act in 1937. The new law endowed the commissioner with instruments to attack specific problems on his own or through his agents in the field, like the trading estates.[11] As a result, government policymakers' commitment to a singular arrangement with the RDO eased considerably. The commissioner did not hesitate to bypass established regional channels in order to achieve subregional goals; as a case in point, he provided targeted assistance for South West Durham, an area suffering from a spate of pit closures, by creating new local promotional organizations and by mobilizing initiatives among local authorities.[12] Although the SA Office maintained contact with the board and repeatedly forced it to shore up its membership base, the halcyon days of the NEDB were over.[13] Nevertheless, the region gained substantially during this period. Between 1936 and 1939, a period of Conservative dominance, the North East, a bastion of Labour support, received 42 percent (£2.44 million) of government-built factories for the special areas.[14]

Corporate pluralism in the North East began to loosen gradually in the postwar period. With the additional powers created by the 1945 Distribution of Industry Act, North East civil servants could shift their attention from the acquisition of information and support to the management of clientele demands and competitive tendencies. Civil servants, hoping to strengthen their claims in Whitehall battles and to deflect the increasingly insistent requests from local and subregional interests to secure formal representation on interdepartmental field administrative committees, invited the RDO and other North East groups

[11] For the most up-to-date account of the role of trading estates, see H. Loebl, *Government Factories and the Origins of British Regional Policy, 1934–48* (Aldershot, Hampshire: Gower Publishing Co., Ltd., 1988).
[12] PRO: LAB8/14.
[13] PRO: BT104/3, 1 June 1937; LAB8/302, 26 February 1940; LAB8/300, 15 March 1940; LAB8/302, 30 April 1940. NEDB, *Annual Report 1939* (Newcastle upon Tyne: NEDB, 1939), 6.
[14] PRO: BT173/6, 15 June 1953.

to engage in regular consultations.[15] The Regional Office of the BoT asked the RDO to draw up a list of priority localities for new industrial development, which placed the organization in an impossible position.[16] Although it stood to gain a pivotal role in the implementation of government policy, unparalleled in the twelve years of government efforts to aid the problem regions, the RDO was asked to choose among its membership. For a voluntary organization lacking executive powers, this was tantamount to a request to self-destruct. In the end, the organization declined the invitation, testimony to the overwhelming need to retain the support of all its members. This failed episode represents the closest approximation of sectoral corporatist patterns in either of the British regions.

New government capabilities in the field of regional policy removed the RDO's principal bargaining chip – monopoly of information – and its internal constitution prevented the organization from taking on the role envisioned by government officials. This was not lost on the RDO, which went to great lengths to demonstrate its continuing indispensability to members.[17] As these appeals began to wear thin, the organization enhanced its research and monitoring capabilities.[18] For lack of a better niche, the RDO improved its capacity to generate alternative interpretations of the regional situation for a government in possession of adequate informational and technical resources. In short, the RDO was on its way to becoming a simple regional lobby, a far cry from its original relationship with government. The effect on the RDO's position was noticeable. Over the next decade and a half, a period of relative prosperity in the region, RDOs found it increasingly difficult to maintain the active financial and in-kind support of their members.

Their increasing distance from government notwithstanding, North East groups continued to derive assistance from regional civil servants, who on numerous occasions fought to protect the region from adverse government decisions.[19] Despite the transformation of group-state relations, the basic policy objectives of North East actors remained stable. Working primarily through the RDO, local and regional actors pursued a maximalist agenda: additions to the assisted-areas map; vigorous pursuit of new firms in the light manufacturing and consumer goods sectors; new infrastructure projects; and overall higher levels of policy benefits

---

[15] PRO: BT208/86, 20 March 1946, BT177/197.
[16] NEDA Minutes, 5 March 1946.
[17] NEDA Minutes, 12 March 1948; NEDA, *Some Notes on the Organization and Activities* (Newcastle upon Tyne: NEDA (1949), 3.
[18] NEDA internal memorandum, 2 August 1945; NEDA Minutes, 6 November 1953; NEDA, *Annual Report 1947–48* (Newcastle upon Tyne: NEDA, 1948), 9.
[19] PRO: BT64/3486, BT173/4, BT177/1393.

to spur the process along. They were also eager to protect the advantaged position conferred on the North East by the new system of positive incentives and negative controls. The have-nots believed their fortunes to be closely bound up with the fortunes of the haves. North East groups kept close tabs on the implementation of IDC controls in the Midlands and the South, and strenuously opposed their relaxation.[20] Regional actors also advanced institutional objectives during this period, including formal ministerial representation for the North East in Whitehall and in Cabinet. These demands reflected a genuine concern with the limitations of Parliament as a vehicle for the transmission of regional demands.[21]

When regional unemployment rose dramatically at the end of the decade and threatened to become an explosive electoral issue, the government undertook a series of actions culminating in the Hailsham Initiative for the North East in 1963.[22] The Conservative government carried the battle directly to the Opposition's electoral strongholds, and sought to link up directly with those actors capable of transforming government assistance into concrete projects: the region's local authorities.[23] The unfolding of the Hailsham Initiative was to sound the death knell of strong corporate pluralism in the region.

The appointment of Viscount Hailsham as special minister for the North East in January 1963 was, in a classic understatement by Prime

[20] These efforts were not always successful; in fact, the 1947 fuel crisis ushered in a decade of relaxed IDC controls, as central government pursued other economic policy objectives.

[21] Repeated attempts to create a standing forum in Parliament to air North East issues met with no success. In 1961, a Conservative MP from Newcastle upon Tyne proposed the creation of a Parliamentary Committee for the North, to be modeled along the lines of the Grand Committee for Welsh Affairs. The Conservative government rejected the request. *Parl. Deb.* (H.C.), 5th ser., 663(1962).

[22] The depth of feeling among government backbenchers from the North was underscored on 17 December 1962, when five Conservative MPs from the region abstained on their government's motion dealing with the growing unemployment problem. *Parl. Deb.* (H.C.), 5th ser., 669.

[23] The General Election of 1959 produced a Conservative majority of 100 seats in the Commons, hardly an impregnable cushion, but also not the kind of razor-thin edge that would lead party strategists to select the North East, one of Labour's strongholds, as the place to hold the line. Nevertheless, the 1959 general election had resulted in a gain of three seats in the region for the Conservatives, from ten to thirteen. This was part of a longer-term trend dating from 1950 (see Table 2.2). In addition, there were eight marginal constituencies in the region, three of which were held by the Labour Party. Thus, the government recognized an opportunity to achieve large inroads into Labour's bastion while making a symbolic point valid for the entire country. However, the disastrous defeat of the Conservatives in the 1964 general election, in which they dropped 4.4 percentage points and six seats to Labour in the North East, marked the end of extraordinary Conservative measures for the region.

Minister Harold Macmillan, "a somewhat novel step."[24] Lacking formal
statutory powers or a ministry of his own, Hailsham sought to coordinate
the activities of Whitehall departments through the power of persuasion.
In these efforts, he received the support of a new interdepartmental
group in Whitehall and a parallel set of officials drawn from regional
offices in Newcastle. The Hailsham Initiative encouraged local authorities to submit project proposals for roads, sewer schemes, land reclamation, and housing, which could then be fed into the Whitehall
machinery by Hailsham and his team. In effect, Hailsham's task was to
lobby the lobby, and to encourage the structured participation and support of local authorities throughout the region. Government officials
bypassed the region's RDO, the North East Development Council, and
spoke directly to local government officials, who were extremely interested in London's overtures. T. Dan Smith, Leader of the Labour-
controlled Newcastle City Council, quipped, "We see [Hailsham] as a
man with £250 million in his pocket." Others stressed the pull Hailsham
could exert: "The North East has been taken into the Cabinet Room."[25]
    The publication of *The North East: A Programme for Regional De-
velopment and Growth* (Cmnd. 2206) in November 1963 was the cap-
stone of the Hailsham Initiative.[26] The plan stressed the need to improve
basic infrastructure and formally introduced the notion of growth zones.
In addition to injecting a large amount of resources into the region (see
Figure 4.2), the Hailsham Plan also gave the North East a considerable
head start in the first few years of the Wilson Cabinet. Above all,
Hailsham's team of regional civil servants was well-positioned to carry
on the formalized tasks of regional planning under the 1964 Labour
government. Nevertheless, the episode marked the official demise of
robust corporate pluralism. By focusing on the eighteen separate local
authorities, each intent on protecting its land, resources, and powers,
government officials undercut severely the efforts of the RDO to maintain its position as regional broker. Enticed by the wish-list approach
of central government, local authorities saw little need to refer decisions
to a voluntary body like the RDO. The Hailsham Initiative resulted in
considerable activity and many projects, but little new machinery and
few incentives for further intraregional cooperation.

[24] H. Macmillan, *At the End of the Day 1961–1963* (London: Macmillan Press,
     Ltd., 1973), 390.
[25] *Newcastle Journal*, 16 January 1963.
[26] United Kingdom, Secretary of State for Industry, Trade, and Regional Devel-
     opment, *The North East* (London: HMSO, 1963). The publication of the White
     Paper coincided with a similar program for Scotland; *Central Scotland: a Pro-
     gramme for Development and Growth* (CMBD 2188) (Edinburgh: HMSO,
     1963).

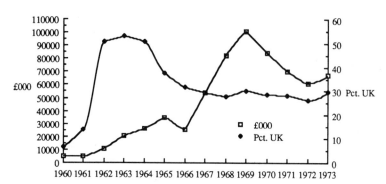

Note: Prices are measured in 1970–71 £.

Source: Northern Region Strategy Team, *Technical Report no. 2*, B. 15.

Figure 4.2. *North East share of regional policy expenditure, 1960–73*

The descent into weak corporate pluralism, 1965–79

The government's decision to create the Northern Economic Planning Council (NEPC) in 1965 ushered in an extended period of competition among several North East organizations, each with pretensions to integrate interests on a regionwide basis and each enjoying close, though separate, relationships with central government. As such, the prevailing pattern of interaction, which ended with the Thatcher election victory in 1979, can best be described as a weak brand of corporate pluralism.

The region as a whole continued to receive the measured support of regional departmental offices. The civil service played a key role in slowing down the rate of pit closures during the 1960s and in presenting the North East's case for large investment projects. As one official active at the time stated, "We were badly hurt by the mine closures, but one recognized that this had to be done. The National Coal Board was not in the business of running a benevolent fund. . . . We did argue very hard to delay certain closures, in order to give time for other policies to speed adjustment of the region."[27] On other fronts, civil servants acted with a great deal more restraint. Although they looked cautiously upon steering investment projects to selected parts of the region in view of the political delicacy of the operation, officials developed a keen sense of the problem areas within their region and actively persuaded firms and

[27] Former civil servant and chairperson of the Northern Regional Economic Planning Board (1966–71), Edinburgh, 20 February 1986. Interview with the author.

investors to settle there.[28] Nevertheless, as a DTI regional official stated with reference to SFA guidelines, "The aim . . . is to apply the policy consistently across the English regions . . . [and] not to help the North East at the expense of other regions."[29] Regional civil servants consistently pushed a broad banding approach to the designation of assisted areas in the region primarily to promote regionwide economic development, although officials hoped to minimize conflicts too.[30] However, officials did not step in actively to rationalize the fragmented organizational landscape that resulted from creation of the NEPC.

The disruptive impact of the planning council grew out of its relationship to central government and the region. NEPC members sat as local notables, not as official representatives of trade unions, industry, local authorities, or subregions. Although appointments to the NEPC were made with a view to incorporating territorial and occupational diversity, council members served as trustees, not delegates.[31] Thus, the council lacked formal representative ties to the region, which diminished its legitimacy in the eyes of the population at large and its competitor organizations. The council's lack of executive powers rendered it ineffectual and largely irrelevant to other regional interests. Furthermore, members were required to sign the Official Secrets Act, which subjected them to the same severe restraints on the use of government information that bind civil servants. This negated a major advantage of the planning council over the RDOs and other individual actors – its direct, continuous access to government ministers and information. Finally, the NEPC relied wholly on civil service data and staff resources to carry out its

[28] "I say unashamedly that there is an element of discrimination." R. Dearing, DTI regional director, NEDC Minutes, 9 April 1973. Evidence of civil service steering to problem areas, as well as the targeted use of advance factory building, is legion, stretching from the 1930s (PRO: HLG30/17, 27 January 1936), through the 1940s (NEDA, *Annual Report 1947–48*), 1950s (PRO: BT173/7, 7 May 1954), 1960s (NEPC Minutes, 3 December 1965), 1970s (NEPC Minutes, 26 January 1978), to the 1980s (senior civil servant, Northern Regional Office of the Department of Trade and Industry, Newcastle upon Tyne, 20 January 1986 – interview with the author).

[29] Civil servant, Northern Regional Office of the Department of Trade and Industry, Newcastle upon Tyne, 27 March 1986. Interview with the author.

[30] NEPC Minutes, 4 February 1966. One of the most divisive intraregional conflicts occurred in the late 1960s, when the government denied SDA status to the Teesside subregion while granting it to nearby areas in Durham and Tyneside. This generated a feud within the RDO that ultimately led to the decision by Teesside County Borough Council to withdraw. Teesside Industrial Development Board, *Annual Report 1964–65* (Middlesbrough: TIDB, 1965), 18; NEDC Minutes, 12 March 1971. Similar problems occurred with the government's development district approach in the early 1960s. *Parl. Deb.* (H.C.), 5th ser., 663(1962).

[31] C. Storer and A. Townsend, *The Northern Economic Planning Council* (London: Regional Studies Association, 1971).

activities. On a wide range of issues, regional civil servants were able to pursue their own agenda with or through the council.[32] Whenever NEPC initiatives showed signs of embarrassing the central government, regional civil servants were quick to moderate or deflect the council's actions. This situation contributed in no small way to the failures of the planning council between 1965 and 1979.

The planning council's first chairperson, T. Dan Smith, viewed his regional responsibilities as threefold: (1) to build channels between local authorities and central government; (2) to bring together interests in the various subregions around a single regional perspective; and (3) to build relationships with other planning council chairpersons in the country.[33] Direct relations between the council and elements of the local power structure failed to materialize, however. In fact, the mere announcement of government intentions to create the council in 1964 provoked a defensive reaction from the major local authorities in the North East. Fearing encroachment on their land-use planning powers and prerogatives, they formed their own group, the North Regional Planning Council (NRPC), to protect their interests. In 1972, seven years after the NEPC's formation, council members were still heard to lament "the apparent lack of understanding among local authorities" of planning council functions.[34] Meetings with MPs were generally poorly attended, and constrained by the obligation of the council to maintain a low political profile.[35] The only coordinating efforts to produce results involved joint meetings with regional officials from the TUC and the CBI, who agreed publicly to improve upon their poor record of industrial relations, which was thought to be a deterrent to companies considering relocation in the region.[36]

Local authorities were not the only actors to react with dismay to the creation of the council. As a body with direct access to government officials, the council threatened the RDO's steadily weakening monopoly of representation. To make matters worse, the RDO suffered a string of membership defections and internal challenges beginning in 1969 that placed its basic functions in question. Dissatisfaction grew over the direction of the organization and its seeming inability to produce results. The main attack came from the local authority members, newly

---

[32] Former civil servant and chairperson of the Northern Regional Economic Planning Board (1966–71), Edinburgh, 20 February 1986. Interview with the author.

[33] Former chairperson of the Northern Planning Council, Newcastle upon Tyne, 5 February 1986. Interview with the author.

[34] NEPC Minutes, 24 November 1972.

[35] NEPC Minutes, 26 January 1968. "A continuous lobbying of MPs might prejudice the Chairman's ready access to Ministers...." NEPC Minutes, 25 May 1978.

[36] T. D. Smith, *Dan Smith* (Newcastle upon Tyne: Oriel Press, Ltd., 1970), 89.

equipped from the 1974 local government reorganization. Larger councils, particularly the City of Newcastle upon Tyne and Tyne and Wear County Council, turned to independent development strategies based on their new powers.[37] By the end of the decade, local authority members, with central government cooperation, had pushed the RDO into a very narrow range of activities focusing on international promotion and marketing. In effect, this period marked the beginning of the end of its role as a principal coordinator of local and regional groups. Needless to say, the precarious position of the RDO did not incline it toward cooperative relations with the planning council.

Despite the competitiveness that characterized relations between the planning council and established local and regional actors, there remained a strong continuity in objectives with the preceding period. Regional economic policy continued to define the agenda, though groups began to stress the need for policies that steered specific kinds of mobile investment to the North East, like high technology, research and development, and corporate headquarters.[38] Industrial objectives exhibited a growing concern with the promotion of indigenous industries and skilled labor reserves, a reflection of the fact that the national pool of footloose industry had dwindled substantially. The new objectives gradually eclipsed the standard palette of infrastructure-related objectives. Groups continued to battle the claims of the prosperous regions and new competition from emerging but as yet nonassisted problem regions. These efforts to the contrary, central government bowed to pressure from aspiring problem regions in 1970 and created the intermediate areas. More important, a permanent relaxation of IDC controls occurred in 1974. These decisions constituted major defeats for the North East and other traditional problem areas.[39] Regional advocates continued to demand another Hailsham as a means of placing North East demands directly on the Cabinet table. The Labour government acceded on two occasions, and appointed an MP to serve as "minister without portfolio"

[37] NEPC Minutes, 25 January 1974. For example, Tyne and Wear County Council moved strongly into local economic development policies with the passage of the 1976 Tyne and Wear Act, a local Act of Parliament that conferred substantial powers on the council to offer development loans and grants. These powers were subsumed and extended by the Inner Urban Areas Act of 1978. See F. Robinson, C. Wren, and J. Goddard, *Economic Development Policies* (Oxford: Clarendon Press, 1987).

[38] Northern Economic Planning Council, *Challenge of the Changing North* (London: HMSO, 1966), 1, 54–5.

[39] "The regions are like the Anglo-Saxon kingdoms, at constant war with one another for survival. Survival of the fittest is the war cry of the South and Midlands." *Newcastle Journal*, 3 April 1969. By 1977, the chairperson of the planning council warned that the region was being outclassed by vigorous publicity drives in the Midlands, and that a counteroffensive was necessary to offset their effect on government policy. NEPC Minutes, 24 November 1977.

responsible for advancing North East claims in Whitehall. Their influence was highly circumscribed, particularly since these appointments were not accompanied by an expansive development program along the lines of the 1963 initiative. Finally, these various organizations continued the practice of remaining studiously nonpartisan. An official with the RDO captured the essence of this approach: "I hope you will . . . maintain the impartiality that we have made traditionally ours since our inception as a regional organization. . . . [We] must not only be strictly nonpolitical but also appear to be nonpolitical. . . . In this way we shall be accepted in every part of the region."[40]

This shared inheritance notwithstanding, the council demonstrated a repeated tendency to adopt positions opposed by other North East groups. For example, the NEPC became the main proponent of growth zones, adopting a position in line with government pronouncements and civil service recommendations. Indeed, the council went so far as to register its opposition to the principle of special development areas and to challenge gently the planning board's practice of steering investment to unemployment trouble spots.[41] These arguments placed the council in an untenable position with respect to other actors in the region. The RDO, initially warm to the idea, had returned along with Northern MPs to principled opposition by 1963 in an effort to counter membership and constituency opposition. Local authorities in low-potential areas like South West Durham, the North Riding, and Northumberland argued that the approach passed death sentences on their communities.[42] The council began to de-emphasize growth zones by the end of 1969, bowing to local opposition and civil service indifference. By the mid-1970s, all major groups in the North East had returned to an uneasy consensus of promoting the region as a whole and the worse-off areas in particular.[43]

By far the most significant disagreement between the planning council and other organizations occurred in the latter half of the 1970s. The bone of contention – Scottish and Welsh devolution – cut to the heart of the organizational fragmentation that had plagued the region since

---

[40] NEDC Minutes, 12 June 1970.
[41] NEPC Minutes, 24 January 1969.
[42] Even the reaffirmation of the black spot approach created internal tensions within the RDO. Teesside interests registered their strong dissatisfaction, linked to their status as one of the few high-growth subregions in the North East. NEDC Minutes, 12 March 1971. These tensions within the RDO were symptomatic of its loosening grip on regional coordination during the 1970s.
[43] NEPC Minutes, 25 July 1969. Despite this fact, much of the development in the region during this period took place in line with the recommendations of the Hailsham Initiative of 1963 and the NEPC's *Outline Strategy for the North* (Newcastle upon Tyne: NEPC, 1969). NEPC Minutes, 23 January 1970.

the early 1960s.[44] Once again, all major regional actors agreed on first principles. Scotland and Wales had benefited in the past from preferential institutional arrangements, such as direct Cabinet representation and more MPs per voter than English regions, and could expect to gain an even greater advantage in the competition for increasingly scarce footloose industry and government assistance with the aid of devolved regional assemblies and development agencies. Therefore, North East actors hoped to replace existing regional bodies with a single organization able to influence investment location decisions in the region, devise a comprehensive regional economic strategy and a mechanism for its implementation, participate in making decisions over public expenditure of relevance to the region, and advise central government on a continuous basis. Unity over means, however, did not follow from unity over long-term goals. The prospect of constitutional reform for Scotland and Wales, heretofore favored parts of the periphery, split North East actors into two blocks, each offering different solutions and pursuing different strategies.

One block formed around North East Labour MPs, who proposed several radical institutional ripostes to the devolutionist threat. Their efforts centered on a series of parliamentary bills to establish a government-funded regional development agency possessing significant powers to attract new industry to the North East. MPs garnered support from the region's major local authorities, the Regional Council of the Labour Party, and the RDO (the North of England Development Council: NoEDC). Given the pervasive strength of Labour in the region, these groups constituted a single partisan block. In 1978, this coalition raised its demands with a proposal to transform the planning council into a democratically elected council of regional representatives with increased powers to coordinate economic development and promotion in the North East.[45] These proposals challenged not only conventional government approaches to regional economic disparities, but the basic distribution of territorial power in the British unitary state.[46]

---

[44] For a general discussion of devolution, see M. Keating and D. Bleiman, *Labour and Scottish Nationalism*.

[45] The Northern Regional Council of the Labour Party, *Let's Pull Together for a Better North* (Newcastle upon Tyne: The Northern Regional Council of the Labour Party, 1978).

[46] These demands echoed the Northern Region Strategy Team's radical proposal for greater regional control over central government's decisions on public expenditure in the North East. Pointing to "the limited degree of freedom available to the region . . . to influence resource allocation in accordance with its own priorities," the report advocated "a comprehensive regional system of administration and resource allocation." Northern Region Strategy Team, *Strategic Plan for the Northern Region*, vols. 1–5 (Newcastle upon Tyne: Hindson Print Group, Ltd., 1977). The radical nature of the regional expenditure proposal,

The planning council for its part advocated an approach to the North East's economic and institutional deficit that built on existing relationships with the Whitehall bureaucracy. It opposed the creation of a regional tier of government in England and a development agency for the North.[47] Instead, the council proposed a slightly enhanced version of itself, complete with an element of democratic representation and an established right to advise and influence central government. The council plumped for limited change because its members valued the close, confidential relationship they enjoyed with government officials. Indeed, the proposals contained in the regional Labour Party's 1978 document placed the planning council in a delicate position, jeopardizing its position with respect to ministers and civil servants. Civil servants were quick to make council members aware of the privileged position of the North East in comparison with other English regions (see Table 4.1). Nationwide changes in the existing structure of regional consultation and representation, they pointed out, would endanger that privileged position.

The main casualty of the devolution debate, oddly enough, was the RDO. By 1977, the chair of the RDO let it be known that his organization would be interested in taking over any devolved powers granted to the region. The RDO's attempt to play the role of vanguard of the devolution movement proved fatal, bringing down upon it the wrath of local authority members. A Durham County Council official stated that the RDO "more or less" transgressed on the powers of the county councils. "We think the [RDO] has a duty to perform. Maybe it has stepped outside the original lines laid down."[48]

Government officials recognized the disastrous political effects of fragmentation, particularly when these competing organizations acted "outside a national context."[49] Nevertheless, the demands from both blocks in the region met with a hostile reception from the government, which was staunchly opposed to any overt strengthening of North East insti-

in combination with the timing of its release (the government was grappling with IMF-imposed expenditure cutbacks), caused the government to shelve the report. According to a DoE official in London, the Northern plan, which challenged core assumptions of government macroeconomic and employment policies, was "the straw that broke the camel's back," and therefore warranted no response. Civil servant, Plans and Regional Policy, Department of the Environment, London, 9 July 1984. Interview with the author.

[47] In 1976, the NoEDC published *A Statement of Claim*, which demanded financing parity with the Welsh and Scottish Development Agencies. The report failed to win the support of the NEPC. NEPC Minutes, 23 September 1976.

[48] *Evening Chronicle*, 10 September 1977.

[49] NEPC Minutes, 27 July 1978. This discomfort can be traced directly to the pressures generated by the devolution debate. Jones and Keating, *Labour and the British State*, 127.

Table 4.1. *British regional policy grants by region (£ million), 1972 to 3/1987*

Region	RDGs	SFA offers	Total	% UK	% Mfg. empl.
Scotland	1658.8	491.3	2150.1	28.8	8.0
Wales	1035.8	356.4	1392.2	18.6	4.0
North East	1497.8	272.5	1770.3	23.7	5.7
Yorkshire and Humberside	354.5	143.2	497.7	6.7	9.5
East Midlands	57.3	43.7	101.0	1.4	8.6
South East	0.0	0.0	0.0	0.0	29.7
South West	106.5	41.2	147.7	2.0	6.5
West Midlands	2.7	51.9	54.6	0.7	12.7
North West	1007.0	346.6	1353.6	18.1	13.5
Northern Ireland	0.0	0.0	0.0	0.0	1.7
Total	5720.4	1746.8	7467.2	100.0	100.0

Notes: % Mfg. Empl. is the percentage of total manufacturing employment contained in the region for 1982. One must interpret these data with some caution. Regional policy grants are not the same as transfer payments from which one can directly infer influence and priorities. In fact, regional policy is ultimately passive, in that firms must apply for assistance voluntarily and then, if awarded a grant, accept it. Thus, the connection between regional share size and influence is tenuous. It can serve as a rough indicator, if one bears in mind that awards are only partially due to the promotion efforts of both regional actors and civil servants.
Sources: United Kingdom, Secretary of State for Trade and Industry, *Industrial Development Act 1982, Annual Report 1985* (London: HMSO, 1985); G. Bentley and J. Mawson, *The Economic Decline of the West Midlands and the Role of Regional Planning (Birmingham: Joint Centre for Regional, Urban, and Local Government Studies, 1985), 19.*

tutions because of the cost, the duplication of effort with existing governmental agencies, and the likely generation of similar demands from other English regions. Although North East MPs proved willing to scuttle, albeit temporarily, the government's devolution bill in 1977, they were unable to gain much from the government in return for a ceasefire. The Labour government defused the radical proposals of its North East MPs through increased Urban Programme aid and a strengthened regional National Enterprise Board office in the North.[50] In response to the planning council's proposals, the Cabinet decided in 1979 to increase the number of council members and to reaffirm the NEPC's role as a consultative body. These reform commitments, largely cosmetic, fell victim to the results of the general election later that year.

[50] R. Guthrie and I. McLean, "Another Part of the Periphery," *Parliamentary Affairs* 31(Spring 1978): 190–200.

The NEPC was abolished along with other planning councils shortly after Margaret Thatcher's victory. Devolution bequeathed to the region a difficult inheritance: a divided regional interest structure combined with an undiminished faith in central government as the ultimate source of solutions to the region's problems. Both would prove to be severe handicaps under the radically changed circumstances brought about by the Thatcherite accession.

Strengthened corporate pluralism without the state, 1979–86
Gloomy prospects for the North East were ushered in by the change of government in 1979. Across the board, London reverted for the first time since the early 1930s to an exclusionary approach to the region. The Thatcher government's intention to rely on market forces threatened to cut off the region from its preferred source of relief – regional economic assistance. Moreover, the disbanding of the planning council left the region bereft of a voice for the North East, and sent a clear message that reform of the country's basic territorial division of power was off the national agenda. The new Conservative government also exposed a political predicament for the region: redress through government via bureaucratic *or* party channels appeared to be little more than a pipe dream. The region's political leverage, historically marginal, was reduced to insignificance by the geographical composition of Thatcher's electoral support coalition. Of the Conservative majority of 339, only six hailed from the North East. Whereas this situation would have posed few problems for the region in the past, the breakdown of consensus over regional policy created an opportunity for the new Tory government to base its regional policy on more overt partisan criteria. The shift to an exclusionary stance with respect to the North East paralleled inclusive overtures to regions like the West Midlands. These political and policy constraints emanating from London eventually prompted a discernible shift in the position of North East actors, which harbored few illusions that the government was sympathetic to the continuing plight of the regional economy.[51] In their efforts, these groups received vital support from regional civil servants, who softened and modified the government's exclusionary stance in key ways. As such, the title of this section is misleading; corporate pluralism emerged without the participation of the central state apparatus but with the continuing involvement of the government's field administration.

With government avenues closed off, North East actors turned in-

---

[51] During a 1985 visit to the region, Thatcher belittled the "moaning Minnies" in the North East and suggested that the region ought "to get its act together." Norman Tebbit, Tory chairperson, echoed these sentiments two months later. *Newcastle Journal*, 7 October 1985.

ward, and began to draft indigenous organizational and policy objectives based on cooperative strategies. Groups exhumed the goal of a regional development agency, yet sought financial and political backing within the region, not from central government. In 1984, the regional CBI and TUC endeavored to replace the discredited RDO with a more powerful organization that would wield control over land and property for development, coordinate regional promotion programs, and arrange financial support packages for investment project. The proposal received only the tacit moral support of central government, which ruled out statutory and financial assistance in view of the pressures for similar treatment likely to arise in other English regions.[52] In the end, the proposal foundered on the radical block formed during the devolution episode. The Regional Council of the Labour Party, the Labour-led local authorities, and the RDO criticized the TUC-CBI model as undemocratic and elitist, and accused proponents of attempting "to hijack the region."[53] In actual fact, their opposition had little to do with democratic etiquette: "Labour can see not only their regional power base going by the board but the establishment by private means of something they have long been advocating is a Government function. . . . The challenge to Labour is whether they now accept these resources are unlikely to come from No. 10 and must be provided from within the region."[54]

Opponents blocked the proposal by withholding vital local authority cooperation, highlighting the veto power of the Labour coalition. A round of further discussions between these groups and the TUC and CBI began in late 1985; regional civil servants served as intermediaries between the opposing camps. The search for a compromise was long and arduous, a symptom of the new breed of organization at issue. In the words of one participant, "Any organization that reduces the sovereignty of any constituent organization is bound to have problems."[55]

In early 1986, negotiations concluded with the formation of the Northern Development Company, Ltd. The difference between the NDC and its paper predecessor is largely a matter of packaging. "We have paid a great deal of attention to the accountability issue, and quite frankly, the NDC is a great deal easier to sell as a result."[56] The NDC set about quickly to consolidate available resources under its control; to this end,

---

[52] Former senior civil servant, Northern Regional Office of the Department of Trade and Industry, 26 March 1986. Interview with the author.
[53] Official with the Northern Regional Council of the Labor Party, Newcastle upon Tyne, 17 March 1986. Interview with the author.
[54] *Newcastle Journal*, 21 May 1985.
[55] Official with the Northern Office of the CBI, Newcastle upon Tyne, 9 December 1985. Interview with the author.
[56] Official with the Northern Regional Office of the TUC, Newcastle upon Tyne, 3 March 1986 and 25 March 1986. Interview with the author.

it absorbed the assets and responsibilities of the RDO,[57] and sought out close relations with the region's divisional offices of the English Industrial Estates Corporation and the New Town Corporations. In areas where the NoEDC had failed or lost credibility, the NDC pushed ahead with the full support of its regionwide membership in regional promotion, investment counseling and market information, export promotion, and networking with government agencies and EC offices in Brussels. Each of these initiatives was accomplished with a level of regional coordination among local authorities, firms, and trade unions never achieved by the NoEDC. In these endeavors, the NDC attained the status of a "one stop shop" for the North East.

With respect to its more controversial objectives, like direct investment, the provision of finance and seed capital, and the direction of regional development, the NDC moved with a great deal less alacrity. The NDC's plan to absorb the assets of English Industrial Estates Corporation, Ltd. and the new towns required an Act of Parliament – a commitment to regionalism that was not forthcoming under any circumstances from the Thatcher Government. Furthermore, local authority members remained unwilling to cede the initiative in local economic development to a strengthened NDC.[58] This ingrained reluctance was stiffened by central government's moral, statutory, and budgetary encouragement of local development initiatives. With subregional alternatives available to local authority members, the NDC was forced to tread warily. Consequently, progress was greatest where internal resistance was the least. While members could only benefit from promotional and marketing activities of the NDC, they felt they had much more to lose in the realm of actual decisions on investment levels and siting. Whether the NDC will overcome the economic tribalism of the region remains an open question to this day.

Despite the overwhelming focus on internal mobilization, groups were unable to ignore Whitehall and Westminster. Given the scarcity of resources in the North East, regional actors like the NDC still had to obtain financial support from central government. Thus, the NDC was

[57] In 1979, the government assumed the major part of the financing of the NoEDC; the relationship between the council and the regional office of the DTI was described in terms of "master" and "servant." Thus, the semihostile takeover of the region's RDO proved less difficult than expected, since the government was willing to cooperate. Civil servant, Northern Regional Office of the Department of Trade and Industry, Newcastle upon Tyne, 6 March 1986. Researcher, Center for Urban and Regional Development Studies, University of Newcastle upon Tyne, Newcastle upon Tyne, 14 March 1986. Interviews with the author.

[58] See Robinson et al., *Economic Development Policies*, for a discussion of local authority economic development policies in the Newcastle upon Tyne metropolitan area.

forced "to boost the North and its emancipation into the enterprise culture and at the same time to make a continuing case for assistance."[59] The juggling act extended to the political arena as well; a principal strategy of NDC organizers was to re-create the strictly nonpartisan stance which predominated in the region before the devolution episode. As an observer warned in 1986, "Unless they are careful, [the NDC] will be a local authority-led, Labour-dominated outfit, and the government will probably walk away from it. It is very important to achieve a [political] balance."[60] The NDC managed to remain studiously apolitical in a region monopolized by Labour, an achievement in which company officials took great pride.

In their efforts to obtain government assistance, North East interests worked through bureaucratic channels, and received the support of regional civil servants in ways that blunted the impact of Thatcherite exclusion. Regional DoE and DTI officials were motivated to play the role of advocate for several reasons. Many had served in the North East prior to the change of government, and continued to adhere to the principle of assisting what they perceived as a chronically depressed regional economy. Several officials arrived after 1979 as exiles from the new regime in Whitehall, which only strengthened the inclination of the regional office to go to bat for the North East.[61]

In 1983–4, the Northern Regional Office of the DTI took the lead in mobilizing a response to the government's proposed cuts in regional aid. DTI officials solicited opinions from groups and combined these with in-house analyses to make the case for the North East as a structurally depressed region. Their goal was to restate the long-standing claims of the region against those of arriviste problem regions like the West Midlands. As a former director of the DTI Regional Office in Newcastle stated, "Regional Offices don't carry much weight with this government or any other, for that matter, if they are alone. They need allies – in this case [the 1983 regional policy review], the private sector in the North."[62] Regional officials also took the unusual step of informing Conservative MPs of a Whitehall proposal to withdraw Newcastle upon Tyne's assisted-area status, which served to close the ranks of the re-

[59] "A New North Getting Back on Track," The Times, 22 April 1988.
[60] Former senior civil servant, Northern Regional Office of the Department of Trade and Industry, phone interview, 26 March 1986. Interview with the author.
[61] On the controversial subject of the politicization of the civil service under Thatcher, see P. Hennessy, Whitehall (London: Secker & Warburg, 1989).
[62] Former senior civil servant, Northern Regional Office of the Department of Trade and Industry, phone interview, 26 March 1986. Additional material from civil servant, Northern Regional Office of the Department of Trade and Industry, Newcastle upon Tyne, 6 March 1986. Interviews with the author.

gion's parliamentary representatives.[63] Regional civil servants helped North East local authorities to tap new sources of assistance provided by the European Regional Development Fund. For example, the Northern DoE set up the Regional Development Programme Working Group in the early 1980s to bring together local government officials to discuss potential projects and EC application procedures. In addition, officials liaised with individual local authorities, advising them on application procedures and project eligibility, and they encouraged local authorities to establish in-house capabilities to monitor EC developments. The view in the regional office paralleled that in London: The ERDF involved a simple resource transfer from the Community to the region.[64]

In other areas, the support proffered by the field administrative apparatus was consistent with broader Thatcherite economic principles. DTI officials believed that the North East's main weakness lay in a market gap; because of the high concentration of branch plants in the region, basic investment decisions were made elsewhere. As a result, officials found it difficult to elicit private sector participation in initiatives like urban development agencies, public-private development partnerships, technology transfer programs, and the like. Operating within these constraints, DTI officials organized cooperative ventures with local authorities and other government departments to create programs like the Newcastle Technology Center and a market advisory service for the region. Their long-term strategy was to encourage the growth of an indigenous, entrepreneurially oriented private sector capable of sustaining regional growth.

What is striking is that these objectives were taken up by many established interest groups in the North East. The NDC concentrated on problems largely unaddressed by previous regional bodies: the lack of an entrepreneurial culture and the prevalence of traditional job skills and outlooks. The changed political environment in London dating from 1979 accounts for the NDC's emphasis on retaining resources in the

[63] Former senior civil servant, Northern Regional Office of the Department of Trade and Industry, phone interview, 26 March 1986. Interview with the author.

[64] The North East's share of UK ERDF expenditure during this period was substantial. Between 1975 and 1986, the region received the equivalent of £354 million: 14.8 percent of the UK total, and third best among UK regions. Commission of the European Communities, *European Regional Development Fund: 12th Annual Report (1986)* (Luxembourg: Office for Official Publications of the European Communities, 1987), 66. Comparable figures for Wales and Scotland are £364 (15.2%) and £572 (23.9%) million. The overall trend for the North East proved worrisome, however, a result of newly eligible regions like the West Midlands. In 1981, the North East received 19 percent of the UK share; in 1986, the figure had dropped to 11.5 percent. Civil servant, Northern Regional Office of the Department of the Environment, Newcastle upon Tyne, 21 February 1986. Interview with the author.

region rather than on traditional requests for additional government handouts. In short, while local and regional actors decried Thatcher's neglect of the North East, many adopted her language, if not her objectives. "There is a strong sense in the region that we had better deal with the government on their terms."[65] Broadly speaking, unity and coherence once again characterized North East initiatives, although in the absence of open support from central government. North East groups achieved corporate pluralism without the state, or more precisely, without the *central* state: Regional civil servants compensated for the dearth of London-based initiatives and resources.

The West Midlands, 1965–86

Comprised of the five counties of Shropshire, Staffordshire, Warwickshire, Hereford and Worcester, and West Midlands, and centering on the city of Birmingham, the West Midlands is distinguished by the structure and (until recently) success of its economy. The region's principal industries, engineering, bicycles, and motor vehicles, emerged in the late nineteenth century and fed on the booming markets of South East England and continental Europe. Over time, the region secured a reputation for the entrepreneurial acumen of its employers, the adaptability of its work force, and an overall economic flexibility. By the interwar years, the West Midlands had become the manufacturing heartland of the country, the engine of British growth and prosperity. Vehicle production was the jewel in the West Midlands crown; the industrial complex built around automobiles included suppliers of components and capital equipment. Until the mid-1960s, this interdependent mix proved to be a powerful growth formula for the region. Unemployment rarely climbed above 1 or 2 percent, growth was high relative to the national average, and investment kept pace with the national rate. But, as a recent study of the region points out, there was a "negative twist" to this success story. Flexible interdependence soon gave way to "focused dependence" on dominant manufacturers in a narrow range of industries.[66]

---

[65] Senior officials with the Northern Development Company, Ltd., Newcastle upon Tyne, 12 July 1989. Interview with the author.

[66] K. Spencer et al., *Crisis in the Industrial Heartland* (Oxford: Clarendon Press, 1986), 10. In 1979, 68 percent of manufacturing output in the region was produced by five manufacturing sectors: vehicles, metal goods, metal manufacture, mechanical engineering, and electrical engineering. These same five sectors accounted for 70 percent of regional employment. Comparable figures at the national level were 45 percent and 49 percent, respectively. West Midlands Economic Planning Council and the West Midlands Planning Authorities Conference, *A Developing Strategy for the West Midlands* (Birmingham: WMEPC–WMPAC, 1979).

After 1966, manufacturing investment in the region began to lag behind the national average and unemployment inched ever upward. The
decline of the automobile industry in the 1970s mercilessly exposed the
region's vulnerability. With unbelievable rapidity, a once buoyant manufacturing mix had become a millstone. Between 1980 and 1983 alone,
over 350,000 jobs in the manufacturing sector were lost, a record that
surpassed even the dismal performance of the traditional problem regions.[67] Viewed in a comparative context, the West Midlands represents
a stark contrast to the North East, in large part because of its comparatively recent, abrupt transition from growth to decline. Patterns of
interaction in the West Midlands are closely related to changes brought
about by this transition. The slow, painstaking process by which consensus emerged during the 1970s, coupled with the halting steps taken
toward regionwide cooperative strategies, presents a very different picture from that in the North East region.

Pluralism reigns, 1965–70
Until 1970, the challenge facing the West Midlands was not to reverse
economic decline, but to manage economic growth and associated planning problems.[68] Local and regional actors pointed to temporary cyclical
fluctuations in the national economy, not to endemic weaknesses in the
region's industrial base, as the cause of the periodic economic recessions
in the region. Amid the chorus of optimism, dissonant voices from within
the business community could be heard. For example, the Birmingham
Chamber of Commerce and Industry lamented the city's chronic inability
to attract new growth industries, while the West Midlands CBI warned
that the regional economy had become unhealthily dependant on the
motor vehicle industry.[69] Still, such gloomy assessments were in no way
indicative of widespread concern about the vulnerabilities of the West
Midlands economy. By most accounts, this was not a problem region.

The legacy of prosperity strongly influenced the way in which local
and regional groups defined and pursued their interests with respect to
each other and to central government. General satisfaction with the
existing political and institutional capabilities of the region reigned, both
among regional groups and civil servants. There were no efforts to forge
cooperative relations among groups along the lines of North East re-

[67] West Midlands Forum of County Councils, *Background Report No. 4* (Birmingham: WMFCC, 1985), 10.
[68] The two official planning studies released during the 1960s painted a rosy picture
of the regional economy, and dealt primarily with problems of land-use planning
and population management. United Kingdom, Department of Economic Affairs, *The West Midlands* (London: HMSO, 1965); West Midlands Economic
Planning Council, *The West Midlands* (London: HMSO, 1967).
[69] *Birmingham Post*, 27 March 1968.

gional development organizations. As one scholar noted, "It is . . . difficult to identify any regional pressure groups in the West Midlands."[70] Satisfaction did not, however, translate into harmony. Within the region, growth sparked an enduring conflict between the rural counties, which placed a premium on urban containment, and Birmingham, which pursued expansion as a means of relieving congestion and overcrowding.[71] A number of voluntary organizations, involving primarily local authorities, arose to handle these issues, and their presence would encourage a pluralist response when economic problems began to surface toward the end of the decade. Moreover, the creation of the planning council had much the same impact on the organizational landscape of the region as in the North East. The region's local authorities reacted swiftly and defensively by forming the West Midlands Planning Authorities Conference (WMPAC).

The assumptions of economic growth permeated the demands placed on government during this period. Central policymakers were asked to recognize the fragility of the region's economic structure, and to safeguard its complex, interdependent webs of large manufacturers and peripheral suppliers.[72] Various business groups cautioned that government disregard for this delicate industrial ecosystem could ultimately kill the goose that laid the golden eggs. Policy objectives focused primarily on macroeconomic, exchange rate, and industrial policies.[73] Where regional policy objectives surfaced, the system of industrial development certificates drew sharp criticism as a major hindrance to economic development in the region. Yet general opposition to IDCs masked deep internal divisions. City of Birmingham officials and business interests decried the impact of controls on the city's ability to retain existing firms and to attract new industries, while shire counties blamed controls for vitiating their arrangements with Birmingham to accommodate its population expansion: Local firms were steered relentlessly by government away from designated "overspill areas" in the region to the development areas in Scotland, Wales, and the North. Oddly enough, subnational actors professed their strong support for the general

---

[70] C. Painter, "Group Interactions and Lobbies in West Midlands Economic Planning, 1965–1972" (Ph.D. dissertation, University of Aston at Birmingham, 1973), 58.

[71] See B. Smith, *The Administration of Industrial Overspill* (Birmingham: Centre for Urban and Regional Development Studies, 1972).

[72] WMEPC's written evidence to the Royal Commission on the Intermediate Areas, WMR/155 Pt. I & II; WMEPC(68)30.

[73] For example, business interest associations monitored hire-purchase controls and interest rate policies, which had a profound impact on the automobile industry. Wilks mentions the "perverse" effects of stop-go macroeconomic policy on the health of the motor industry in the 1960s and 1970s. Wilks, *Industrial Policy and the Motor Industry*, 38.

objectives of regional policy – a sign of their stalwart confidence in the
health of the regional economy.[74] Throughout this period, the main
advocacy organizations in the region saw no compelling reason to object
to the exclusionary stance of the central government.

Pluralism in spite of it all, 1971–9

As the West Midlands slid into economic decline during the 1970s, a
slow, conflictual reappraisal among local and regional groups commenced. Whereas North East interests could draw on a common definition of the problem and a shared set of long-range objectives dating
back to the 1930s, comparable groups in the Midlands had to forge a
consensus among actors who strongly disagreed about the nature of the
problem, or whether one even existed. Despite efforts to the contrary,
groups were able neither to unify on a regional basis nor to change the
exclusionary stance of central government.

The planning council led the first significant break with the prevailing
assumptions of growth. Its 1971 report, *The West Midlands: An Economic Appraisal*, "blew the whistle on the region," and marked the first
step in the development of a new consensus over the structural problems
of the regional economy.[75] The study drew attention to the lack of
economic adaptation in recent decades, the region's dependence on a
narrow range of industries, and the rapid rise in the regional unemployment rate, which in 1971 had matched the national average for the
first time. Government IDC policies aggravated these weaknesses by
locking the region into a stagnating industrial structure.[76] The council
recommended the adoption of a positive economic policy for the West
Midlands to bring about "an adjustment in the resource allocation between regions."[77] This analysis initiated a fierce intraregional debate,
pitting industry, labor, and urban local authorities against the majority
of the shire counties led by WMPAC, which rejected the pessimistic
forecasts of the council.[78] At this juncture, the planning council had

---

[74] West Midlands Economic Planning Council Document 68/30; Birmingham
Chamber of Commerce and Industry, "Evidence to the Hunt Committee on
Intermediate Areas" (Birmingham: mimeo, 1968).

[75] Senior civil servant, West Midlands Office of the Department of the Environment, Birmingham, 12 February 1986. Interview with the author. See West
Midlands Economic Planning Council, *The West Midlands* (London: HMSO,
1971).

[76] Spencer et al., *Crisis in the Industrial Heartland*, dispute this claim on empirical
grounds (p. 127). The *perception* among subnational actors, however, was (and
remains) strong.

[77] Painter, "Group Interactions," 181.

[78] WMPAC placed the regional economy in the midst of a transitional phase,
during which any overdependence on manufacturing industry would be corrected by a shift into services under conditions of continued economic growth.

developed into the sole platform for the expression of producer group (as opposed to local authority) interests in the region.[79] This position would not last, however. Indeed, the publication of *Appraisal* marked the beginning of a period of "embarrassed decline" for the council. "[Council members] became somewhat unpopular figures. . . . No one wanted to hear that the West Midlands was on the slide."[80]

By the end of the decade, opinion in the West Midlands had converged substantially in the face of mounting urban problems and the lack of resilience in the regional economy exposed by the OPEC crisis. Between 1975 and 1979, the planning council, WMPAC, and producer groups gravitated toward a common position: "The West Midlands . . . could no longer afford to see its declining resources siphoned off for the benefit of other parts of the United Kingdom."[81] In short, indifference to government neglect was a luxury the region could no longer afford. These organizations were careful not to request regional policy assistance, preferring to avoid identification with the traditional problem areas. Regional policy was the problem, not the solution. Instead, they advocated the further relaxation of IDC controls as well as sectoral schemes to rejuvenate manufacturing industry and increased Urban Programme aid.[82] The overall goal was economic regeneration for the entire region, coupled with urban regeneration for the decaying inner cities. This position enabled groups to begin to bridge the divisions caused by the long period of economic growth.

The regional office of the DoE played two key roles in bringing about a convergence of interest among these disparate actors. First, it provided the impetus for a reevaluation of the region's situation within government circles. The DoE waged a rear-guard action in Whitehall, advanced by the judicious use of statistics and analysis, with the planning council as the sometimes witting, sometimes unwitting mouthpiece. "[The council] was especially useful as a means of getting civil service opinions in under the cloak to London."[83] Indeed, the main planning documents issued by the council, including *Appraisal*, were the products of DoE in-house analysis. Second, the DoE worked actively to accelerate the

West Midlands Regional Study, *A Developing Strategy for the West Midlands* (Birmingham: WMRS, 1971), 22.

[79] Painter, "Group Interactions." Senior civil servant, West Midlands Office of the Department of the Environment, Birmingham, 12 February 1986. Interview with the author.

[80] Senior civil servant, West Midlands Office of the Department of the Environment, Birmingham, 12 February 1986. Interview with the author.

[81] Minutes of the West Midlands Economic Planning Council, 3 February 1976.

[82] West Midlands Planning Authorities Conference, *A Developing Strategy for the West Midlands* (Birmingham: WMPAC, 1980).

[83] Civil servant, West Midlands Regional Office of the Department of the Environment, Birmingham, 12 February 1986. Interview with the author.

process of consensus-building among indigenous actors. Its willingness to play both roles grew out of its responsibilities for the urban problems of the region and its regular contacts with hard-hit local authorities. As the strongest department in the region, the DoE was well positioned to accomplish both objectives.[84] The principal vehicle for the generation of a modicum of regional consensus was the West Midlands Regional Strategy Review. The strategy review brought together the WMEPC, WMPAC, and regional government officials in an effort to iron out the differences in planning analyses of the region and to provide a monitoring capacity for the resulting plan. The arrangement led to a rapid admission that a problem did in fact exist; in 1976, the participants reported that "the Region seemed to have lost the strong industrial advantage it appeared to have at 1958."[85]

DoE efforts were ultimately constrained by fierce opposition from its headquarters in London as well as from the regional and central offices of the DTI. The region's long history as a growth region, and its crucial role within national regional policy as a source of steerable investment projects for the depressed areas, influenced the positions adopted by other government departments. For example, the regional office of the DTI remained committed to the cyclical view of the regional economy well into the late 1970s, adopting a position in line with its headquarters.[86] DTI intransigence related in no small way to policy divisions at the national level between the urban responsibilities of the DoE and the regional policy interests of the DTI. In the absence of a Whitehall decision to the contrary, the West Midlands DoE could expect no assistance from its DTI counterpart to focus attention on the growing economic problems of the inner cities, particularly if this involved direct support for industry or increased local authority powers. The issues of departmental turf and the inviolability of regional policy assumptions were paramount, and as a result, the overall exclusionary stance of government vis-à-vis the West Midlands was maintained.

---

[84] The DoE was official head of the planning board and the largest spender of discretionary resources in the region, totaling some £50–£60 million annually. By way of contrast, the DTI had virtually no discretionary resources until 1984. Senior civil servant, West Midlands Office of the Department of the Environment, Birmingham, 12 February 1986. Interview with the author.

[85] Joint Monitoring Steering Group, *A Developing Strategy for the West Midlands* (Birmingham: JMSG, 1976), 37. For detailed accounts of the actions of these actors, known collectively as the Joint Monitoring Strategy Group (JMSG), see J. Mawson and C. Skelcher, "Updating the West Midlands Regional Strategy," *Town Planning Review* 51(1980): 152–70. See the bibliography for a full list of reports published by the JMSG.

[86] Civil servant, West Midlands Office of the Department of Trade and Industry, Birmingham, 22 January 1986. Interview with the author. WMEPC Steering Committee Minutes, 24 July 1978. WMEPB Minutes, 10 November 1972. DoE internal memoranda, 2/1977.

As far as the goal of fomenting cooperative approaches among subnational actors was concerned, DoE officials were held back by their overarching allegiance to central government. For example, planning council requests for greater autonomy, which coincided with the national devolution debates, found little favor with the DoE.[87] More significant, the limitations of the strategy review surfaced in 1979, when regional civil servants refused to underwrite a set of controversial policy recommendations put forward by the nongovernmental participants. Since these officials had provided much of the analysis and a good part of the write-up, they were placed in a sensitive position. As one official exclaimed, "Government could hardly sign an advocacy document to itself!"[88] In the end, two separate reports were published, one under the auspices of government, the other by the council and WMPAC.[89] Both drew on a common analysis and interpretation of the region's problems, but they differed markedly in the scope of their recommendations.

In sum, although key industrial sectors in the West Midlands received a great deal of government attention during the 1970s,[90] the *regional* claims of these groups generally fell on deaf ears in Whitehall. The West Midlands continued to be treated by central government as a source of mobile investment for the country's traditional assisted areas, a view which caused much consternation in the region. In the words of one local notable, "The West Midlands should have been treated as a seed bed rather than a quarry."[91] And as long as Conservative and Labour governments were unwilling to acknowledge the structural economic problems of the West Midlands, local and regional groups could do little to address the mounting economic trends. Labour governments proved especially unwilling to reevaluate the region's status, since any changes would call into question the party's commitment to the traditional problem regions and to Labour's core electoral base there. In fact, the lack of regional unity enabled government policymakers to offer localities and subregions partial, largely symbolic responses requiring only administrative modifications of existing policies. As a DTI regional civil servant explained, governments of both parties were able to "pick off"

---

[87] WMEPB Minutes, 8 February 1977.
[88] Senior civil servant, West Midlands Office of the Department of the Environment, Birmingham, 12 February 1986. Interview with the author.
[89] JMSG, *A Developing Strategy for the West Midlands* (Birmingham: JMSG, 1979); WMEPC–WMPAC, *A Developing Strategy for the West Midlands*. In 1980, WMPAC published an update of the strategy under its own auspices; see WMPAC, *A Developing Strategy for the West Midlands* (Birmingham: WMPAC, 1980).
[90] Three decades of government assistance to the vehicle industry are outlined in Wilks, *Industrial Policy and the Motor Industry*.
[91] Minutes of the West Midlands Economic Planning Council, 8 April 1975.

the West Midlands with ease.[92] The success of *divide et impera* was reflected in the failure of organized collective action prior to 1979.

For much of this period, the principal point of access for West Midlands' interests went through parliamentary channels. This was in effect a default option, since the region contained no assisted areas to speak of and therefore its principal advocacy organizations – regional offices of central government, local authority organizations, producer groups – remained outside the formal regional policy-making process. Although the Commons remained the only visible forum for airing regional grievances, the effectiveness of the West Midlands lobby was hampered by severe partisan divisions. "There has never really been a regional lobby in Parliament. . . . Collectively, you can't get them to do anything."[93] The competitive nature of party politics contributed to the atomization of MP efforts on behalf of the region.

Planning council chairpersons attempted unsuccessfully throughout the decade to use their position to integrate and coordinate the various groups in the region. Although the lingering absence of regional consensus was a factor, the root cause of the council's failure lay in perceptions of its weakness and even irrelevance, for identical reasons as in the North East. The conflictual state of industrial relations at the time proved to be infertile ground for the council's efforts at matchmaking between the TUC and the CBI.[94] The council fared just as poorly with the region's elected representatives; between 1965 and 1972, it arranged just a single meeting with West Midlands MPs. Thereafter, regular joint meetings were often poorly attended, and party conflict between Labour and Conservative members often necessitated separate sessions, which defeated the underlying purpose of these initiatives.[95]

The most spectacular failure to promote a cohesive cooperative strategy occurred in the late 1970s. Consultations conducted by the planning council with the major interests in the region revealed a need for more effective political lobbying on behalf of the West Midlands. There was also limited support for unified promotion of the region in domestic and

---

[92] Civil servant, West Midlands Office of the Department of Trade and Industry, Birmingham, 22 January 1986. Interview with the author.

[93] Senior civil servant, West Midlands Office of the Department of the Environment, Birmingham, 12 February 1986. Confirmed by senior civil servant, Northern Regional Office of the Department of the Environment, Newcastle upon Tyne, 3 March 1986. Interviews with the author.

[94] WMEPC correspondence to West Midlands CBI, 7 March 1977.

[95] One such meeting in June 1977 drew twelve MPs (seven Conservative, five Labour), which was described as a good turnout. The region at the time sent a total of fifty-five MPs to the House of Commons. Senior civil servant, West Midlands Office of the Department of the Environment, Birmingham, 12 February 1986. Interview with the author. WMEPC Correspondence, 21 July 1978.

international markets.[96] The council, along with the support of other
groups, proposed the creation of a regional development and promotional agency (the West Midlands Industrial and Economic Development Agency: WMIEDA) similar to those in other British regions. This
provoked the vehement opposition of local authorities, which favored
the conversion of an existing body like the council or WMPAC, since
these were known quantities and therefore posed little threat to their
own prerogatives. Still unconvinced of the urgency of the situation and
of the benefits of pooling resources, local authorities responded defensively and competitively. Nothing that central government did during
this period encouraged them to act otherwise. Consequently, the
WMIEDA proposal was dead in the water by mid-1979. Thus, although
substantial progress had been made in forging a regional consensus on
the nature of the problem and the required remedies, the West Midlands
entered the Thatcher era as it had entered the decade of the 1970s:
internally divided and neglected by London. However, unlike the North
East, the West Midlands welcomed the Thatcher revolution with open
arms.

Corporate pluralism emerges, 1979–86
Shortly after the election in 1979, serious national policy initiatives began
to parallel earnest cooperative initiatives at the regional level. This can
be attributed to several factors: the accelerated decline of the regional
economy after 1979, which forced the main interests in the region to
set aside their differences and act together; the presence of an institutional vacuum in the region as a result of the disbanding of the planning
council[97]; and the presence of Margaret Thatcher in No. 10 Downing
Street. Many groups, especially business, saw in Thatcher a golden
opportunity to weaken drastically if not eliminate regional economic
policy. The end product was the emergence of corporate pluralist relations between national and subnational actors for the first time in the
West Midlands.

Early on, central government commenced a shift from an exclusionary
to an inclusive stance vis-à-vis the West Midlands. In 1981, the government abolished IDC controls, a largely symbolic act designed to allay

---

[96] WMEPC Minutes, 22 January 1979.
[97] Senior civil servant, West Midlands Office of the Department of the Environment, Birmingham, 12 February 1986. Interview with the author. Birmingham
Chamber of Industry and Commerce, *Regional Industrial Development* (Birmingham: BCIC, 1984), 8. Regarding the planning council, one former member
stated, "I have never seen a body which was so disparaged while it was around,
and yet so longed after [sic] once it was gone." Official with the West Midlands
Regional Council of the TUC, Birmingham, 6 February 1986. Interview with
the author.

the resentment emanating from the South and the Midlands. The government built upon this action in March 1983 with the appointment of John Butcher, Conservative MP from Coventry South West, as junior minister in the DTI with special responsibilities for the West Midlands. Some hailed the announcement of an "unofficial minister" for the region as "a milestone in the government's thinking, . . . public recognition of the fact that a serious problem existed in the West Midlands," while others dismissed it as "simply a publicity drive."[98] Government officials in London put together the Butcher appointment on short notice, with little advance warning for regional officials or interest groups. No extra money was provided for policy purposes. Butcher hosted seminars for businesspersons and luncheons for junior achievers, and in the course of twenty months as unofficial minister, he presided over a modest number of projects, including a Team for Innovation, whose job it was to promote local take-up of DTI sectoral policies, and the coordination of public and private financing of small factory and workshop units in the region. The government's targeted response betrayed an awareness of the considerable number of marginal seats in the region: six Labour marginals and seven Conservative. With the core of its 1979 majority in the South and the Midlands, and the 1983 general election looming on the horizon, the government adopted a high profile, low-budget approach to economic crisis in the West Midlands.

Despite its tentativeness, the Butcher episode created a forceful political momentum that led to another milestone the following year. In 1984, the government announced that a portion of the West Midlands surrounding the Birmingham metropolitan area would be granted intermediate-area status in a slimmed down regional-policy program. This decision, the outcome of hard-fought battles between civil service defenders of the traditional depressed regions and advocates of the new problem areas,[99] marked the final stage in the transformation of the West Midland's status in government regional policies. No longer a seed bed or a quarry, the region now found itself in the same league, though not on a par, with long-standing problem regions like the North East.

Regional groups both reacted to and influenced this sequence of

---

[98] Official with the Birmingham Chamber of Industry and Commerce, Birmingham, 27 February 1986. Civil servant, West Midlands Office of the Department of Trade and Industry, Birmingham, 22 January 1986. Interviews with the author.

[99] DTI officials in London, wary of the high Exchequer costs of designating large parts of the region with the highest concentration of manufacturing industry in the country, opted for a restricted boundary designation. Designating the entire West Midlands "would have wrecked the budget." Senior civil servant, West Midlands Office of the Department of the Environment, Birmingham, 12 February 1986. Interview with the author.

events. Shortly after the election in 1979, the principal organizations in the West Midlands took up the issue of regional cooperation with increased vigor. In 1981, WMPAC was replaced by the West Midlands Forum of County Councils (WMFCC), a body with a larger brief focusing primarily on economic issues and government policy. Collaborative efforts between the principal local and regional actors culminated in 1983 with the creation of the West Midlands Regional Economic Consortium (WMREC), the first organization to bring together under a single roof the full range of regional actors: the WMFCC; the Regional Council of the TUC; the Regional CBI; and the West Midlands Regional Group of Chambers of Commerce. The West Midlands Industrial Development Association (WMIDA), a promotional body assigned the task of attracting foreign and domestic investors, followed soon thereafter.

New and shifting objectives accompanied the new organizational structures. Soon after the government announced its review of regional policy in 1983, West Midlands groups began to advocate not just the removal of IDC controls, but the complete replacement of regional policy with sectoral manufacturing schemes. In 1984, regional actors abandoned this position in response to the government's decision not to abolish regional policy, and in an about-face called for maximum inclusion of the West Midlands in the assisted-areas map.[100] Despite their public embrace of regional policy, West Midlands groups continued to place primary emphasis on developing indigenous manufacturing and service industries by means of targeted sectoral policies financed by central government.

Regional groups pursued these objectives through both bureaucratic and party channels. The CBI and the Birmingham Chamber of Industry and Commerce (BCIC) used direct political connections to government ministers to put across the region's case. These contacts, however, paralleled an apolitical stance adopted by the consortium.[101] Although the

---

[100] See inter alia Birmingham Chamber of Industry and Commerce, *Regional Industrial Development*; West Midlands Forum of County Councils, *Regenerating the Region* (Birmingham: WMFCC, 1985); West Midlands Regional Economic Consortium, *Regional Industrial Development* (Birmingham: 1984); West Midlands County Council, *Regional Industrial Development: Response of the County Council of the West Midlands* (Birmingham: WMCC, 1984); and Confederation of British Industry (West Midlands), *Regional Industrial Development (Cmnd. 9111)* (Birmingham: 1984).

[101] Official with the West Midlands Forum of County Councils; Birmingham, 13 February 1986. Official with the West Midlands Office of the CBI, Birmingham, 26 February 1986. Official with the West Midlands Regional Council of the TUC, Birmingham, 6 February 1986. Interviews with the author. Members credit the multitrack approach with a great deal of efficacy; it "increased immeasurably the nuisance factor from the region." Official with the Birmingham Chamber of Industry and Commerce, Birmingham, 27 February 1986. Interview with the author.

consortium collaborated sporadically with regional MPs, who were waging their own campaign in Parliament, its avenue of choice led through DoE and DTI regional offices to Whitehall in view of the potential for intraregional conflict. In the aftermath of the government's reappraisal of the situation in the West Midlands, bureaucratic channels opened wide to groups – a direct contrast to past periods.

As in the North East, regional civil servants actively assisted the organizational and lobbying efforts of West Midlands groups. By 1980, the DoE had succeeded in bringing the regional offices of the DTI and the Department of Employment around to its view of the regional economy.[102] The overt decline of the economy after 1980 simplified its task of effecting changes in favor of the West Midlands, while the DoE's responsibility for urban policy provided it with a platform to make the case for the extension of regional policy benefits to the region. Officials argued effectively in Whitehall that the success of urban policy, a priority of the Thatcher government, was contingent upon the placement of the West Midlands on a comparable footing with the traditional problem regions. Little could be done to encourage the creation of manufacturing jobs in Birmingham and other cities if new investment continued to be steered toward problem regions in the North, Scotland, and Wales. DoE officials played the political card too, pointing out to ministers the political sensitivity of neglecting areas with high concentrations of Conservative marginal seats.[103]

Regional government departments sought to use regional groups to improve their own hand in Whitehall skirmishes. They threw their weight behind the lobbying efforts of the consortium, the CBI, and the BCIC, making it clear to other regional groups "which horse ministers were backing, to quash the separatist aspirations...being fostered."[104] In particular, the DoE sought to marginalize the WMFCC, which, because of a narrow membership base confined to the shire counties, was thought to be incapable of attracting the widespread regional support necessary to sway ministers' minds. Officials also kept regional actors apprised of the government's policy review, and sought to bring group demands in line with what was achievable. For example, both Butcher and regional civil servants sent clear signals to groups that the government was re-

[102] Civil servant, West Midlands Office of the Department of Trade and Industry, Birmingham, 22 January 1986. Interview with the author.

[103] DoE internal memorandum, 9/1984. Civil servant, West Midlands Regional Office of the Department of the Environment, Birmingham, 12 February 1986. Civil servant, Northern Regional Office of the Department of Trade and Industry, Newcastle upon Tyne, 6 March 1986. Interviews with the author.

[104] Civil servant, West Midlands Office of the Department of Trade and Industry, Birmingham, 22 January 1986. Interview with the author. DoE internal memoranda, 3/1983 and 9/1984.

luctant to abolish regional policy; this information prompted the group U-turn outlined before.[105] Officials were keen to help their cause at the subregional level as well. For example, civil servants hoped to secure assisted-area boundaries that would promote cooperation among local authorities. This objective applied in particular to the Black Country; officials argued that if the subregion were split into assisted and non-assisted areas, the result would be to increase conflict and fragmentation precisely where joint efforts were most needed.

Government officials continued to play an advocacy role after the 1984 regional policy decision. The DoE maintained its focus on the Black Country, ensuring that a constant stream of ministers found their way to this subregion. With the West Midlands assisted area eligible for ERDF assistance, DoE officials began to solicit actively individual and joint project proposals from local authorities. During this period, the DoE achieved a measure of success in tapping this source of Community largesse for the region.[106] Although the meteoric rise of the West Midlands share can be traced in part to pent-up demand, it was also the result of the DoE's aggressive stance.

The impact of group cohesiveness in the West Midlands remains an open question. According to interest group representatives, solidarity led to the Butcher appointment as well as to the regional policy decisions of 1984. Civil servants were quick to pour cold water on these assertions. "They were actually pushing on an open door. . . . In fact, you could argue that the lobby failed because it did not come close to achieving its stated objectives – a shift from regional to discretionary sectoral aid, and failing that, development-area status for the region."[107] Regional unity was a necessary but not sufficient cause of government actions, insofar as it concentrated the minds of wavering government ministers in the run-up to the 1983 election.

By the end of the period in question, a marked shift away from a regional to a subregional, even local, focus was underway. In 1985,

---

[105] Official with the West Midlands Office of the CBI; Birmingham, 26 February 1986. Interview with the author.

[106] Although the region received only 4.7 percent of the UK share between 1975 and 1986, this figure is not reflective of the dramatic changes realized toward the end of the period of study. In 1985, the West Midlands received an amount two and one-half times that garnered by the North East. The 1986 UK allotment for the West Midlands reached 12 percent, as against a North East share of 11.5 percent. All figures from Commission of the European Communities, *European Regional Development Fund: Annual Reports.*

[107] Senior civil servant, West Midlands Office of the Department of the Environment, Birmingham, 12 February 1986. Interview with the author. The West Midlands Intermediate Area was expected to attract a modest £5.6 million in SFA awards, an amount described as "peanuts" by one observer. Official with the West Midlands Forum of County Councils, Birmingham, 13 February 1986. Interview with the author.

several consortium members, led by the CBI, the TUC, and the urban local authorities, turned their attention to the creation of a private sector development agency for the inner urban areas of the region. Proponents of the urban development agency were aware from the start that they could count on little more than the moral support of the Thatcher Government, for reasons similar to the North East case.[108] In the process, the consortium revealed itself as a loosely organized affair, with few if any powers of coordination over its members. This resulted in large part from the status of its members as individual service organizations. Each had to be be seen by its own membership to be doing something, and if the consortium had become the sole initiator on regional economic matters, its constituent organizations would have encountered internal difficulties. This, coupled with the consortium's weak resource base, meant that its power to lead was severely circumscribed. What is more, government officials displayed little willingness to use the consortium as the principal channel for contacts with regional groups. The fragility of regionalism was also reflected in the constitution of WMIDA. Because of considerable opposition from local authorities and business groups over the implications of a high-profile lobbying role, the association eventually emerged as a body devoted solely to the international promotion of the region, with a only modicum of coordinating powers and no formal lobbying brief.[109] Indeed, many local authorities proceeded with their own economic development programs, free from overarching regional coordination.[110]

Although these developments were consistent with long-standing public and private efforts to rebuild the urban areas, the implications for continued *regional* cooperative strategies were highly unfavorable. After all, by 1984, shire interests had been won over to a regionwide approach by the promise of regionwide assistance under a revamped (or even abolished) regional policy. The government's decision to draw the boundaries of the intermediate area around the urban core disrupted this consensus and laid the groundwork for a reactivation of the fault lines dating from the 1960s and 1970s. Since shire interests were heavily represented on the WMFCC – a key member of the consortium – proponents of the urban development agency were aware that they risked sacrificing regional unity via the consortium in order to focus on the pressing urban problems of the region. The West Midlands CBI and

---

[108] Civil servant, West Midlands Regional Office of the Department of the Environment, Birmingham, 12 February 1986. Interview with the author.
[109] CBI (West Midlands) Consultative Papers, 30 March 1983 and 25 April 1983.
[110] The West Midlands County Council, now defunct, launched its development strategy in 1981; this culminated in the creation of an enterprise board in 1982. See Spencer et al., *Crisis in the Industrial Heartland*, 144–54.

Central actors

Inclusive   Exclusionary

	Inclusive	Exclusionary
Cooperative	NE2 WM3	NE4 WM2
Non-cooperative	NE3	NE1 WM1

Local/regional actors

NE1: pre-1934; pluralism
NE2: 1934–65; corporate pluralism
NE3: 1965–79; corporate pluralism
NE4: 1979–86; corporate pluralism
WM1: 1945–70; pluralism
WM2: 1971–79; pluralism
WM3: 1979–86; corporate pluralism

Figure 4.3. *Strategy mixes and patterns of interaction in the British regions*

TUC simply followed the government's lead. As a CBI official stated, "It is in the end a matter of horses for courses."[111]

Explaining the patterns

What accounts for the mosaic of continuity and change observed in these two cases (see Figure 4.3)? While a thorough evaluation of the outcomes must await the results of the next chapter, we are in a position to explore their more striking aspects. There is ample evidence that national and subnational actors interpreted the options available to them in ways very similar to those posited in the earlier theoretical chapters.

During an identifiable period in each region, groups shifted from noncooperative to cooperative strategies. The rationale behind these shifts involved perceptions of structural political and economic weakness in the British political economy. Subnational actors believed that regionwide cooperation would further their economic objectives – playing the mobile investment market – *and* political objectives – gaining resources from Whitehall. The preferred approach aimed at the creation of a development organization capable of mobilizing the scarce and widely dispersed economic and organizational resources in the regions, and of coordinating their use both at home and at the edges of government policy-making circles. Of course, desire did not always translate into deeds. Cooperative efforts were subject to disintegrative forces from within the regions and from without.

---

[111] Official with the West Midlands Office of the CBI, Birmingham, 26 February 1986. Interview with the author.

Table 4.2. *Temporal shifts in the regional hierarchy, Britain*

		North East		West Midlands	
		1928	1986	1960	1986
	HIGH	local authorities	local authorities trade unions business	local authorities business	local authorities business trade unions
Relative importance	MEDIUM	trade unions business MPs	political parties MPs	trade unions MPs	MPs
	LOW	political parties		political parties	political parties

One of the main problems that plagued cooperative initiatives was the parochialism of powerful local authorities. British central-local relations grant local governments unparalleled legitimacy and access to resources at the subnational level: (1) They are the only regional actors with democratic credentials; (2) they serve as agents of many government policies and programs; and (3) they retain, as a matter of legal right, control over land, planning powers, and tax revenues. These attributes placed local authorities at the top of the regional hierarchy (see Table 4.2). Indeed, group interactions in both regions bear the indelible imprint of local authority participation. For example, local authority representatives dominated the REPCs and the executive and plenary councils of the regional development organizations. Similarly, local authorities contributed the bulk of membership subscriptions to the RDOs. And finally, local authorities maintained independent voices in economic matters through their own umbrella associations.

When combined with the relative weakness of other actors in the regions like organized labor and business, the position of local authorities endowed them with a veto power over cooperative efforts. Examples are legion. Local authorities blocked the 1984 TUC-CBI proposal in the North East and the attempt at the end of the 1970s to establish a RDO in the West Midlands by challenging the democratic representativeness of these bodies and their powers to encroach upon the prerogatives of local government. The increased statutory planning powers granted to county councils and borough councils in the 1960s and the reorganization of local government in 1974 created new incentives for larger local authorities to go it alone – that is, to opt out of, refuse to enter into, or otherwise limit the constraints placed on them by cooperative initiatives in both regions. Although many students of British local government rightly question the ultimate significance of these powers, the resulting changes had a dramatic effect on the balance of power within the regions.

Groups intent on organizing the periphery from below reduced intraregional conflict by pursuing "fair shares" objectives and by using apolitical bureaucratic channels. To be sure, parliamentary representatives tried to keep the plight of their regions on the agenda of the House of Commons by the assiduous use of written and oral questions and formal debates. Furthermore, they lobbied departmental ministers and civil servants in London on matters of concern to the region.[112] However, despite the cohesion of the Northern Group of Labour MPs, they were too small numerically and overly loyal to influence outcomes in the Commons.[113] For their part, West Midlands MPs demonstrated an overall lack of regional cohesiveness, which limited the effectiveness of their large parliamentary contingent. Whatever the case, MP participation in cooperative regional initiatives was sporadic, a condition expressly sought by local government, labor, business, and regional development organizations.

Where groups succeeded in overcoming disintegrative tendencies, government officials usually played the key role by pursuing inclusive strategies with respect to their group environment. The rationale behind inclusion shifted in line with the changing resource needs of central government. Where such strategies were in operation, some form of regionwide coordination – corporate pluralism – usually resulted. The decision to provide government support for the North East Development Board grew out of the needs of the special-areas commissioner to acquire information and to generate policy demands that could be fed quickly into the new government machinery. In return, the board gained government financial support coupled with a visible role in the policy implementation process, which reduced its dependence on parochial members. In a similar fashion, civil servants

[112] R. Guthrie, "An Inquiry into the Effectiveness of the Contribution to the Region of Northern MPs as Regional Representatives in Parliament, with Special Reference to the Period February 1974 to December 1976" (M.S. thesis, University of Newcastle upon Tyne, 1978). The Northern Group of Labor MPs met regularly to discuss regional affairs, while Conservative MPs from the region had no such parliamentary grouping.

[113] Only once has the party mechanism been employed with effect – in the late 1970s, when Northern Labour MPs were able to secure concessions from the Labour government in return for their support of the Scottish and Welsh devolution proposals. The conjuncture of several unusual conditions made this possible: a minority government and a proposal that, in equal measures, threatened Northern interests while representing a core part of the party's election manifesto.

in the West Midlands, with Whitehall backing, moved quickly in the period 1983–4 to organize the periphery in response to the changed evaluation of the regional economy's prospects and to the need for rapid, visible results. The success of the consortium, albeit short-lived, was due in no small part to their efforts.

Government officials, particularly those at the regional level, who adopted inclusive strategies were aware of the potentially disruptive effects of regional policy and sought to minimize those effects where possible. For example, the practice of designating assisted and nonassisted areas within a region often generated intraregional competition among localities and their representatives. To the extent that a region was carved up into haves and have-nots, inclusive approaches based on group coordination and unity proved difficult to achieve. As a result, regional civil servants generally pushed for assisted-areas that were coterminous with the boundaries of the region, or at a minimum with the parts targeted for coordinated action.

Government actors on occasion pursued explicitly exclusionary strategies with respect to groups. The most obvious case is the West Midlands. Whitehall refused to acknowledge the existence of structural economic problems in the region until the early 1980s in large part because of the pivotal position assigned to the West Midlands in national regional policy. The deliberate lack of intervention by government officials allowed internal conflicts to dominate the regional agenda. Hints of this can be seen in the North East, too. Although government officials continued to take an interest in the structure of group interaction between 1965 and 1979, their commitment to inclusion in no way matched the intensity of the 1930s, when government capabilities were at their weakest. As their policy capabilities waxed and their dependence on policy clienteles waned, central government officials began to disengage, however slowly. The Thatcher Government represented the final culmination of government approaches toward groups in the North East: from inclusion, to selective inclusion, to full exclusion.

Regions did not always bear the full brunt of exclusionary government approaches, a finding which confirms once again the conceptual dangers of treating "The State" as a monolithic actor. At critical junctures, regional civil servants provided assistance and resources in ways that softened or even counteracted the general line of policy set in London; examples include the North East after 1979 and the West Midlands during the 1970s. Whether regional civil servants acted purely as agents of central government, as regional advocates ("going native"), or as some combination thereof proved to be of vital importance to the co-operative efforts of subnational groups. Despite their lack of control over key resources, the "regional outposts of central government" provided essential points of contact for local and regional groups.[114]

The sectional centralism characteristic of the British policy-making process affected two aspects of group-state relations: (1) the extent of access for groups; and (2) the stability of cooperative arrangements established between groups and central government. As to the former, the compartmentalization of the nationalized industries constrained the effective reach of groups in the North East. Rationalization policies for the National Coal Board and the British Steel Corporation were formulated well away from the RDO and planning council. Despite repeated attempts, they were unable to secure policy coordination with these government-owned industries, or even to receive advance warning of pit and plant closures.[115] Regarding the stability of cooperative arrangements, the Urban Programme encouraged new patterns of public-private interaction that cut across emergent cooperative arrangements between subnational actors in both regions. Government ministries, above all the DoE regional offices, forged closer relationships with the principal beneficiaries, which encouraged the adoption of noncooperative strategies among large local authorities.

Subnational actors sought to wield influence at the national level primarily through regional civil servants. To the extent that groups provided these officials with the proper building blocks and materials, regional influence became possible. The periods of cohesion in the North East – strong corporate pluralism – also tended to be those periods when the region extracted the most from central government. Conversely, pluralism reigned in the West Midlands for many years, and resulted in a notably weak influence on central government. These examples underscore the key contribution of central government to the politics of regional decline. In the North East, where the association with regional policy is of the longest duration, the tight fit between group objectives and those of government policy is unmistakable. Regional actors embraced the practice of bringing work to unemployed workers and of using the prosperous regions as investment spawning ponds well

---

[114] Keating and Rhodes, "The Status of Regional Government," 51.
[115] "[Big] public bodies such as Britrail or the National Coal Board were tending to develop themselves . . . into completely self-contained bodies. It was thought that this policy was wrong and that such organizations were in fact the very bodies which should properly set an example to others in carrying out the Government's policy of making the fullest use of the industrial potential of each of the Development Areas." NEDA Minutes, 21 April 1949. The planning council and the RDO had to content themselves with organizing their own impact studies of the major areas affected by BSC closures in the late 1960s and 1970s. They participated in campaigns to influence BSC investment decisions, but they did so as outside lobbyists. NEPC Minutes, 26 January 1968, 19 May 1972, 27 July 1973.

into the early 1980s.[116] The decline of regional policy and the rise of local economic development programs in the 1980s prompted tangible shifts in both regions, particularly the North East. As long as central government sustained a political and budgetary commitment, regional policy defined the realm of the possible for North East interests.[117] Only the breakdown of political consensus over regional policy in the late 1970s and the expenditure reductions introduced after 1979 spurred North East groups to reevaluate their policy objectives and ultimately to switch to an indigenous development approach. Similar adjustments took place in the West Midlands. Thus, the agenda-setting effect of central government's decentralization of penury in the 1980s is visible in both regions. Not only does central government play an important role in structuring relationships between groups, it also has a tangible impact on the content of those relationships.

The findings suggest variable patterns of interaction clustered primarily around bureaucratic channels. In short, a governmental logic appears to dominate. What do these preliminary conclusions signify about the role of partisan logic? In the North East, subnational actors, with several notable exceptions, tended to eschew partisan overtures for fear of disrupting regionwide cooperative initiatives. In effect, coalitional objectives in the regions severely constrained the emergence of a partisan logic from below. Those instances in which politicization occurred, as in the late 1970s, revealed a second major constraint acting on partisan logic that flowed from above, specifically the national political parties. The North East was unable to change its position within the cross-party consensus on regional policy because regional interests were totally without leverage on either political party. In fact, the region found itself in the worst of all possible political worlds: It was of little use to the Conservatives in a national election strategy, and it was completely in the Labour Party's pocket. "Under the Labour Party, this region can be taken for granted; under the Conservatives, there is no reason to

---

[116] As the president of the Board of Trade informed the RDO in the early 1960s, "[I can] put fish into the stream, but it [is] up to the individual regions to land them." NEDA Quarterly Meeting; 6 March 1961.

[117] A regional civil servant serving in the early 1950s described this dependence in colorful terms: "I doubt whether anyone . . . can conceive the blind reliance and faith which the populations of the erstwhile 'distressed' areas still place in the Government's ability . . . to save them from the misery and destitution which they suffered in the '30s, and which they believe may descend on them again at any time. . . . It must be remembered that, rightly or wrongly, inhabitants of the [Development Areas] look on the Distribution of Industry Act as their lifeboats." PRO: BT177/1393, 19 November 1952.

suspect that resources will be wasted in hopelessly irretrievable areas."[118] The West Midlands, hamstrung by the national consensus on regional policy during the 1970s, found itself in a very different position at the end of the decade. At a time when its problems were driving regional interests into each other's arms, the Midlands became a key electoral "swing region" in the eyes of a Thatcher Cabinet willing to make partisan regional policy. This seems to suggest that the importance of political symmetry is not necessarily whether a region is "in" or "out" of office, but whether the region holds the key to No. 10 Downing Street. On this basis, regions are either favored or not. The shift of the partisan cycle in regional policy allowed certain actors in the West Midlands, principally business groups, to plead their case for the region through Conservative Party channels without undue fear of tearing apart the nascent regional coalition headed by the consortium.

As a final remark on these preliminary findings, the patterns point out the differing constraints that acted upon the two national political parties. During the heyday of consensus, Labour was condemned to a solid (skeptics would say perfunctory) commitment to regional policy to placate its electoral strongholds, but the party experienced great difficulty making an opening to erstwhile prosperous regions like the West Midlands for fear of jeopardizing that prior commitment. The Conservatives, on the other hand, enjoyed much greater flexibility: Forays into the traditional problem regions could only benefit them politically, and concessions to regions like the West Midlands would not lose them support elsewhere that they did not already have. The consortium played on this flexibility to good effect. With the complete breakdown of the national consensus over regional policy after 1979 and the resulting loss of monopoly status by the traditional problem regions, party political channels accommodated the delivery of regional policy benefits to regions provided they played a role in the electoral calculus of the governing party. Under Thatcher, inclusive approaches by government became increasingly contingent upon the electoral utility of the region.

---

[118] Civil servant, Northern Regional Office of the Department of Trade and Industry, Newcastle upon Tyne, 6 March 1986. Interview with the author.

5 The German Länder

The German cases share broad similarities. Regional responses to decline in the Saarland and North Rhine–Westphalia were rarely region-wide in scope, were inherently politicized, and remained well-insulated from the effects of federal policy initiatives. As such, they depart in key respects from the patterns of interaction uncovered in Britain. While theoretically significant differences between the German Länder emerge, the common elements are more striking, and can be traced to the presence of regional governmental institutions, engaged political parties, and a highly institutionalized, multilateral policy-making framework, each of which is wholly absent in the British regions. These factors create distinctive resource distributions among subnational actors and greater latitude for responses bearing the imprint of a partisan logic.

The Saarland, 1960–86

The Saarland is the smallest and youngest of the original German Länder, having joined the Federal Republic officially in 1959. The origins of the state's economic travails are a matter of scholarly and political controversy. The debate pits those who emphasize political factors – unstable boundaries,[1] unfair treatment at the hands of the French, and late incorporation into the Federal Republic's economy – against those who point to the constraining role of economic and structural factors like poor quality coking coal, outmoded production methods, and the late take-up of new technology.[2] In any event, the Land's decline can be traced back to the turn of the century, by which time the coal and iron-working industries in the region had lost production and market battles with competitors in the Rhine–Ruhr area, as well as those in nearby Lorraine and Luxembourg. The Saarland is a typical mining region whose economy has always been based on coal and steel. The primary coal fields are in the eastern part of the region, while the main steel-producing concerns are found along a centrally located industrial axis in the shape of a "V," with Neunkirchen at the eastern tip, Völklingen at the western tip, and Saarbrücken (the state capital) situated

---

[1] The region has changed hands between Germany and France a total of four times since the late seventeenth century.
[2] R. Latz, *Die saarländische Schwerindustrie und ihre Nachbarreviere, 1878–1938* (Saarbrücken: Saarbrücker Druckerei und Verlag, 1985).

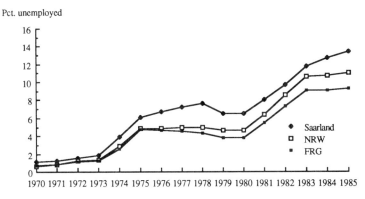

Source: Statistisches Landesamt des Saarlandes.

Figure 5.1. *Unemployment in the Saarland, NRW, and the Federal Republic*

at the angle. In 1957, the percentage of the total work force employed in coal mining was 36.3 percent, while those engaged in iron, steel, and metalworking industries made up a further 42.7 percent.[3] The relative concentration of these two industries in the region remains far above the national average in spite of the severe contractions of the last two decades.

The Land's historical handicaps have been aggravated by two postincorporation blows to its industrial economy. The first of these occurred during the 1960s in the coal-mining sector. Production plummeted, pits were closed, and tens of thousands lost their jobs. Between 1960 and 1970, the number of mining concerns fell by one-third, from twenty-seven to eighteen, while the number of jobs declined from 55,750 to just under 27,000. The second blow occurred in 1974, and initiated the long, ongoing decline of the steel leg of the Saar economy. The crisis in steel paralleled the earlier experiences with coal: rationalization, resulting in reduced capacity, reduced employment, and serious ripple effects for the regional economy. Between 1977 and 1985, employment in the Saar steel industry dropped by approximately 28 percent, representing a loss of over 15,000 jobs.[4] The decline of coal and steel led to serious economic and financial consequences for the Saarland. Whereas the unemployment rate rarely rose above 1 percent during the 1960s, Saar rates outran the national average after 1970 (see Figure 5.1).

---

[3] Statistisches Landesamt des Saarlandes.
[4] Arbeitskammer des Saarlandes, *1986 Daten zur Lage der Arbeitnehmer im Saarland* (Dillingen/Saar: Krüger Druck & Verlag, GmbH., 1986), 45.

By the mid–1980s, unemployment was the highest of any Land in the country. Regional growth rates were consistently below average, with attendant fiscal strains on the state and local governments. As a direct result of its economic travails, the Saarland state government amassed the highest per capita debt ratio of any German Bundesland between 1970 and 1986.[5]

Saar elites were in general agreement about the long-range solutions to the Land's problems. First, policies should seek to preserve and strengthen the core industrial base of the economy. Second, priority should be given to the improvement of the region's public infrastructure, such as transportation and sites for new industrial development. And finally, the economy should be diversified, primarily through the creation of a light industrial sector comprised of small and medium-sized firms.[6] Yet if politics in the Saarland was about economic decline, economic policy was largely a matter of politics. Political parties and other or- ganizations clashed over the pace at which these objectives were pur- sued, subregional and local development priorities, and the proper division of labor between federal and state policymakers. The patterns of interaction between center and periphery fall into four distinct periods.

Dependent development and regional pluralism, 1957–69
The Saarland's early history witnessed growing political conflict between state government and opposition parties over the appropriate policy approach to the regional economy. Although the main political parties and economic interest groups proved capable of joining together on occasion to lobby the federal government, intra-Land relationships re- mained decidedly competitive. The CDU-led state government followed a laissez-faire economic program for most of the period, leaving subre- gional actors to their own, unintegrated devices. Tentative moves toward interventionism by the CDU coincided with Germany's first major eco- nomic recession in 1966–7. The crisis prompted additional demands for federal assistance, which ultimately came with a price tag: matching policy efforts on the part of the state government. These new initiatives brought few if any changes in the relationship of state government actors to subregional groups and organizations, however.

The Saarland's late incorporation into the Federal Republic structured the debate about the regional economy until 1966, albeit with decreasing force. The CDU, in power for the duration of the period, argued that

---

[5] Von Voss and Friedrich, *Das Nord-Süd-Gefälle*, 123.
[6] A fourth goal was to open up new markets in Germany to indigenous firms in the immediate aftermath of the state's incorporation in 1957. By 1964, this objective had disappeared from public discourse.

Saar firms, denied ready access to German markets during the period of French control, were competing at a disadvantage with firms whose market positions had been forged during the peak years of the *Wirtschaftswunder*. Although the CDU acknowledged the structural imbalance of the region's economy, it held that the situation was temporary and therefore not comparable to the country's standard problem regions. As the *Ministerpräsident* stated categorically in 1957, "The Saar is surely not a problem region such as those found in the border areas of the Bavarian forest or the zonal border areas. However, we suffer from difficulties of a unique nature, . . . ones that surely entitle us to similar exceptional treatment."[7]

The state government placed the primary responsibility for these problems at Bonn's doorstep, and requested commensurate financial assistance in the form of infrastructure development and market assistance for private firms. Bonn was asked to step in where the Land could not, in view of the severe financial constraints on independent state action. The regional government drew on the support of the opposition parties, including its principal opponent, the SPD, as well as the major economic interests in the Land: the Saar Chamber of Industry and Commerce (Industrie- und Handelskammer des Saarlandes: IHK-Saar), and the Saar Chamber of Labor (Arbeitskammer des Saarlandes: AK-Saar).[8]

Extraordinary claims on federal resources drew strength from the argument that the sovereignty and viability of the Land would be placed in jeopardy if it were forced to respond alone. Direct appeals to Article 72 of the Basic Law accompanied these requests. The strategy was based on a tangible piece of reality: The Saarland was plagued by a weak tax base, a high proportion of public fixed costs relative to the size of the state, and the largest state debt in the country. Saar officials buttressed these arguments with functionalist rationales, as in a 1966 statement by the economics minister: "[It] is important to bear in mind that each economic region . . . can only play a complementary function with respect to the overall national economy. For the most part, this role has been denied to the Saarland because of its historical past."[9]

Party linkages represented the main avenue for Saar attempts to crack

---

[7] Plenary Session of the Landtag of the Saarland, 12 June 1957, 1055.
[8] The AK-Saar is one of two chambers of labor in the entire country; the other is in the city-state of Bremen. On matters relating to the regional economy and regional policy, the AK-Saar plays a much more visible role than the DGB-Landesbezirk Saar. The DGB, according to an AK-Saar spokesperson, is "not always in a position to make suggestions on regional economic issues." Nevertheless, cooperation between the DGB and the AK-Saar is close. Senior official, Arbeitskammer des Saarlandes, Saarbrücken, 12 November 1986. Interview with the author.
[9] Proceedings of the Economics Committee of the Landtag of the Saarland, 13 January 1966.

the federal treasury. Although the Bundestag was the scene of occasional initiatives by Saar MPs, the small size of the delegation (eight) and the general limits on parliamentary influence relegated that institution to a minor role, a situation which remained operative throughout the period of study. The principal partisan channels linked government and opposition in the Saarland with their political counterparts in Bonn, either directly to ministerial offices or through the Bundesrat. For several years after 1957, Saar government officials played on the desire of the CDU/CSU-FDP coalition in Bonn to support the majority Christian Democratic governing party in the new state. Although the CDU had emerged as the leading party in the Saarland, its hold on power was by no means assured.[10] Federal aid for the newcomers constituted a small price for ensuring the survival of a friendly ally, both in federal electoral matters and in Bundesrat proceedings.[11]

The first formal request for federal aid surfaced in late 1957. The "Memorandum of the Saar Government to the Federal Government," a joint statement of the political parties and industrial interest groups in the Saarland, produced tangible results.[12] Between 1956 and 1961, the federal government provided approximately 2.8 billion DM in transitional assistance to help the Saarland overcome difficulties associated with late incorporation. Of this total, approximately 500 million DM went to economic and industrial policies. In a related 1963 decision, Bonn extended federal assisted-area status to St. Wendel, an area lying inside the Saar coal fields. Technically, St. Wendel did not meet the selection criteria of federal regional policy, but was allowed in as an exception because of the problems there and the limited capacity of the Saarland government to respond on its own.[13] By 1966, two more assisted areas had been added: the city of Lebach, and the area surrounding Sulzbach, Neunkirchen, and Schmelz.

The CDU government's approach did not go completely unchallenged. Beginning in 1963, the SPD's Landtagsfraktion (state parlia-

[10] G. Bauer, "Die CDU im Saarland" (Ph.D. dissertation, Universität des Saarlandes, 1981).

[11] Similar calculations appeared as late as 1985. "Shortly before the 1985 state elections, the federal government announced a three year, 300 million DM aid package for the Saarland. There is a direct connection between this action and the fact that the CDU government was fighting for its life. There is now a much lower chance of success in negotiations with Bonn, since the next state elections are three years away." Senior official, Arbeitskammer des Saarlandes, Saarbrücken, 12 November 1986. Interview with the author.

[12] Landesregierung des Saarlandes, *Memorandum der Regierung des Saarlandes an die Bundesregierung vom 13. November 1957* (Saarbrücken: Malstatt-Burbacher Handelsdruckerei GmbH., 1957).

[13] The IHK-Saar described the incorporation of St. Wendel as the beginning of a conscious regional policy in the Saarland. Industrie- und Handelskammer des Saarlandes, *Saarwirtschaft 1973* (Saarbrücken: IHK-Saar, 1973), 7.

mentary caucus) called a series of parliamentary debates to discuss the geographical impact of rationalization measures in the coal industry. Motivated by close political and personnel ties to the trade unions, the SPD demanded state initiatives to preserve jobs and to expand alternative employment opportunities for laid-off workers. MPs focused on the areas most dependent on coal mining, particularly the towns of St. Wendel and Neunkirchen. The SPD welcomed federal regional assistance, and called for additional assisted areas in the eastern Saar. More controversial was the party's attempt to persuade the state government to plan investment, employment, and land-use targets at the Land level. SPD officials called specifically for direct state government involvement in the rationalization under way in the eastern mining areas and for new Land policies to attract footloose industries.

While the state government openly supported the opposition's demands for additional help from Bonn, it rejected the SPD's insistence on an independent state contribution to the resolution of the coal crisis as unnecessary, given that federal policy was sufficient, and as impossible, since the Land was financially strapped. The SPD's demands challenged the government's noninterventionist stance and its efforts to treat the Saarland's economy as a seamless whole. The minister of economics responded in 1963, "We have a comparatively small state. If we now begin to regard problems of economic development by county or even township, we surely run the risk of adopting the particularism of the local authority perspective. I find this extremely worrisome."[14] Granting prior claim to a territorial fragment of the regional market like the eastern Saarland would set a bad precedent, leaving the government open to a flood of subregional claims.

Nevertheless, the Land government declared the focus of federal regional policy on the eastern Saar to be fully in keeping with its statewide spatial priorities; indeed, it facilitated the safeguarding of the Saarland's *Montan* (coal and steel) core.[15] The state government's response to the crisis in the eastern Saar reflected a high degree of continuity with past rhetoric and practice. Officials explicitly declined to create programs to provide financial assistance to attract new firms, or even to collect information relevant to firms considering a move into the Saarland. Citing the presence of full employment and the limits to interventionist policies, *Ministerpräsident* Röder argued that the state must refrain from an attraction-of-industry policy that encouraged "a murderous struggle between the old and the new" over labor, markets, and sites.[16] Government officials were able to argue that the market was taking care of itself,

---

[14] Plenary Session of the Landtag of the Saarland, 24 May 1963, 1305.
[15] Plenary Session of the Landtag of the Saarland, 15 January 1964, 1618.
[16] Plenary Session of the Landtag of the Saarland, 19 July 1965, 12.

since miners released from closed pits were opting for early retirement, transferring to more profitable mines, or shifting into other industrial employment. As a result, Land efforts to attract new industry proceeded on an ad hoc basis, drawing on general expenditure funds and seconded staff from the ministries of economics and the interior.[17] The conservative governments of this period relied on a self-styled division of labor, in which the state provided basic infrastructure and an appropriate business climate while local authorities developed sites, and private industry created new employment opportunities.[18]

The apparent complacency of the CDU state government was shattered by the national recession of 1966–7. One in ten Saar manufacturing jobs disappeared, compared to a national rate of one in fourteen.[19] In April 1967, the CDU cabinet presented a resolution to the state parliament outlining its intention to seek expanded federal assistance.[20] The list of specific demands included sectoral aid for the coal industry, new investment in steel production, and assistance for a long-range program to create 50,000 new jobs in the Land by 1980. The principal demand outside of regional policy was for a federally funded waterway, the Saar–Pfalz canal. In this endeavor, the state government enjoyed the full backing of opposition parties and industrial interests. Arguing that the coal and steel industries were disadvantaged by the lack of ready access to German and international markets, Land interests pushed for the construction of a seventy-seven-mile canal connecting the Saar River at Saarbrücken with the Rhine just above Mannheim. The issue of the waterway, which would not be fully resolved until a 1973 Bonn Cabinet decision, epitomized the efforts of the CDU government to rectify what it viewed as basic infrastructural weaknesses in the Saar regional economy. The state government also acknowledged the special claims of the eastern Saarland, and pledged to concentrate federal and state resources on those areas.

Lobbying efforts directed at the federal government were based on more complex party political relationships than in years past. Shifts in

---

[17] The interior minister rejected the need for a special budgetary item to promote local infrastructure projects, arguing that his ministry was quite capable of carrying out these tasks through existing departmental arrangements. Plenary Session of the Landtag of the Saarland, 15 January 1964, 1623.

[18] "The attraction of industry requires certain preconditions, which local government is primarily responsible for creating." CDU spokesperson, Plenary Session of the Landtag of the Saarland, 30 January 1962, 572. Similar government statements can be found well into 1965.

[19] Chef der Staatskanzlei, *Landesentwicklungsprogramm Saar, Teil 2* (Saarbrücken, 1984), 781.

[20] Landesregierung des Saarlandes, *Das Saarland: 10 Jahre nach seiner Eingliederung in die Bundesrepublik Deutschland, Bilanz und Aufgabe* (Saarbrücken, 1967).

voter preferences had produced new governing coalitions at both the federal and state levels. In Bonn, the CDU's hegemonic grip on power had gradually weakened, giving way partially in 1966 to the SPD-CDU Grand Coalition and completely in 1969 to a SPD-FDP government. In Saarbrücken, the CDU had been forced to bring the FDP into the cabinet in the face of significant gains by the Social Democrats. As a result, at least two vertical party linkages were employed, albeit competitively, both of which increased the potential leverage that Saar parties could exercise over central government policy-making. One linked the governing SPD in Bonn with the opposition SPD in the Saarland, the other joined the junior coalition partner FDP to its similarly situated provincial colleagues. Although the federal coalition members were motivated by different calculations – the SPD to bolster its sister party in opposition, the FDP to strengthen its colleague's voice within the Saar's governing coalition – their intentions were complementary as far as the Saarland's economic case is concerned.[21]

The federal government's response unfolded over the next two years. Beyond the *Kohlegesetz* of 1968, Bonn provided close to 100 million DM in general infrastructure funding between 1967 and 1968.[22] The most ambitious package was drawn up in February 1969, when the Bonn government announced the *Strukturprogramm Saar*. The result of almost eighteen months of negotiations between the federal government and the state governments of the Saarland and Rhineland–Palatinate, this program committed the federal government to the construction of a waterway for the Saarland and to a set of flanking measures designed to improve the industrial structure of the region.[23] These measures eventually became the *Aktionsprogramm Saar–Westpfalz*, which represented a dramatic upgrading of the federal regional policy effort in the Saarland. The *Aktionsprogramm*'s goal for the Saarland was to create 50,000 jobs over a five year period; the federal government pledged over 40 million DM for Saar areas, an amount that tripled federal regional assistance for the Land.

Developments on the federal front paralleled a moderate degree of interventionism at home. The 1967 state budget contained, for the first

---

[21] Evidence consists of the competitive credit taking by the SPD opposition and the FDP coalition members for successful partisan lobbying efforts in Bonn. Plenary Session of the Landtag of the Saarland, 7 November 1975.

[22] IHK-Saar, *Saarwirtschaft 1973*, 13. These came under two so-called *Konjunkturprogramme*, which were expansionist public works programs undertaken by the federal government, but regionalized to aid particularly hard-hit areas in the Saarland, the Ruhr, and the zonal border areas.

[23] Rhineland–Palatinate was involved in these matters because of the canal proposal. In 1973, the Bund decided to proceed with the "canalization" of the Saar River, instead of the more expensive Saar–Pfalz canal.

time, a specific item for regional assistance: a 1.0 million DM fund to help local authorities in federal assisted areas to recondition industrial sites for prospective industrial developers. Ministers, while pledging themselves to act on behalf of the entire Land, stated that the fund would go primarily to the hard-hit coal areas.[24] In 1969, the government published the *Strukturprogramm Saar*, which was intended to serve as a ten-year planning horizon for economic development in the region. In addition, the bureaucratic apparatus within government was modified to facilitate efforts to attract mobile investment. A special division in charge of economic development was created within the Economics Ministry. In addition, the main promotional body for the Saarland, the Gesellschaft für Wirtschaftsförderung Saar, was reorganized to support the government's general economic and regional policies, as well as to coordinate the promotional efforts of Saar local authorities. And finally, the government established a subsidiary company of the state's Investitionskreditbank AG with an initial capitalization of 2.0 million DM to provide investment counseling and financing to new firms and indigenous firms wishing to expand operations.[25]

All in all, these Land initiatives were comparatively modest. Most were undertaken to ease negotiations with Bonn, or to enable the Saar government to implement the newly acquired federal assistance more efficiently. This was clearly the case with the *Strukturprogramm Saar*, which arose out of the federal government's demand that the Land formulate concrete development objectives and priorities if it wished to receive federal assistance.[26] Although the need to curry favor in Bonn moved the CDU government periodically to mobilize a public unity of purpose among political and economic actors in the Land, relations between government departments, parties, producer groups, and local authorities remained unintegrated, exceptionally fluid, and prone to party politicization.

Inclusion and the achievement of weak corporate pluralism, 1970–7

During this period, the Land government used the political insulation provided by federal regional policies to treat the Saarland's economic problems as a unitary whole, which had a significant impact on its relations to nongovernmental groups and interests. The CDU and its parliamentary spokespersons cautioned against a snowballing of com-

---

[24] Proceedings of the Economics Committee of the Landtag of the Saarland, 16 December 1966.
[25] Plenary Session of the Landtag of the Saarland, 3 July 1968, 1679.
[26] Plenary Session of the Landtag of the Saarland, 5 November 1975, 134.

petitive subregional claims, decrying it as expensive and inefficient parish-pump politics.[27] In the main, Land officials deflected local and parliamentary pressures for regional policy aid by simply pointing to the rigid constraints set down in the new joint policy-making arrangements at the federal level, especially the use of transparent eligibility criteria and finite budgetary allotments.[28] Blaming Bonn, other Länder, and the GRW procedure allowed them to shrug off demands from local authorities, parliamentary representatives, and other parochial interests.

Officials in the Economics Ministry consulted regularly with the IHK and the Arbeitskammer about general principles of federal and state regional policy. However, neither the AK-Saar nor the IHK-Saar exercised any influence whatsoever on the GRW process in the Land, a situation that continued into the following period. Their contribution was to mobilize a policy consensus in the private sector, and to voice support for or opposition to specific policy measures undertaken by the state government. Government officials established informal, regular contacts with individual local authorities to monitor the existing economic situation and the capacity for take-up of regional policy benefits at the local level.[29] These relationships were normally bilateral, involving the ministry and individual localities, and were transitory in nature. In short, the pattern of relations moved to a fragile form of corporate pluralism during this period.

State governments were unwilling to entertain further changes because of a string of economic and political successes during this period. Between 1968 and 1973, the Saarland posted one of the best records of any Land in the attraction of industry and the creation of additional jobs. Close to 40,000 new jobs were created, of which 25,000 came from new firms in the area.[30] When the Bund replaced the various *Aktionsprogramme* with the GRW in 1971–2, the Saarland's gains from 1969 were incorporated into the new policy, a significant coup for the state

---

[27] Plenary Session of the Landtag of the Saarland, 27 September 1978, 2595.

[28] Members of the Structure Policy–Industrial Policy Division, Saar Ministry of Economics, Saarbrücken, 11 November 1986. Interview with the author.

[29] This latter point relates primarily to the ability of local authorities to undertake infrastructure improvement projects, financed on a matching funds basis through state and national regional policies. This ability is in part a function of available land – if the local authority cannot acquire land, it cannot develop it – and of the financial status of the authority.

[30] IHK-Saar, *Saarwirtschaft 1973*, 22. The Saarland's real growth of GDP in 1970 was the highest of any other Bundesland. Arbeitskammer des Saarlandes, *Bericht an die Regierung des Saarlandes 1971* (Saarbrücken: AK-Saar, 1971), 19. The halcyon days of the Saar economy, to the extent one can even speak in those terms, lasted until 1975. Arbeitskammer des Saarlandes, *Bericht an die Regierung des Saarlandes 1982* (Saarbrücken: AK-Saar, 1982), 125.

government. In fact, until 1981 the Land enjoyed advantages comparable to the zonal border areas: assisted-area status sui generis, and a
proportionally higher share of GRW budget outlays than other Länder.

Thus, the Saar government was content to allow federal regional
policy to carry the burden of the state's response to regional economic
crisis. In 1970, the CDU unabashedly proclaimed the federal *Aktionsprogramm* as the Saarland's development program. Aside from the
creation in 1970 of an investment fund to finance local authority infrastructure projects, the regional dimension of state government policy
remained minimal.[31] Government ministers consistently rejected opposition demands for the creation of a state-funded regional policy, and
justified its limited initiatives with the argument that additional expenditure was neither necessary nor possible.

With the GRW in place, the exercise of party political leverage on
the Bund grew more infrequent, though it by no means disappeared.
Indeed, the policy achievements of this period led Saar policymakers
to adopt an approach oriented toward incremental improvements to the
status quo. Although its problem areas were similar to those in NRW
or Bremen, the Saarland refused to side with these Länder in their
attempts to open up the GRW to the emerging industrial problem regions of the country. For example, the Saarland openly opposed NRW's
1978 Bundesrat initiative to extend the Investment Allowance Act to
all high unemployment areas, regardless of their status vis-à-vis the
GRW. As part of an effort to derail the NRW proposal, the Saarland
suggested an increase in the award rates for those areas already covered
by the GRW – namely, the entire Saarland. Demands for special treatment based on the Land's historical handicaps remained a standard part
of state policymakers' repertoire, although these were beginning to de-
value as time wore on.[32]

Saar reformers were not completely silent during this period. They
pursued two reform proposals throughout the 1970s: (1) the abolishment
of the SPO principle in the Land, by having the entire state declared a
SPO; and (2) the strengthening of the GRW's regulation of Länder
regional policies, so as to limit the extent to which other state programs
undercut GRW goals and the Saar's privileged place within them. Neither objective met with any notable degree of success. As a GRW
participant interested mainly in protecting its *Sonderstatus*, the Saarland

---

[31] The fund set aside approximately 38 million DM out of GRW funds and other
federal transfers. The SPD criticized the government for this budgetary sleight-
of-hand. Plenary Session of the Landtag of the Saarland, 17 February 1971,
384.

[32] Senior civil servant, Saar Staatskanzlei, Saarbrücken, 11 November 1986. Interview with the author.

had more in common with the largely rural states, particularly those with a priori assisted areas like the zonal border areas (i.e., Bavaria, Lower Saxony). It assiduously courted the support of the federal government representatives in the PA: "Without the federal government, nothing flies at all."[33]

The emergence of consensus and strong corporate pluralism, 1977–86

Two contextual developments distinguish this period from previous ones. First, the pool of mobile investment, which had contributed to the successful attraction of industry in the Saarland during the early 1970s, disappeared by the middle of the decade.[34] Second, a severe crisis in the steel industry erupted. The dramatic rise in unemployment, coupled with the deleterious effects on the wider Saar economy, threatened to overwhelm the government's preferred reliance on federal regional policy. Indeed, the steel crisis virtually determined the state's approach to regional problems. Between 1980 and 1985, the Land spent close to 1.5 billion DM on sectoral support for the steel industry. In the same period, federal and state regional policy expenditure totaled approximately 770 million DM.[35] In response to this combination of sectoral and political crisis, Saar governments of both right and left attempted to generate alternative policy approaches by upgrading existing relations between public and private actors along sturdier corporate pluralist lines.

In March 1977, ministers drafted yet another memorandum intended for the Bonn coalition partners.[36] The list of demands, buttressed by a functionalist rationale outlining the national economic and security risks of a collapse of steel, included a special GRW program for the steel areas, direct federal assistance to restructure the industry, social policies to promote the early pensioning and retraining of laid-off steelworkers, special programs for towns in the eastern Saarland, and general transfers

---

[33] Members of the Structure Policy–Industrial Policy Division, Saar Ministry of Economics, Saarbrücken, 11 November 1986. Interview with the author. Hence the shock, even feelings of betrayal, when the federal government announced its intention to cut GRW expenditure in 1981. Saar ministers believed that their "faithfulness to the Bund" in the PA had not been acknowledged. Plenary Session of the Landtag of the Saarland, 10 December 1980, 399.

[34] In 1975 and 1976, a total of 23 new firms, employing 530 people, settled in the Saarland. The comparable figures for 1971–72 were 27 firms, 5,837 people. In 1968 alone, 18 firms employing 8,788 people were brought to the Saarland. H. Georgi and V. Giersch, *Neue Betriebe an der Saar* (Merzig: Merziger Druckerei und Verlag GmbH, 1977), 14.

[35] Landesregierung des Saarlandes, *Saar-Memorandum 1986* (Saarbrücken, 1986), 24–8.

[36] Landesregierung des Saarlandes, *Memorandum der Regierung des Saarlandes an die Regierung der BRD vom 28.3.1977* (Saarbrücken, 1977).

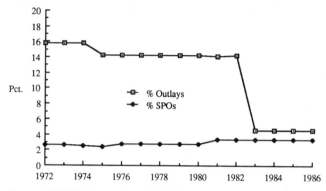

Source: GRW *Rahmenpläne*, 1972–86.

Figure 5.2. *The Saarland's share of GRW outlays and Schwerpunktorte*

to cover the state's additional budget outlays in the crisis. The estimated cost of these measures was 500–600 million DM. The results, announced by the federal government in December, were substantial. The total package of aid was over 400 million DM. One quarter financed a special GRW program for the steel areas, to last from 1978 to 1981. Additional assistance included a 2.7 million DM annual increase in urban development grants for the city of Neunkirchen in the eastern Saarland, which bore the brunt of layoffs and capacity reduction in the steel industry.[37]

Thereafter, the news from Bonn grew progressively gloomier. The sole positive development was a 1981 PA decision to grant a one-time extension of the Saar's special steel program from 1982 to 1985. However, what Bonn gave with one hand it took away with the other (see Figure 5.2). In 1981, the Land suffered a 70 percent cut in funding for its assisted areas, effective in the 1983 framework plan.[38] This reduced severely the Saarland's capacity to pursue its regional economic objectives, in view of the Land's total reliance on the GRW. This setback was followed by the loss in 1986 of the remaining component of the Saar's *Sonderstatus:* its a priori claim to inclusion in the program. Like other assisted areas in the country, the Saarland was required to satisfy the aggregate indicator values set by the GRW. With the complete loss of its special status, Saar officials, in contrast to previous periods, discovered a compelling interest in such GRW reforms as the weight given

---

[37] Plenary Session of the Landtag of the Saarland, 14 December 1977, 1939.

[38] The large size of the cut, which the government imposed in order to bring the Saarland in line with the per capita shares of other Länder, is an indication of just how special the Saarland's *Sonderstatus* was.

to the unemployment indicators and the relevance of the infrastructure indicator.[39]

The continuing crisis in steel intensified the pressure for home-gown political initiatives from Saarbrücken, while drastically reduced federal support prompted political elites to look to new policy approaches and to locate alternative sources of funding for the old ones. This period marked the emergence of coordination among Saar political and economic actors in several policy areas, a conscious response on the part of the state government to its worsening resource dependence. State officials sought to bring together trade unions and employers to work out socially and politically acceptable rationalization measures in the steel industry. The resulting "political regulation cartels" were primarily sectoral in composition, and excluded local authorities affected by plant closures and massive redundancies. "Neunkirchen, Saarbrücken, and Völklingen did not take part in the political regulation cartel. Accordingly, their interests were scarcely represented, and they found themselves in an isolated position when dealing with the long-term problems of regional decline. Their role . . . has been a passive one."[40] Though not explicitly territorial, these cartels nonetheless became a vital part of the state's objective of maintaining the industrial core of the regional economy.

Changes in the field of regional policy were no less dramatic. After much public soul-searching, the CDU government responded to GRW cuts in 1983 by taking a momentous step: the creation of a Land-funded regional policy program. The scope of this initiative must again be described as extremely constrained, a reflection of the dearth of financial resources available to the government. The policy guidelines followed those of the GRW to the letter, reflecting a desire simply to compensate for GRW cuts. Even more telling, the bulk of the funds for the program, initially set at 39.0 million DM, were taken from the investment fund for local authorities, severely depleting that program in the process.[41] In defense of their actions, ministers described the program as "a justifiable compromise between the financially defensible and the economically indispensable."[42]

Saar governments also increased expenditure in related policy areas like the promotion of the indigenous small and medium-sized firm sectors.[43] The new SPD government, led by Oskar Lafontaine, took office

---

[39] Landesregierung des Saarlandes, *Saar-Memorandum 1986*, 25.
[40] Esser and Väth, "Overcoming the Steel Crisis," 657.
[41] SPD opposition members accused the government of robbing Peter to pay Paul. Plenary Session of the Landtag of the Saarland, 10 November 1982, 1608.
[42] Plenary Session of the Landtag of the Saarland, 14 December 1982.
[43] *Mittelstandsförderung* became a regular feature of government rhetoric and policy during the mid-1970s. Between 1981 and 1986, the amount of money

in 1985 and immediately attempted to shift the focus of policy to technology development, particularly as it relates to the environment.[44] The
IHK followed the lead established by the state government, providing
information and seconded personnel to a handful of publicly funded
technology initiatives like the Zentrale für Produktivität und Technol-
ogie Saar e.V. (ZPT), financed by the Land, and an innovation and
technology center set by the city government of Saarbrücken.

Beginning in the early 1980s, Saar parties engaged in a competitive
search for alternatives at the supranational level. Cooperative ventures
with bordering regions in France and Luxembourg were sought with an
eye to improving infrastructure, tourism, and investment opportunities
in the Saar–Lor–Lux area. Above all, Saar government and opposition
targeted the EC as a means of closing the financing gap created by Bonn
actions. In 1983, the SPD opposition spearheaded efforts to access new
sources of ERDF aid, effectively pressuring the CDU-led government
into similar action. Coordinated efforts on the part of Land politicians
and Euro-MPs resulted in a number of large grants and loans from the
European Social Fund and the ERDF. In 1984, the Saarland became
the first German Land to be awarded ERDF funds earmarked for regions
with critical steel problems. Between 1975 and 1986, the Saarland received approximately 11 percent of the total German allotment. When
translated into a per capita share of the German allotment, the Saarland's figure is second highest among the states, excluding West Berlin.[45]
A measure of the vital importance that Saar officials attached to the EC
is revealed by the fact that the Saarland in 1985 was the first German
Bundesland to set up its own monitoring and lobbying office in Brussels,
an act soon copied by other states, including NRW, Hamburg, and
Bavaria. Although the Saarland's take from the ERDF paled in comparison with the 1.3 billion DM received from national regional policy
since 1972,[46] Community assistance gained in relevance as national
sources declined. As an IHK official stated, "At a time when money is

spent on programs to assist small and medium-sized firms almost doubled (1981:
13.9 million DM; 1986: 26.7 million DM). Chef der Staatskanzlei, *Landesentwicklungsprogramm Saar, Teil 2*, 819.

[44] Critics charged that the shift in emphasis was mainly rhetorical, a function of
the financial straitjacket in which the Land found itself. The main objectives
of the Land's economic policies continued to be carried out largely through the
GRW. Senior civil servant, Saar Staatskanzlei, Saarbrücken, 11 November 1986.
Senior official, Industrie- und Handelskammer des Saarlandes, Saarbrücken,
12 November 1986. Members of the Structure Policy–Industrial Policy Division,
Saar Ministry of Economics, Saarbrücken, 11 November 1986. Interviews with
the author.

[45] Commission of the European Communities, *European Regional Development
Fund: 13th Annual Report (1987)*, 63 and 67.

[46] Source: Bundesamt für gewerbliche Wirtschaft.

ever more difficult to acquire from Bonn, the EC becomes an additional source of cash, pure and simple."[47]

In sum, the sectoral concertation in the steel industry combined with cooperative relations among subregional actors in the realm of technology policy represented a marked departure from the pale brand of corporate pluralism prevalent during the preceding period. Steel crisis and GRW cutbacks created new resource deficits for Saar policymakers, and ad hockery no longer satisfied their policy needs.

North Rhine–Westphalia, 1955–86

North Rhine–Westphalia, in contrast to the Saarland, is the largest and most populous of the German states. In 1984, 28 percent of the German population lived in the state and 27 percent of the country's GDP was produced there.[48] The state encompasses several urban concentrations, including Cologne, Düsseldorf, and Bonn, the seat of government in the Federal Republic. The economic landscape of NRW is a product of Germany's late industrialization. Its centerpiece is the Ruhrgebiet, a jumble of pits, plants, and settlements along the Ruhr Valley that provided the principal impetus for German industrialization.[49] The state's contribution to postwar reconstruction during the 1950s and early 1960s can only be described as pivotal. Germany's *Wirtschaftswunder* was in many respects a miracle of the North Rhine–Westphalia economy.

The existence of diverse centers of economic activity distinguishes NRW from more one-sided regional economies like the Saarland. Nevertheless, the broad emphasis on manufacturing and extractive industries translated into a vulnerability no less worrisome for regional and national elites.[50] Events since the late 1950s, particularly the mounting economic

---

[47] Senior official, Industrie- und Handelskammer des Saarlandes, Saarbrücken, 12 November 1986. Interview with the author.

[48] J. J. Hesse, "Wirtschaft und Strukturpolitik in Nordrhein-Westfalen," in *Nordrhein-Westfalen*, ed. Landeszentrale für politische Bildung Nordrhein-Westfalen (Köln: Verlag W. Kohlhammer, 1984), 210.

[49] The Ruhrgebiet is an area of approximately 1,600 square miles bounded by the Ruhr, Emscher, and Lippe rivers. In the present study, this area will be referred to by any one of a number of names: Ruhrgebiet, Ruhr, Ruhr Valley, and Revier. The political and economic literature on the Ruhrgebiet is voluminous. Excellent works on the postwar situation include H. Adamsen, *Investitionshilfe für die Ruhr* (Wuppertal: Peter Hammer Verlag GmbH, 1981); D. Petzina and W. Euchner, ed., *Wirtschaftspolitik im britischen Besatzungsgebiet 1945–1949* (Düsseldorf: Schwann Verlag, 1984); and U. Bochum, *Industrie und Region* (Frankfurt a.M.: Peter Lang, 1984).

[50] In 1961, manufacturing employment represented 56.2 percent of the state's total employed; in 1981, the figure stood at 52.9 percent. Figures for the national level were 48.1 and 44.3 percent, respectively. In 1984, the regional economy contributed 90 percent of the nation's domestic coal extraction and 60 percent of German steel production. Hesse, "Wirtschaft und Strukturpolitik," 211–15.

Table 5.1. *Annual gross domestic product, various Länder*

Land	(Billion DM; 1980 prices)		
	1970	1977	1985
North Rhine–Westphalia	324.1 (28.6)	378.6 (27.8)	417.9 (26.6)
Bavaria	179.3 (15.8)	224.9 (16.5)	279.1 (17.8)
Baden–Württemberg	175.1 (15.5)	213.0 (15.6)	247.5 (15.8)
Saarland	17.1 (1.5)	20.5 (1.5)	24.0 (1.5)
Federal Republic	1132.8	1361.8	1569.7

Note: Figures in parentheses indicate the Land's GDP as a percentage of federal GDP.
Source: Statistisches Landesamt Baden–Württemberg.

crises in coal and steel, conspired to expose that vulnerability. In comparison with the Saarland, NRW's economic problems appear to be not a matter of degree, but of kind. Nevertheless, observers and policy-makers interpreted the crisis in light of the state's past performance; by these standards (as in the case of the West Midlands), the problems were serious indeed. In terms of the state's percentage contribution to the national gross domestic product, the decrease, though not over-whelming, established a disconcerting trend (see Table 5.1). Unemployment also emerged as a serious problem in the 1980s, particularly in the industrial areas based on coal and steel like the Ruhr Valley. From just over a half percentage point in 1970, the unemployment rate in NRW consistently outstripped the national average after the mid-1970s, and reached an all-time high in 1985 at 11.0 percent (see Figure 5.1).

Like the Saarland, political and economic elites shared a consensus over the Land's economic problems. Yet the translation of this consensus into concrete political responses was the subject of intense political conflict. Whereas Saar responses bore the mark of twenty-six years of Christian Democratic hegemony, the situation was reversed in NRW, where governments led by the SPD held power continuously after 1966.[51]

[51] For discussions of the political history of NRW, see the following: U. von Alemann, ed., *Parteien und Wahlen in Nordrhein-Westfalen* (Köln: Verlag W. Kohlhammer, 1985); W. Först, *Kleine Geschichte Nordrhein-Westfalens* (Düsseldorf: Droste Verlag GmbH, 1986); D. von Herz, *Die Politik des verspäteten*

Nevertheless, the pattern of relations among private and public actors in NRW across the entire period bears a striking resemblance to the Saarland.

The politics of decline and fragmentation, 1955–69

In just under a decade, NRW underwent an abrupt transformation from prosperity to penury. Distributional conflicts between parties and subregions marked this transition period, as did a generally exclusionary approach by the federal government. The resulting pattern of intra-Land relations verged on untrammeled pluralism. Although the Land won official recognition of its special industrial problem areas from the federal government in 1968, little if any coordination of regional, subregional, and local interests followed thereafter.

The 1950s marked the zenith of prosperity in NRW. With major industrial centers like the Ruhrgebiet operating at full capacity and full employment, political and economic elites kept economic soul-searching to a minimum. Policy objectives during this decade, the subject of widespread consensus between CDU-led governments and the SPD opposition, revolved around the tasks of postwar reconstruction: to rebuild the urban and industrial centers of the Land; to secure a steady supply of foodstuffs and raw materials; and to gain a measure of independence from Allied control.[52] Reconstruction objectives of a territorial nature aimed to improve the social and economic situation in the state's war-torn rural periphery. The state government enacted the *Grenzland–Kreditprogramm* in 1948, which targeted selected border areas near Belgium and the Netherlands, and two additional programs in the 1950s, the *Ostwestfalen–Kreditprogramm* and the *Randgebiete–Kreditprogramm*. Each program provided incentives for the attraction of new firms and for the improvement of infrastructure in these largely rural areas.[53]

In 1958, crisis hit the NRW coalfields for the first time. Parliamentary debates from this period reflected a growing concern among all political parties about structural vulnerabilities in the Land's economy and the deterioration of its heavy manufacturing and extractive industries. The coal crisis presented NRW with a new type of problem area: the mono-

---

Machtwechsels (Meisenheim am Glam: Verlag Anton Hain, 1970); F. Keinemann, *Von Arnold zu Steinhoff und Meyers* (Münster: Kommissionsverlag, 1973); H. Kühn, *Aufbau und Bewährung* (Hamburg: Hoffmann und Campe, 1981); F. Meyers, *gez. Dr. Meyers* (Düsseldorf: Droste Verlag, 1982); Landeszentrale für politische Bildung Nordrhein-Westfalen, *Nordrhein-Westfalen*.
[52] Adamsen, *Investitionshilfe*; Petzina and Euchner, *Wirtschaftspolitik im britischen Besatzungsgebiet*.
[53] See Minister für Wirtschaft, Mittelstand, und Verkehr des Landes Nordrhein-Westfalen, *Denkschrift* (Düsseldorf, 1964).

structural industrial areas in the Ruhrgebiet. In response, the CDU-led government pressed for sectoral aid from Bonn, and succeeded in eliciting a federal response that focused on a managed reduction of capacity in the coal industry and a mitigation of the resulting social hardships experienced by laid-off workers. NRW elites, like their Saar counterparts, employed all-party resolutions and separate ties to national political parties in government and opposition to secure a favorable response from the federal government. For example, the state parliamentary coal caucus (*Kohlefraktion*) pressured the Bonn government repeatedly for action on the Ruhr's behalf.[54] Bundestag MPs from NRW often used debating opportunities to highlight the demands and problems of their Land and constituencies. The Bundestag arena proved to be of limited value, a fact not confined to this particular period. Referring to the SPD *Fraktion* in the Bundestag, a NRW official explained, "They are ready to support the Ruhr by sponsoring debates or parliamentary questions, but it is clear that these MPs are also interested in ensuring that their own constituencies receive equal air time. Thus, it is difficult for a region like the Ruhr to claim the national parliamentary agenda on a consistent basis."[55] In any event, between 1958 and 1966, approximately 2.5 billion DM flowed to the coalfields in the Ruhr, under some fifty different programs. Of that total, the Land's contribution reached a modest 82 million DM.[56]

In 1959, the Land's interior minister promised impending action to attract new firms to the Ruhrgebiet, a statement that marked the first explicit commitment by the state government to aid the new problem areas in NRW.[57] Reconciling this new commitment to the monostructural areas with existing regional policies proved to be politically contentious. Christian Democratic MPs from the rural periphery vigorously defended their programs against the claims of the industrial areas, and sought to ensure that the amount of money allocated to the Ruhr remained nominal in proportion to expenditure on the classic problem areas. In the face of strong political pressure, the state government responded warily. While the government chose to avoid an uncontrolled market solution to the crisis in the coalfields (*passive Sanierung*, or passive readjustment), it interpreted the situation as a sectoral problem with local spatial implications.[58] Accordingly, policy sought to mitigate

[54] Kühn, *Aufbau und Bewährung*, 224–5. The use of the joint party resolution was repeated in the early 1980s, as the Land government sought federal support for the steel producing areas in the state.
[55] Senior civil servant, NRW Ministry of Economics, Düsseldorf, 29 October 1986. Interview with the author.
[56] Schaaf, *Ruhrbergbau und Sozialdemokratie*, 68.
[57] Plenary Session of the Landtag of NRW, 16 December 1959, 933.
[58] In fact, ministerial statements from the period suggest that the various measures

the duress of unemployed miners and of local governments, which faced tax revenue losses as pits and plants closed.[59] Thus, the thrust of these measures was primarily local and social. Ongoing programs for the rural areas provided the model for the government's response: to create new employment opportunities in the Ruhr, primarily through the attraction of new industry. In addition, the Land promised to aid local government efforts to acquire and develop unused industrial sites and to improve infrastructure, since local authorities were to serve as the principal agents in the attraction of industry to problem areas.[60] A publicly funded promotional organization was established to publicize the new regional programs to the private sector. Defenders of NRW's rural periphery were successful in the end, however; Ruhr areas were allocated an amount equal to one fifth of the allotments for these other areas. In later years, the imbalance diminished only marginally. For example, the 1962 budget set aside 38 million DM for regional policy measures, of which 10 million DM was earmarked for the coal-producing areas.

The SPD, with strong electoral ties to the Ruhr, criticized vehemently the government's measured response. The party's parliamentary *Fraktion* called a series of debates on the situation in the coal-mining areas, drawing attention to the plight of miners and local authorities in particular. As such, the party shared the official interpretation of the problem as a collection of local crises. The SPD's position began to change in 1963, when statistical evidence suggesting that the state's economic performance had fallen behind that of the other Bundesländer surfaced for the first time. The SPD called for a new set of spatial priorities centering on the core industrial areas and for a more interventionist approach overall. In short, the Social Democrats began to distinguish themselves from their political opponents in government.

In 1966, the crisis in the coalfields entered a new, more desperate phase. On the eve of scheduled state elections, the Land government formally acknowledged "the economic and social upheaval" caused by the crisis of the monostructural industrial areas.[61] This confession was accompanied by the creation of a special fund to aid local authorities in their ongoing efforts to attract industry. The eleventh hour conversion, however, could not avert a poor electoral showing by the CDU-FDP coalition. In the Ruhr, the CDU dropped 5.5 percentage points

designed to address the crisis in the Ruhr were viewed as necessary to convince miners of the need to accept rationalization measures as peacefully as possible. Plenary Session of the Landtag of NRW, 16 December 1959, 933.

[59] Schriftenreihe des Ministerpräsidenten des Landes Nordrhein-Westfalen, *Vorschläge zur Strukturverbesserung förderungsbedürftiger Gebiete in Nordrhein-Westfalen* (Düsseldorf: Ed. Lintz Kg. Verlag, 1960), 44–5.

[60] Plenary Session of the Landtag of NRW, 17 February 1960, 1153.

[61] Plenary Session of the Landtag of NRW, 26 July 1966, 12–13.

from its 1962 results (39% to 34.5%), while the SPD picked up 6.8
percentage points (52.4% to 59.2%). Studies of the 1966 state election
reveal the electorate's general sense of unease about the state of the
NRW economy, and the degree to which the CDU was held responsible.[62]

With the accession of the Social Democrats to power later that year,
the priorities of the state government changed dramatically. Although
existing policy instruments remained intact, the SPD-FDP coalition
moved quickly to reverse the spatial bias set by the outgoing CDU
government. In the words of an official party spokesperson, "When the
Ruhr is sick, then aid for the Grenzland, or Ostwestfalen, or [other
areas] is of little use. The heart of this state is ailing, and therefore the
chief emphasis of the state's economic and structural policies must lie
there."[63] Priority for the Ruhr expressed itself in several ways. The state
government was able to secure the inclusion of the investment premium
in the 1968 federal *Kohlegesetz* (§32 of the act), a regional component
benefiting the Revier. The sweeping changes in federal coal and energy
policy, outlined in Chapter 3, were due in no small part to the active
support of the SPD economics minister in Bonn, Karl Schiller. The
Ruhrgebiet also began to receive the lion's share of state regional aid.
In addition to increased assistance to Ruhr local authorities, the SPD-
led government created a new 54 million DM budget item to attract
new industries to the Ruhr. Regional programs for the traditional assisted areas were slashed to 10 million DM. The amount of Land-
financed sectoral and regional aid for the Ruhr reached 40 percent of
the state's total in 1967, and 45 percent in 1968.[64]

The creation of a special Land program for the Ruhr, the *Entwick-
lungsprogramm Ruhrgebiet* (EPR), provided the most visible evidence
of this conscious shift in spatial priorities. Announced late in 1967, the
EPR combined a number of budget items into a loosely coordinated
development program designed to last from 1968 to 1973. A major goal
of the EPR was to break the hold of Ruhr coal owners on undeveloped
real estate, which was needed to attract new industries. Identified by
officials and economists alike as the major bottleneck affecting industrial
diversification in the Ruhr during the 1950s and 1960s, the scarcity of
land presented the government with a dilemma involving the sanctity
of property rights and the limits of state intervention in facilitating

[62] Von Aleman, *Parteien und Wahlen*, 206. This is not to suggest that the election
results were driven by specific voter concerns about regional problems or policy.
Preelection polls confirm that the most important issues for voters were inflation,
housing, and road construction. Fabritius, *Politik und Wahlen*, 83; von Herz,
Die Politik des verspäteten Machtwechsels, 72.
[63] Plenary Session of the Landtag of NRW, 17 January 1967, 140.
[64] Plenary Session of the Landtag of NRW, 12 December 1968, 915.

regional development.[65] Total EPR outlays, financed by both the state and federal governments, reached 8.4 billion DM. Despite the considerable amount of activity, few permanent contacts between state officials and subregional interests in the Ruhr were employed during the EPR exercise. The initiative took the form of an in-house effort on the part of the Land government to channel benefits to this key industrial part of the state, and the program paid little attention to the structure of interests on the receiving end.

Favoritism for the Ruhr provoked a strong response from the CDU opposition, which began to champion the claims of what it described as equally deserving but politically less central areas like Ostwestfalen and the Westmünsterland. Both of these areas were strongholds of electoral support for the CDU; for example, in the 1966 election, the CDU posted pluralities of between 47 and 73 percent in Westmünsterland. Between 1967 and 1970, the party formed working groups to study the problems of these areas, and published a series of development plans for various subregions in NRW including the Ruhrgebiet.[66] The SPD-led government, ever-sensitive to charges of spatial favoritism, continually stressed to the Landtag and to the press that preferential treatment for the Ruhr was temporary, and that any extra aid was additional to, not in place of, the amount set aside for the rest of the Land. To counter the growing criticism, the SPD announced its intention to have the areas championed by the CDU designated in the federal government's regional program, a goal which ultimately proved unattainable. The announcement of the EPR in 1967 accentuated the appearance of imbalance. After a series of pitched Landtag debates, the *Ministerpräsident* announced the government's intention to act.[67] Highly publicized tours of these areas by state officials and extensive consultations with local interests preceded an increase in budgetary outlays for programs benefiting the noncoal areas by 12 million DM, to a total of 22 million DM.[68] Despite such

[65] Bochum, *Industrie und Region*, 149. This problem was not resolved until the early 1980s, and highlights one of the principal self-imposed constraints on government intervention in the distribution of industry. See Rhein-Ruhr-Institut für Sozialforschung und Politikberatung e.V. (RISP), *Begleitforschung zum Aktionsprogramm Ruhr* (Duisburg: RISP, 1984), 39.
[66] The leader of the CDU opposition, Franz Meyers, pointed out with considerable irony that his party's announcement was followed a fortnight later by the creation of similar groups in the SPD *Fraktion*. Plenary Session of the Landtag of NRW, 17 January 1968, 1014.
[67] Plenary Session of the Landtag of NRW, 1 October 1968, 1518.
[68] Plenary Session of the Landtag of NRW, 25 November 1969. This change took place six months before the 1970 state elections. Whether these electoral calculations paid any dividends is debatable. In the Westmünsterland, for example, CDU gains, compared to 1966, were below its Land-wide average (+2.9 percentage points compared to +3.5 percentage points), while in Ostwestfalen its gains were above average (+6.8 compared to +3.5). The biggest surprise,

backsliding, the spatial priorities pursued by NRW governments changed permanently during this period.

On the eve of the creation of the GRW framework, relations among NRW actors and between NRW and the federal government remained competitive and pluralistic. Land initiatives to redress spatial imbalances in the regional economy, which invariably emanated from state governmental institutions, more often than not proceeded according to calculations of partisan advantage. These attributes of national-subnational relations began to change with the far-reaching reform of federal regional policy inaugurated at the end of the decade.

Inclusion and the emergence of weak corporate pluralism, 1970–7

The federal government's decision to introduce joint regional policy-making in 1969–70 brought about significant changes in the intraregional relations of NRW actors and the policy objectives of the Land government. By moving to an inclusive stance and endowing the Land government with new statutory responsibilities and powers, Bonn created a new set of incentives for state government officials and new constraints for local and subregional actors. A governmental logic soon displaced the more overt partisan characteristics of interactor relationships, both within NRW and between the state and the federal government.

Regarding intra-Land relationships, participation in the GRW led state officials in the Ministry of Economics to install a procedure to process requests for assistance. Applications were gathered at the ministry, and then sent on to the chamber of commerce responsible for the area in which the proposed project would be located. The IHK evaluated the application according to several criteria, including economic compatibility with the existing mix of industry in the area, and then submitted its recommendations to the Economics Ministry, where final decisions were made.[69] It is possible to make too much of these evaluation pro-

---

however, occurred in the Ruhrgebiet, which rewarded the SPD government with above average *losses* (-3.9 compared to -3.4). The heavy imprint of national political issues, which swamped the Land debate, is identified by scholars as the main reason for this result. Von Herz, *Die Politik des verspäteten Machtwechsels*.

[69] The procedure remains in place to this day. Since early 1986, the DGB has participated in a similar screening process. Applications are forwarded to the appropriate local trade union office, where officials check the applicant's record on job safety, collective bargaining, and other shop-floor related issues. An opinion on the application is then returned to the Economics Ministry by way of the Landesbezirk headquarters. It is interesting to note the narrow range of issues that concern DGB local offices. Questions pertaining to the overall impact on the local economy, or other development related issues, are simply not pursued. These are left either to the IHK or to the Economics Ministry to handle.

cedures; indeed, their resemblance to sectoral corporatism is wholly superficial. In the first place, rejection by the chambers was virtually unheard of.[70] Second, the IHKs did not have input into key areas of the policy-making process, namely the selection of assisted areas and the setting of subsidy levels. These decisions were made entirely by the PA at the national level, and by the Economics Ministry at the state level. According to an official with the state IHK association, assisted-area designation took place according to established criteria, "so there is no real room for influence: Either you are in or you are out."[71] Since each IHK was responsible for its own bailiwick, and nothing more, the system did not lend itself to the formation of blocks or groupings that might seek to influence the process on a pan-local basis.

The government sought to use the insulation afforded by the GRW to promote its particular spatial priorities and to strengthen its bargaining position in the PA, both of which are described below. The lack of formal input by local authorities, IHKs, trade unions, and party parliamentary caucuses translated into considerable leeway in determining objectives, and state officials were keen to preserve their freedom.[72] Pressures for inclusion in the GRW or state regional programs were usually rebuffed with reference to the intractable bargaining situation in the PA. In other words, blaming Bonn provided state officials with an extremely effective and thus oft-used means of managing the explosion of localistic demands typically generated by regional economic policy.[73] More important, the state ministries became involved in shifting bilateral relationships with local interests, especially local governments, over the allocation of regional policy benefits. To further their goals in the PA, NRW officials often employed local interests selectively as allies. In exchange for detailed information on the local economic situation and coordinated political support for the Land's policy objectives, localities received a pledge by the state government – conditioned as always by inflexible GRW parameters – to press their case in the PA. Like the Saarland, the patterns of interaction during this period approximated a loose form of corporate pluralism.

---

[70] Official with the Association of NRW Chambers of Industry and Commerce, Düsseldorf, 3 November 1986. Interview with the author.

[71] Ibid.

[72] In turn, Land officials were subject to the relatively inflexible set of constraints set down in the GRW legislation and PA decision-making procedures. Senior civil servant, NRW Ministry of Economics, Düsseldorf, 29 October 1986. Senior civil servant, NRW Ministry of Economics, Düsseldorf, 31 October 1986. Interviews with the author.

[73] These pressures were considerable. One official referred to "drawers full of letters" from local authorities and Landtag MPs requesting favorable consideration in the annual GRW application round. Senior civil servant, NRW Ministry of Economics, Düsseldorf, 29 October 1986. Interview with the author.

During this period, the GRW determined the Land's regional policy goals almost completely. NRW officials initially sought to increase their share of assisted areas and funding allotments. Since the federal government had simply incorporated existing assisted areas into the *Aktionsprogramme* and the GRW framework, NRW's share was of course meager. Small area coverage translated into small funding allotments, such that the Land started off in 1969 with a mere 3 million DM of the 266 million DM provided out of federal coffers and just 31 of the 312 SPOs.[74] NRW officials were well aware of the inadequacies of the new framework, but chose to climb on board anyway. The principal incentive to join was the investment allowance. Since all federal assisted areas, not just SPOs, were eligible for this automatic grant, NRW officials hoped to gain an additional 42 million DM in assistance per year.[75] Concerns about the GRW's ingredients and methods of preparation accompanied the basic dissatisfaction with the size of the pie. The state government's long-range objective was to change the selection criteria to accommodate the high-unemployment *Montan* areas, which represented the modal spatial problem in NRW. These areas, concentrated in the Revier, suffered under the relative weights accorded to income levels and infrastructure as compared with that for employment. NRW efforts to have large areas in the Ruhr and the Westmünsterland included in the GRW began with its first application in 1972.

In 1976, NRW officials initiated a four-prong effort to reform the GRW. First, they sought to introduce current data for the calculation of the various indicator values. NRW argued that the old data from the late 1960s failed to reflect the existing situation in many of the Land's regional labor markets, particularly where regional income levels and gross domestic product were concerned. Second, officials pressed for the elimination of the infrastructure indicator and an upgrading of the weight assigned to employment indicators. They argued that the infrastructure indicator penalized urban industrial areas like the Ruhr and favored the more rural, less developed parts of the country. NRW introduced a proposal to include a value for long-term unemployment on the list of selection indicators. Third, the NRW government lobbied in the Bundesrat for a new investment-allowance law to make high unemployment areas automatically eligible for assistance, regardless of whether they resided within an approved *Aktionsprogramm*. Finally, NRW pushed repeatedly for special assistance through the GRW for the emerging crisis in the steel-producing areas of the Land.

[74] Under the terms of the GRW, the federal contribution of 3 million DM was matched by an equal amount provided by the Land.
[75] Proceedings of the Economics Committee of the Landtag of NRW, 18 March 1971, 4.

These objectives met with considerable resistance in the PA, particularly from Länder with rural economic problems and with zonal border
areas. The NRW government sought to build majorities in the PA among
similarly situated Länder to achieve its objectives. Still, the government's approach was rarely if ever based on exploiting party political
differences. Rather, NRW used precedent successfully, endeavoring to
portray its demands in the spirit of fairness and equal treatment. In
other words, like cases should be treated alike.[76] The approach worked
well during this particular period, when concessions could be won without harming the interests of other participants. Selective relations with
subregional actors were used effectively by the NRW government; for
example, the NRW Ministry of Economics cultivated close ties with
officials from the city of Gelsenkirchen, an unemployment black spot
in the Ruhr, to coordinate a lobbying effort to change the GRW's
indicator package to the Land's advantage. The city was enlisted by the
state to press its case in Bonn for assisted status as a hard-hit unemployment area, an effort that ultimately bore fruit in 1984.[77]

On occasion, NRW resorted to openly conflictual strategies in the
PA. The clearest example took place in 1977, when officials played a
game of brinksmanship with the federal government and other states
over the issue of the data upon which selection indicators were calculated. The federal government and seven Länder expressed their support
for retaining the old 1966 data base. NRW's proposal to employ new
data from 1974–5 would have resulted in the expulsion of fifteen labor
market regions from the GRW, concentrated in Lower Saxony, Baden–
Württemberg, and Schleswig–Holstein. Most of the newly eligible areas
would have been in NRW.[78] Unhappy with the foot dragging of its PA
colleagues, the NRW delegation, backed by a formal cabinet decision
in Düsseldorf, threatened to restructure its own regional program in
accordance with the new data and indicator weights – a virtual unilateral
declaration of independence from the GRW. The purpose of the threat,

---

[76] These strategies remained relevant in the 1980s. For example, the argument
for a special GRW program for NRW steel areas was strengthened considerably
by reference to the special program for the Saarland in 1978 and specifically to
the federal government's public commitment to aid similar areas in the future.
Plenary Session of the Landtag of NRW, Vorlage 9/668, 7 December 1981, 3.

[77] The city was admitted to GRW status as an exception, requiring no sacrifices
from other Land participants. Indeed, NRW had to remove two existing SPOs
in order to collect the requisite support. The success of the Gelsenkirchen
initiative typified the decision-making dynamics of the PA, in which each Land
could effect change so long as costs were not imposed on other participants,
but were internalized. Senior official, City of Gelsenkirchen (NRW), Gelsenkirchen, 8 December 1986. Interview with the author.

[78] Proceedings of the Economics Committee of the Landtag of NRW, 14 September 1977, 2.

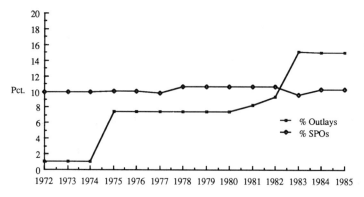

Source: GRW Rahmenpläne, 1972–86.

Figure 5.3. North Rhine–Westphalia's share of GRW outlays and Schwerpunktorte

in the opinion of state officials, was to precipitate a response in the PA.[79]

NRW's "as if provisions" (Als-ob-Regelung) prompted Bonn to call a special PA session in December 1977. In exchange for a NRW commitment to withdraw its threat, the Bund and a majority of the Länder agreed to grant assisted-area status to three NRW areas, and to undertake a reform of the selection criteria within three years. The NRW areas were admitted on the basis of new data values, while the rest of the GRW areas continued to operate under the old system. NRW agreed to the compromise largely because Bavaria had threatened to lodge a complaint in Brussels if NRW went ahead with the Als-ob-Regelung, and NRW officials were aware that they would need the support of the federal government to fend off an EC regulatory challenge.[80] In sum, NRW played on the fragility of the GRW consensus to achieve some movement in the PA. A NRW defection would have dealt a serious blow to the program's aspirations to blanket the country with a uniform assistance framework.

By 1975, the Land had won a measure of redress on the distributional issue (see Figure 5.3). NRW's quota reached 22 million DM out of a total of 294 million DM. Improved access to GRW resources had other advantageous affects for state policymakers; above all, it enabled them to concentrate their regional policy programs on specific problem areas,

[79] Proceedings of the Economics Committee of the Landtag of NRW, 5 October 1977, 2.
[80] Proceedings of the Economics Committee of the Landtag of NRW, 23 November 1977, 3; ibid., 15 December 1977, 3.

in particular the Ruhr.[81] The purpose of state regional policy, in the opinion of government officials, was to compensate for changes in the GRW. Those areas deselected in the PA were as a matter of stated policy picked up by the Land program. Furthermore, problem areas not covered by the GRW were incorporated as Land assisted areas. The Ruhr was the main beneficiary of these programs, receiving close to 40 percent of the state's regional assistance.

The forced march to strengthened corporate pluralism, 1978–86

During this period, a shift in emphasis away from a sole reliance on regional policy occurred. NRW began to employ a broader range of policies to address its regional problems, including technology policy, programs to assist small and medium-sized firms, and job training and employment programs. According to one official, support for these alternative economic programs developed to a certain extent at the expense of regional policies in the Land.[82] Robust corporate pluralist relationships between state government actors and subregional and local groups accompanied these changes in policy emphasis.

Several mutually reinforcing developments brought about the shift in policy priorities and group relationships. In the first place, the main prerequisite for a successful regional policy – a large pool of mobile investment – gradually disappeared over the course of the decade.[83] Second, government officials concluded that conventional regional policies were incapable of addressing the problems of the Land, in particular the need to retain jobs and improve competitiveness. If the future of the NRW economy lay in a technologically advanced *Montan* core flanked by a thriving and innovative small firm sector, then regional

[81] Land programs took their cue from the GRW. Differences surfaced in the award levels: The highest award in a state assisted area could not exceed 10 percent, which corresponded to the lowest award in the federal designated areas. A lower preference assisted area existed, too, in which eligible firms were entitled to a maximum 7.5 percent investment grant on proposed projects. The total value of grants disbursed under Land regional policy between 1972 and 1985 was 899 million DM; comparable figures for the GRW and the investment-allowance program were 657 million DM and 437 million DM, respectively. The figure for the investment allowance includes the years 1969 to 1971. Landesamt für Datenverarbeitung und Statistik Nordrhein-Westfalen.

[82] Senior civil servant, NRW Ministry of Economics, Düsseldorf, 29 October 1986. Interview with the author. The 1984 budget contained a cut in outlays for Land regional policies, reflecting the government's shift in priorities. Plenary Session of the Landtag of NRW, 11 January 1984.

[83] An official with the DGB-Landesbezirk NRW estimated that by 1986, there were no more than 10,000 jobs nationwide in any given year that could be secured through attraction of industry policies. Official with DGB-Landesbezirk, NRW, Düsseldorf, 2 December 1986. Interview with the author.

policy could contribute to these objectives, but it had to be accompanied by other instruments.[84] Finally, like the Saarland, NRW officials had to cope with deep cutbacks in the scope and level of its GRW allotment. This latter point warrants additional comment.

By 1981, the Land had achieved many of its GRW reform objectives. Although the proposal to reform the Investment Allowance Act continued to languish in the Bundesrat, and the abolition of the infrastructure indicator ran up against intractable opposition in the PA, the NRW government secured advantageous changes in the selection criteria. The government also received a federal commitment to establish a special GRW steel program for the Ruhr beginning in 1982.[85] Nevertheless, NRW's share of GRW expenditure remained below average (see Table 5.2), and the unfavorable situation was compounded by the federal expenditure cutbacks of the 1980s. In 1986, the PA approved the removal of NRW assisted areas that contained a total population of 2.6 million; the total population in deselected areas for the rest of the country was 1.2 million.[86]

In the 1980s, the advantage within the PA shifted back to the rural Länder – a situation described by one NRW official as "extraordinarily imbalanced. . . . The *Montanblock* is simply too small." Since logrolling in the PA became much less prevalent during this period, NRW's traditional strategies were much less effective. Furthermore, there was a party political dimension to its travails that could not be overlooked; a problem of political asymmetry emerged for the Land under the Kohl Cabinet. As a senior civil servant in the NRW Ministry of Economics reasoned, "The difference between the Brandt–Schmidt and Kohl eras is that the economic problems facing NRW during the former were not nearly as dire as they are now. The lack of a sympathetic government in Bonn makes for very difficult times, in view of the financial stringencies facing the Düsseldorf government."[87]

Further complicating the situation, the capacity of the Land to use its own regional programs to compensate for these cutbacks contracted

---

[84] "Regional policy simply cannot be overburdened with demands for results. It cannot take the place of general fiscal policy, industrial policy, technology policy, and other such programs. Rather, it fulfills a definite, complementary task." Minister of Economics, Proceedings of the Economics Committee of the Landtag of NRW, 5 December 1984, 14.

[85] Here, as elsewhere, the NRW government did not realize all its objectives. Having proposed large parts of the Ruhr for the new steel program, Land officials had to be content with just three townships.

[86] Senior civil servant, NRW Ministry of Economics, Düsseldorf, 29 October 1986. Interview with the author.

[87] All quotes from senior civil servant, NRW Ministry of Economics, Düsseldorf, 29 October 1986. Interview with the author.

Table 5.2. *German regional policy grants (DM million) 1/1972 to*
6/1986, by state

Land	Total grants	Pct. infrast.	% GRW pop.	% GRW grants	Total investment
Schleswig–Holstein	1215.96	51.3	12.1	13.5	14551.13
Hamburg	0	0	0	0	0
Lower Saxony	1860.77	50.1	23.3	20.7	38932.22
Bremen	150.77	82.7	0.8	1.7	1464.36
North Rhine–Westphalia	728.47	12.2	17.4	8.1	19791.21
Hesse	681.14	46.2	8.0	7.6	11155.53
Rhineland–Palatinate	769.35	30.8	10.1	8.6	12103.13
Saarland	1273.51	49.7	5.9	14.2	10945.58
Baden–Württemberg	287.15	51.4	1.1	3.2	8313.77
Bavaria	2021.10	61.2	21.4	22.5	37041.89
Total	8988.22	48.3	100.0	100.0	154298.84
Zonal Border Areas	3377.01	53.1	38.0	37.6	54547.56

Notes: Total grants are awards paid out under the various GRW schemes. *Pct. infrast.* is the percentage of *Total grants* allotted to infrastructure. *% GRW pop.* is the percentage of the nation's population in Land assisted areas in 1981. *% GRW grants* is the percentage of *Total grants* awarded to the Land. *Total investment* indicates the value of investment projects financed by GRW grants. The zonal border areas are comprised of parts of Schleswig–Holstein, Hesse, Lower Saxony, and Bavaria.
Source: Bundesamt für gewerbliche Wirtschaft.

in the face of internal fiscal constraints as well as the increasingly assertive role adopted by the European Commission. In 1983, the European Commission filed a legal challenge under Article 93 of the Rome Treaty to the status of several NRW assisted areas defined in federal and state regional policies on the grounds that they contravened the Community's assistance criteria based on unemployment rates and infrastructure development. NRW officials took their case to the PA, seeking a united front to resist the perceived encroachment by the commission. However, their request fell on deaf ears, since the rural Länder and the federal government wished to resolve the problem quickly and without fuss. Lacking the support of its fellow PA members, NRW acceded to the commission's threat. The episode had a chilling effect on regional policy-making in NRW, whose officials grew increasingly reluctant to schedule many areas in the Land regional program. From the standpoint of state government policymakers, the Brussels injunction resulted in a direct transfer of Land sovereignty to Brussels. For all intents and purposes, the state's own regional policies required preapproval in Brussels.[88]

Despite these constraints, NRW policymakers stepped up efforts to acquire financial assistance from Brussels, particularly for the steel industry.[89] Individual local authorities in the Land began to look to the EC as well, seeking contact with Brussels officials either directly or through Euro-MPs. However, the Land government did not promote these inquiries with much vigor.[90] Generally speaking, NRW efforts to tap the ERDF revealed much more hesitancy than those launched in the Saarland. According to state officials, EC assistance played "a complementary role to state and federal policies."[91] This is perplexing, given that the ratio of NRW's share of ERDF funds to its share of national regional assistance from Bonn was much larger than in the Saarland during this period: approximately 1 to 5. Between 1975 and 1986, NRW received 161.5 million DM in ERDF assistance: 9.7 percent of the German share over the same period. This translated into a per capita share of 12 ecus, ninth best of the ten *Flachenländer* (here meaning contiguous Länder).[92]

One reason behind the diffident position adopted by Land policymakers concerned the sovereignty disputes outlined before. However, the effects of the ERDF extended beyond the loss of policy-making autonomy for regional officials. State policymakers were forced to cope with a proliferation of demands for assistance from crisis-prone subregions and localities – demands generated by the commission's factfinding and promotional delegations. According to a federal official, the commission often attempted to bypass the Land governments and negotiate directly with local authorities: "The EC tells these local authorities that the money is there for the taking, provided they can acquire assisted-area status. As a result, the letters from local officials and chambers of commerce start flowing into the state governments, and ulti-

[88] Proceedings of the Economics Committee of the Landtag of NRW, APr 9/880, 16 March 1983, 6–7.
[89] A 100 million DM, four-year program for subregions affected by steel rationalization measures commenced in 1984. The program was financed 50–50 by the EC and the Land. Between 1981 and 1984, a total of 2.4 billion DM in EC assistance found its way to NRW. This figure includes European Coal and Steel Community assistance, energy subsidies, European Social Fund assistance, and ERDF expenditure. Minister für Wirtschaft, Mittelstand, und Verkehr des Landes Nordrhein-Westfalen, *Information der Landesregierung* 554/8/85, 2 August 1985.
[90] Senior official, City of Gelsenkirchen (NRW), Gelsenkirchen, 8 December 1986. Interview with the author.
[91] Minister für Wirtschaft, Mittelstand, und Verkehr des Landes Nordrhein-Westfalen, *Information der Landesregierung.*
[92] Commission of the European Communities, *European Regional Development Fund: 12th Annual Report (1986)*, 63 and 67.

mately to Bonn. The EC is setting in motion political activity incompatible with the principles of a federal system."[93]

Unlike the tiny Saarland, NRW contains numerous economic subregions that retain their distinctiveness. Therefore, even under the best of circumstances its officials faced an ongoing problem of managing diverse and competing territorial economic demands. The intrusion of the Community between the Land and its localities exacerbated the internal distributive conflicts confronting Land policymakers. In effect, the new assertiveness of EC regional policy officials disturbed the splendid isolation of NRW officials. To NRW officials, the EC appeared as a double-edged sword: an alternative yet elusive source of largesse to an increasingly unresponsive central government, and an additional source of constraints on independent action. In response, the Land government moved to improve communication with the commission by establishing a NRW information bureau in Brussels staffed with a permanent contingent of Land officials.

As part of the broader response to the changed circumstances of the 1980s, NRW governments, like the Saarland, formed political regulation cartels to confront the steel crisis in the Land. State officials repeatedly sought to bring together the trade unions and owners to work out socially and politically acceptable solutions to industry rationalization, concentrated above all in the Ruhr.[94] Alongside these networks linking state officials, unions, and employers in the Ruhr, the government sought to mobilize broader initiatives to combat the economic problems of this key subregion, including another special program: the *Aktionsprogramm Ruhrgebiet* (APR).

The APR originated in a two-day conference held in Castrop-Rauxel between state officials and Ruhr groups. The goal of the conference was to gather suggestions, to mobilize resources, and to build political support for a state program to aid the area.[95] Concerted efforts on the part of state officials to reach out to subregional and local actors distinguished this initiative from its predecessor, the EPR. Two Ruhr organizations in particular were closely involved in the consultation process: the Kommunalverband Ruhrgebiet (KVR), which brings together the local authorities in the area to promote joint action on a number of different fronts,[96] and the Industrie- und Handelskammern des Ruhrgebiets, an

---

[93] Civil servant with the Planungsausschuβ, Federal Economics Ministry, Bonn, 4 December 1986. Interview with the author.

[94] Esser and Väth, "Overcoming the Steel Crisis," 663–87.

[95] A. Schlieper, *150 Jahre Ruhrgebiet* (Düsseldorf: Schwann Verlag, 1986). Senior official, Kommunalverband Ruhrgebiet, Essen, 18 November 1986. Interview with the author.

[96] These included land use planning, conservation of the area's natural resources, waste disposal, and promotional activities. The KVR was formed in 1979 to

association of the Revier's chambers of commerce. The conference represented an extraordinary exercise in collaboration between state officials and groups from this historically well-organized subregion.[97] According to organizers and participants, the conference created a great deal of pressure among Ruhr interests to present a common front. Furthermore, by giving local and subregional actors an opportunity to criticize government policy and put forward their own suggestions, the government in effect bound the participants to the results of the conference. State policymakers also kept demands from expanding uncontrollably; for example, they rejected Ruhr efforts to create a standing conference in the subregion, hoping to head off similar requests from other subregions in NRW.

The resulting program pumped over 6.9 billion DM into the subregion under a number of different programs, with the federal government financing approximately 21 percent of the total.[98] The thrust of the APR reflected the state's shifting approach to regional problems, in addition to its newfound need for the direct participation of subregional interests. The main planks of the program were technology promotion, employment and training measures, and environmental improvements to the area, and these priorities were mirrored in the division of responsibility among Land ministries for the APR. The principal sponsors were the Ministry for Environmental Protection, Spatial Planning, and Agriculture and the Ministry for Labor, while the Ministry of Economics played a relatively minor role.[99]

For several reasons, the government's focus on the Ruhr did not spark the divisiveness of earlier periods. First, the GRW provided cover for the Land government, insofar as the main subregional contenders for attention, like Ostwestfalen and the Westmünsterland, were already designated federal assisted areas. Though Revier towns and cities were the objects of the Land's strenuous efforts to change the GRW, and a substantial portion of regional policy expenditure ended up there (see

replace its lineal predecessor, the Siedlungsverband Ruhrkohlenbezirk, a similar body formed in the early 1920s. Toward the end of the 1970s, the SVR sought a higher profile role and fell victim to Land and local authority opposition, both of which actively sought its demise and replacement with the considerably weaker KVR. Senior civil servant, NRW Ministry of Economics, Düsseldorf, 24 October 1986. Interview with the author.

[97] Observers attribute the prevalence of subregional group activity in the Ruhr to the unique economic structure of the area, which has produced a uniform problem load for interests unmatched in any of the Land's other subregions. Senior civil servant, NRW Ministry of Economics, Düsseldorf, 24 October 1986. Interview with the author.

[98] Landesregierung NRW, *Politik für das Ruhrgebiet* (Düsseldorf, 1979), 67.

[99] Senior official, Kommunalverband Ruhrgebiet, Essen, 18 November 1986. Senior civil servant, NRW Staatskanzlei, Düsseldorf, 27 November 1986. Interviews with the author.

Table 5.3. *Bias in favor of the Ruhr in federal and state regional policies, 1969–85*

Program	Payments (Mio. DM)	% Land total	Total investment value (Mio. DM)	% Land total
Land program	345.36	38.4	5901.4	39.4
GRW	203.67	31.0	3019.9	34.4
GRW steel program	*	*	4186.8	100.0
Investment allowance	*	*	7541.3	44.5
Total	*	*	20649.4	46.0

*Data incomplete.
Source: Landesamt für Datenverarbeitung und Statistik Nordrhein-Westfalens.

Table 5.3), the appearance of zero-sum conflict between the Ruhr and other areas was kept to a minimum. Officials cultivated this appearance, too; for example, they declined to create a special ministerial division to oversee the Ruhr in view of the competitive demands this would generate.[100] Second, the scale of the problems in the Ruhr, particularly after 1979, was unrivaled. "Job losses in the Ruhrgebiet number in the tens of thousands, those in the Westmünsterland in the hundreds," quipped one Economics Ministry civil servant.[101] Finally, the CDU had a strong interest in not being seen to be anti-Ruhr, since to win back power in the Land, the party had to reverse a string of abysmal electoral performances there.[102] The party tried to play all the relevant subregional angles by consistently advocating more aid for the Ruhr while accusing the government of continued indifference to the problems of Ostwestfalen. In the run-up to the Ruhr conference, the CDU established a number of working groups to study the problems of various subregions, and proposed that the government create standing subregional conferences.[103]

This is not to suggest that the Ruhr was politically sacrosanct. In fact, perceptions of the Land's problems were gradually shifting to a statewide focus. In 1985, seven IHKs from the prosperous areas along the Rhine criticized the state government's practice of aiding the economically

[100] Senior civil servant, NRW Ministry of Economics, Düsseldorf, 24 October 1986. Interview with the author.
[101] Senior civil servant, NRW Ministry of Economics, Düsseldorf, 31 October 1986. Interview with the author.
[102] CDU results in the Ruhr for the 1975, 1980, and 1985 state elections were 37.2%, 33.9%, and 28.0%, respectively. Von Aleman, *Parteien und Wahlen*, 206.
[103] Proceedings of the Economics Committee of the Landtag of NRW, 29 August 1979.

weaker areas of NRW, and proposed a growth-oriented principle of regional assistance.[104] The government declined to extend the APR when it expired in 1983, reflecting the dual concerns of minimizing the appearance of bias and of addressing the widening scope of the Land's problems. Nevertheless, the Ruhr continued to pull in the lion's share of the state's technology and innovation policy benefits. These programs were in effect tailor-made for the Ruhr, only the bias was not as overt as it was in earlier periods.[105]

In addition to the concern with steel and the Ruhr, the state government began to employ a broader range of policies, including small-firms policy, job training and employment programs, and – the main recipient of government's political and financial capital – technology policy.[106] The government introduced a host of technology innovation and transfer programs in the areas of energy, steel, coal, and small firms. The reasons behind the *Gewichtsverlagerung* (shift in priorities) are illuminating. First, technology policy, unlike regional policy, was largely unregulated by the federal government, which left state officials leeway to develop independent approaches. "We are a lot freer in this policy area [and] are able to steer developments to a greater extent."[107] In contrast to conventional regional policy, state policymakers were free to tailor technology programs to the needs of specific subregions, as in environmental technology for the Ruhr and wood-processing technology for Ostwestfalen. Second, technology policy did not require the state to pick and choose among localities and subregions. Since the goal was to diffuse new technologies throughout the Land's economy, the policy generated far fewer political burdens than orthodox regional policies. Responsibility for drafting and implementing these programs resided primarily with local authorities, universities, and the IHKs. The Land government played a facilitative role. In effect, the state government gave a lightly regulated free hand to local initiative during this period, and local actors were happy to oblige. With considerable regularity, small sets of contiguous local authorities formed loose coalitions, called *Aktionsgemeinschaften*, to coordinate promotion policies or to make a case for aid to state officials. Local governments engaged in a wide variety of activities designed to attract industry to their areas.[108]

[104] *Handelsblatt*, 14 January 1985.
[105] Senior civil servant, NRW Staatskanzlei, Düsseldorf, 27 November 1986. Interview with the author.
[106] Official with the Economic Performance Monitoring Division, NRW Ministry of Economics, Düsseldorf, 30 October 1986. Interview with the author.
[107] Senior civil servant, NRW Staatskanzlei, Düsseldorf, 27 November 1986. Interview with the author.
[108] These included promotion, which was accomplished most often by a local development agency. There were sixty-nine in the state – one for virtually every

In general, the growing emphasis on technology policy translated into a wider scope of initiative for the Land's local actors. Technology programs exploded onto the NRW local scene "like mushrooms out of the ground," with the IHKs as pace setters.[109] Self help took the form of cooperative initiatives between local governments, local savings institutions (*Stadtsparkassen*), and IHKs – a reflection of their "skin tight interest" in promoting a flourishing local economy. Local authorities' general interest in the preservation of the local tax and employment base overlapped with the IHK's interest in preserving a healthy membership and therefore local economy.[110] Public-private technology centers and parks soon blanketed the state, particularly in areas near major universities: in Aachen, Dortmund, Gelsenkirchen, Siegen, Essen, Paderborn, Duisburg, Bochum, Wuppertal, Bonn.[111] Active IHKs like those in Dortmund and Aachen created a measurable territorial effect in their localities by increasing the take-up of existing state and federal technology programs. "[Technology transfer programs], though not regional policy, are being created on a geographical basis, and have enabled certain areas to take advantage of other state economic programs, thus creating a regional effect."[112]

In sum, under adverse economic and political conditions, NRW policymakers discovered the need to create stronger policy-making networks with public and private actors at the subregional level, and implemented their own decentralization of penury in the process. "The state simply cannot solve all of NRW's problems on its own. It must seek to mobilize resources and initiative at lower administrative and political levels."[113] Facing declining federal support and lacking adequate resources and capabilities to address the worsening problems of the Land, officials reorganized state policies, priorities, practices, *and* relations with subregional clienteles. The result: a multitude of coop-

major city and township. M. Littlechild, "Germany: The Economic Promotion Agencies for North Rhine–Westphalia and for the Borken District," in *Regional Development Agencies in Europe*, ed. D. Yuill (Aldershot, Hampshire: Gower Publishing Co., Ltd., 1982), 171. Other activities were the clearing of sites for development and the provision of tax and infrastructure incentives to interested firms.
[109] *Westdeutsche Allgemeine Zeitung*, 25 September 1984. Official with the Association of NRW Chambers of Industry and Commerce, Düsseldorf, 3 November 1986. Interview with the author.
[110] Ibid.
[111] On the role of business in this process, see J. Anderson, "Business Associations and the Decentralization of Penury: Functional Groups and Territorial Interests," *Governance* 4(January 1991): 67–93.
[112] Senior official, Kommunalverband Ruhrgebiet, Essen, 18 November 1986. Interview with the author.
[113] Official, SPD Parliamentary *Fraktion* (NRW), Düsseldorf, 28 November 1986. Interview with the author.

Table 5.4. *Temporal shifts in the regional hierarchy, Federal Republic of Germany*

		Saarland		North–Rhine Westphalia	
		1957	1986	1955	1986
	HIGH	state ministries political parties	state ministries political parties	state ministries political parties business	state ministries political parties business
Relative importance	MEDIUM	MPs business trade unions	business trade unions/ MPs local authorities	MPs local authorities	local authorities trade unions
	LOW	local authorities		trade unions	MPs

erative links to subregional and local actors organized along both spatial and sectoral lines.

Explaining the patterns

Federalism creates two factors of great importance to German patterns of group-state interaction: a formal government at the regional level, and a key role for political parties therein. With their capacity to generate political and financial resources, state government institutions resemble small-scale central governments, and this renders them preeminent among various organizational interests in the Land. Furthermore, the competition for political power at the state level places political parties in a prominent position within each region (see Table 5.4). Parties seek to capture regional governments, and when successful find themselves in a position to influence the distribution of resources to subregions and localities.

The dominance of state institutions and political parties influenced strongly patterns of actor interactions (see Figure 5.4). Regionwide efforts of nonstate public and private actors to create cooperative linkages are generally absent, a fact that distinguishes the German cases from their British counterparts. Indeed, the ongoing efforts of local authorities, IHKs, and other local actors to protect and to develop their economies contributed to the formation of subregional and local parliamentary coalitions, lending in the process a certain stability to

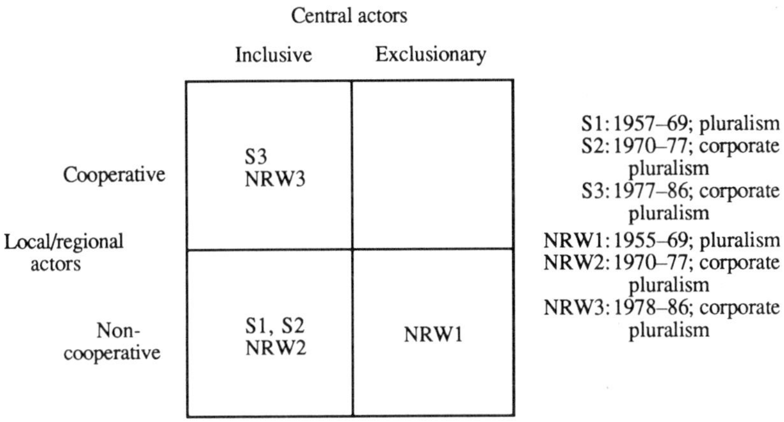

Central actors

Inclusive   Exclusionary

	Inclusive	Exclusionary
Cooperative	S3 NRW3	
Non- cooperative	S1, S2 NRW2	NRW1

Local/regional
actors

S1: 1957–69; pluralism
S2: 1970–77; corporate
     pluralism
S3: 1977–86; corporate
     pluralism
NRW1: 1955–69; pluralism
NRW2: 1970–77; corporate
     pluralism
NRW3: 1978–86; corporate
     pluralism

Figure 5.4. *Strategy mixes and patterns of interaction in the German Länder*

pluralist tendencies within the Land. Competitive party politics at the Land level further encouraged pluralist, zero-sum competition between subregional coalitions. However, these coalitions and their state parliamentary representatives were sealed off almost entirely from ministerial channels of access – a situation expressly created by state government officials. Transitions from pluralist to corporate pluralist relations correspond to instances where Land officials chose to or were forced to employ these coalitions instrumentally to further Land objectives.

Prior to the installation of the GRW in 1970, state government decisions to take independent policy initiatives turned on a partisan logic involving the interplay between parties in power and key subregional electoral coalitions. During this period, attempts to influence Bonn policies took place primarily through party political connections, which provided potential channels of influence for parties both in and out of government. Despite the prevalence of partisan conflict during this period, there were strong incentives for the symbolic demonstration of intraparty and cross-party unity at the state level. Of the two cases, the Saarland best exemplifies the phenomenon. State political parties, using their links to the national organizations, directed a string of memoranda at the federal government with considerable success. Party linkages were also employed with effect in NRW. In 1966, the SPD government sought to address the coal crisis by obtaining federal assistance. Although negotiations with Bonn proceeded through official meetings with ministerial officials and the like, backstage contacts between SPD leaders at state and national levels eased the process considerably.[114] It should be

---

[114] Fabritius, *Politik und Wahlen*, 31.

noted that partisan connections did not always bring benefits to the provinces. For example, the Saar FDP, in the wake of its poor showing in state and federal elections in 1980, was unable to forestall the economic policy reorientation of the Bonn FDP, which led the federal push to cut subsidy policies of great importance to the Saarland.[115]

With Bonn's adoption of the inclusive GRW framework in 1969, the main channel of access to the federal policy-making arena shifted to the bureaucracy. Indeed, the classic federal linkage between state and federal levels – the Bundesrat – soon played a very minor role for party and government officials in the Länder. Moreover, NRW and Saar officials rarely worked through the Bundestag to achieve their policy objectives, although they continued to use the lower house to publicize the problems of a particular subregion or of the Land itself. With the GRW reforms, public and private actors in the Länder confronted new opportunities and constraints, which had the paradoxical effect of depoliticizing the vertical and to some degree the horizontal dimensions of Land policy-making, centralizing initiative in the state governments, and limiting their autonomy in this policy area. The GRW created a baseline for state governments, which enabled them to defuse internal conflicts between representatives of rural and industrial problem areas. As a case in point, the GRW's use of stable *Aktionsprogramme* (i.e., collections of regional labor markets) and variable SPOs shifted debate in NRW from the partisan subject of subregions, prevalent in the 1960s, to the technical question of including or excluding individual localities. Policy formulation in the PA took place in a closed, bureaucratic environment in which the Länder gained continuous access to informational and statutory resources, and this contributed to strong Land government control over relations with subregional actors.

The complexity of the GRW policy-making process offered state officials effective means of deflecting requests and demands from local authorities, parliamentary representatives, and other local and subregional interests. Saar and NRW Economics Ministries stood in splendid isolation at the center of their respective regional policy universes. Given the information gathering capacity of the Land governments, coupled with the general successes of the GRW, there was no need to bring in local and subnational actors into the process at the Land level. In effect, neither Saarbrücken nor Düsseldorf was compelled to organize its periphery on a permanent basis during the 1970s, and both were capable of riding out the intense intraregional conflicts that permeate cooperative initiatives in Britain. In comparison to the immediately preceding period

[115] Proceedings of the Economics Committee of the Landtag of NRW, 14 November 1980.

in each Land, the pattern of actor relations shifted to a tepid corporate pluralism as state officials responded to the incentive structure created by the GRW. Governments in both Länder made and unmade relationships with subregional groups as the situation warranted.

The combination of steel crisis and GRW cutbacks after 1977 prompted parallel Land responses involving the introduction of stable, bilateral relationships between state ministries and nonoverlapping sets of actors at the subregional and local levels. Crisis cartels in steel, drawing together state, business, and trade union officials, were formed to manage rationalization and investment programs with tangible spatial impacts. Land governments fashioned corporate pluralist relations with key subregional actors to compensate for an objective increase in their resource dependence, specifically the loss of regional policy benefits and decline in their policy-making autonomy.[116] Governments and parties in the Saarland and NRW sought alternatives to the GRW, and constructed new policy relationships with IHKs, universities, local governments, and other actors. The politicization of the GRW played a visible role in this search for alternatives; with the accession to power of the CDU/CSU-FDP coalition in 1983, both states experienced difficulties in making a case for special assistance "The *Montan* Länder can no longer expect to benefit to the extent they did under the Brandt and Schmidt coalitions."[117]

The two Länder were not equally capable in this regard, a function of their differing resource bases. Over the entire duration of the period, the Saarland faced severe financial constraints arising out of its small tax base, high proportion of governmental fixed costs, and costly obligations with respect to rationalization measures in coal and steel. NRW governments were comparatively better off, although the situation worsened dramatically in the 1980s.[118] Despite these differences, the patterns of interaction are surprisingly similar across both cases.

Nevertheless, these differences highlight the variable agenda-setting effect of federal policy, a clear parallel to the British cases. The Saarland was highly dependent on federal largesse of all forms, and not surprisingly, the impact of central government policies and processes was great-

---

[116] This underscores an interesting feature of German regional policy. Unlike Britain, where government retrenchment in the 1980s brought about a shift from inclusive to exclusionary approaches in certain regions, the German federal government maintained its inclusive policy approach, complete with restrictions on Land initiatives, while undertaking similar drastic reductions in regional assistance.

[117] Official, SPD Parliamentary *Fraktion* (NRW), Düsseldorf, 28 November 1986. Interview with the author.

[118] Von Voss, *Das Nord-Süd-Gefälle*, 123. Senior Civil Servant, NRW Ministry of Economics, Düsseldorf, 31 October 1986. Interview with the author.

est there. Governmental regional policy initiatives acted as both a spur to and a brake on the Land's efforts to deal with its economic problems. The CDU's increased interventionism at the end of the 1960s was due in large part to the federal government's insistence. The limited moves toward a pro-active policy between 1967 and 1982 were kept in check by the demonstrable success of federal regional policy. Indeed, until 1982, Saar government officials were able to use the considerable advantages conferred on them by federal policy to postpone the development of their own policy initiatives. In contrast to other Bundesländer, participation in the GRW did not prompt Saar governments to concentrate their own resources on specific problem areas. Only with the federal government's retreat from regional policy in the 1980s was a reluctant Saar Cabinet exposed to pressures for action. For states such as NRW, Bavaria, or Rhineland–Palatinate, the GRW provided a baseline from which state governments sought to improvise and to extend their own policy efforts. Bonn regional policy presented NRW officials with more in the way of constraints than opportunities, in view of the line-up of Länder interests in the PA. Despite its success in obtaining a larger share of the GRW pie and advantageous modifications of the selection criteria, much of the state government's actions during the 1970s and 1980s were taken with an eye to compensating for or circumventing altogether the perceived inadequacies of federal policy.

Unlike Britain's experience, the formulation and implementation of federal policies did not exercise a direct impact on the relationships among actors within the Länder. Because Bonn lacks its own means of implementing federal policies, regional governments stand positioned as gatekeepers between federal impulses and subregional actors. As a result, intraregional interactions were decoupled from central initiatives. For example, sectional centralism had no appreciable impact on intraregional relations because Land officials were in a position to compensate for any fragmenting impulses from the center. Where fragmentation existed, it was usually the result of intentional actions taken by state government officials. The significance of decoupling is taken up in greater detail in Chapter 6.

What role did partisan politics play in the German cases? Although vertical party linkages lost much of their utility with the inauguration of the GRW, party politics remained a fact of life *within* the Länder themselves. Government and opposition parties collided frequently over the priority accorded to regional economic development issues, as well as over the pace and timing of responses to decline. In NRW, general evidence for an electoral dimension to regional economic issues can be gleaned from a simple analysis of Landtag debates. Between 1958 and 1985, there were 171 debates on regional economic issues: an average of 0.70 debates per month in session. If a state election phase is defined as the period from January of the preceding year to a state election (normally held in May or June), then one would expect 56.3 debates during election phase months. The actual figure is 80, which suggests a connection between the timing of elections and the calling of regionally relevant debates. State officials announced all major initiatives for the Ruhr Valley within one to two years of a state election.[119]

A comparable electoral connection is not evident in the Saarland. Between 1961 and 1985, there were 98 Landtag debates dealing with regional economic issues: 0.44 debates per month. One would expect 23.1 debates during election phases; in actual fact, 22 debates took place. Overt subregional prioritization as a function of party political competition is more difficult to substantiate in the case of the Saarland; the Land is too small to contain a number of distinct subregions. Any spatial bias is attributable to the simple geography of industrial settlement in the Saarland, which produces imbalances in the problem load facing government officials.[120] Indeed, once the CDU government acknowledged the special needs of the eastern Saar in 1967, party conflict shifted to the appropriate scope and level of government policy initiatives. Still, on the basis of the earlier discussion, it is difficult to escape the conclusion that partisan politics generates much of the sound and fury of Saar regional economic policy.

As a case in point, the absence or tentativeness of Saar initiatives during the 1960s was directly linked to the composition of the CDU's political support coalition. The party enjoyed close financial, social, and political ties to major industrial employers in the region, which gave the latter substantial influence over the content of government regional policy. CDU politicians were reluctant to pursue an aggressive policy to attract industry because of the disruptions it might cause in an otherwise stable labor market. New firms, less willing to abide by the prevailing wage structure in the region's traditional heavy industries, would have bid average wage costs up. As a result, the government pursued a policy of "protecting the labor market."[121] The CDU in North Rhine–Westphalia displayed a similar reluctance to grant the Ruhr a status equal to the rural problem areas; large industrial firms had no interest in competing for scarce labor in the 1950s and 1960s, and they

---

[119] One official acknowledged that the APR was attributable in large part to "the political and economic centrality of the Ruhrgebiet." Senior civil servant, NRW Staatskanzlei, Düsseldorf, 27 November 1986. Interview with the author.

[120] Of the total amount of GRW expenditure in the Saarland, 43.3 percent went to the eastern Saarland; 47.0 percent of the policy-created jobs were located there too. Saarland Ministry of Economics.

[121] Senior official, Arbeitskammer des Saarlandes, Saarbrücken, 12 November 1986. Interview with the author.

were successful in preventing or circumventing government efforts to free land for the attraction of light manufacturing industry well into the late 1960s.[122] Stasis gave way to action in 1966, when the newly elected SPD government targeted the Ruhr. Like the Saarland, the mere appearance of crisis in NRW's industrial heartland was not enough to bring about a concerted government response; unlike the Saarland, party political turnover contributed directly to a change in the policy stance of the state government.

Thus, in the German cases we discovered similar patterns of interaction arising out of the decline of the regional economy. With these findings fresh in our minds, it is time to bring them together with the results of Chapter 4. Many contrasts with the previous chapter's findings are already evident, and the fact that the German patterns surfaced under a markedly different distribution of resources among actors must weigh heavily in our comparative analysis.

[122] Official with DGB–Landesbezirk, NRW, Düsseldorf, 2 December 1986. Interview with the author. Bochum, *Industrie und Region*, 168. "Full employment in the Land was a fact of life until 1966, which lessened the pressure to come up with immediate solutions. The politicians could afford to wait." Official with the Economic Performance Monitoring Division, NRW Ministry of Economics, Düsseldorf, 30 October 1986. Interview with the author.

6   The territorial imperative: political logic interprets problem logic

Rumors of the death of territorial politics are greatly exaggerated. Indeed, politics about territory fought out across territory would appear to be an omnipresent feature of advanced industrial democracies. Equipped with evidence gleaned from the British and German case comparisons, we are now in a position to return to the original questions formulated in Chapter 2. Do the approaches adopted by national and subnational actors combine to produce the predicted patterns of interaction? How can one account for any divergence between actual and predicted outcomes? Whatever the resulting patterns uncovered in the British and German regions, what caused them and what are their political consequences? More importantly, can any regularities in the territorial imperative be traced to the influence of problem and political logics? After these questions have been addressed, the discussion then turns to several broader conceptual issues. A principal objective of this book has been to explore the relative importance of constitutional orders as bona fide institutions. In light of the findings, we need to assess the utility of such a perspective, and to speculate about future lines of research. Finally, we return to mesopolitics and its relative merits as a focus of analysis. To the extent that politics at the mesolevel takes place under a markedly different set of constraints and opportunities than those operative in national politics, do we need to reformulate prevailing ideas in the literature, many of which are based on an exclusive concern with the national level? Are conventional perspectives on British or German politics, or for that matter comparative political economy, in need of revision?

Patterns of interaction between center and periphery: the empirical evidence

Chapters 4 and 5 document the extent to which resource dependence influences the selection of cooperative and autarchic strategies by subnational actors and national government officials in both countries. The issue before us is whether distinctive strategy mixtures generate the pluralist, corporate pluralist, and corporatist patterns of interaction depicted in Figure 2.2. The most striking feature of Figures 4.3 and 5.4 is the sheer variability of mixes and outcomes. Individual regions do not exhibit unvarying patterns over time. Furthermore, the British cases

187

Central actors

	Inclusive	Exclusionary
Cooperative	sectoral corporatism *4 corporate pluralism*	corporate pluralism *1 corporate pluralism* *1 pluralism*
Non-cooperative	corporate pluralism *3 corporate pluralism* *1 pluralism*	pluralism *3 pluralism*

Local/regional actors

Note: Framework predicts 53.8 percent of the cases correctly.

Figure 6.1. *Patterns of interaction: predicted and actual outcomes*

reveal differentiation that is not constant across cases at the same point in time. In toto, we find intranational differences within a single policy sector, an outcome that is not consistent with conventional analyses of European group-state relations, which tend to predict uniformity within national policy sectors.[1] As the following sections will show, these differences arise from the variable ability of central governments to treat their peripheries in a differentiated manner on the bases of the spatial-political location of the areas in question. In other cases, differences are the produce of spatial variations in the political capabilities of subnational actors. The evidence suggests the possibility of similar complexity in other policy sectors. Perhaps a spatial dimension – defined in terms of the geographical distribution of economic and political resources valued by central elites, for example – must be incorporated into the concept of policy sectors. In such a manner, one might accommodate other cases in which patterns of interaction between state and nonstate actors vary intrasectorally.

The relationship between predicted and actual outcomes, depicted in Figure 6.1, is strong in certain directions and tenuous in others. The model performs quite ably in accounting for the emergence of pluralist relations. Whenever subnational noncooperative approaches met with

---

[1] For a review of this literature, see Jordan and Richardson, *Government and Pressure Groups.*

an exclusionary stance by central government, pluralism resulted without fail. Although commendable, the model's accuracy should hardly provoke surprise. Since the analytical framework focuses on the behavior of purposive organizations, it stands to reason that some element of intent, either on the part of national or subnational actors, is required to move beyond pluralism to more structured interactions.

On the other hand, the model performs miserably in predicting the emergence of sectoral corporatism. In the four cases where regional cooperative approaches met with central inclusiveness, corporate pluralism emerged. This is consistent, but not the pattern anticipated by the model. Such open slippage between predicted and actual outcomes, although certainly troubling, actually illuminates important dimensions of the politics of regional decline and is therefore worthy of further elaboration. As we shall see, a thorough exploration of the source of these discrepancies leads not only to a useful revision of the original model's predictions, but to several nuances that distinguish the German from the British cases and are of direct relevance to the discussion of problem and political logic.

Even when subnational and national approaches were mutually reinforcing, the most any region could achieve was strong corporate pluralism. These results are disconcerting from a theoretical standpoint, since the recurrent mix of cooperative and inclusive approaches should have provided optimal conditions for mesolevel corporatism to flourish. Yet if we look behind the outcomes to the actual case evidence, the reasons for the predictive failures are not only self-evident, but point to immutable structural factors in this problem area that rule out the corporatist variant. These constraints consist of an explicit lack of intent to generate corporatist relations on the part of central officials and, more important, an absence of organizational capability among the actors that inhabit the regional level.

In both countries, central government officials sought at critical times to organize the periphery, either to improve the delivery of policy benefits or to manage demands, yet they generally stopped well short of bringing subnational actors into the intimate arrangements characteristic of sectoral corporatism. To be sure, since the early 1970s the German states have participated directly in the federal policy-making process. At no time, however, has Bonn sought to extend the web of relations to groups and organizations below the Land governments. As such, German regional policy-making is a highly institutionalized and multilateral *intergovernmental* arrangement, but it is not corporatist.

Much more significantly, the constellation and capabilities of actors at the regional level conspire to render territorial expressions of corporatism inoperable. As a case in point, the British government's only attempt to coax a subnational organization into a corporatist relationship, which occurred in the North East in 1946, foundered on the inability of the regional umbrella association to play the part. Corporatist bargaining requires organizations that can control members and make allocative choices among them. For a regional development organization interested in cultivating the support of institutional members possessing their own resource bases and skeptical of the benefits of cooperation, this proved to be an impossible task. Although such British regional weaknesses are not fully replicated in Germany – state governments are eminently capable actors – corporatism from below has not emerged there either. Subregional and local actors suffer from similar resource constraints and tenuous representational monopolies, and are prevented from interacting directly with the federal government by the absence of a national field administration and by the intergovernmental exclusivity of the GRW. Thus, in the absence of a lead from Land governments, the corporatist option lies dormant. In short, the failed British episode is emblematic of an inherent limitation on the corporatist alternative. It is impossible for central government or subnational actors to reduce substantially the variety of actors in a given region, in view of the institutionalized heterogeneity of the group environment. Representatives of local authorities, trade unions, business associations, and political parties cannot and will not merge their organizational identities. Moreover, local, subregional, and regional actors are not in a position to receive grants of representational monopoly from government and the obligations these normally entail.

Such limitations apply most clearly to local authority umbrella associations that seek to play a pan-local role in the regional economy. Although individual local authorities in Britain and Germany have interacted with a variety of organizations to counter the effects of decline, and have banded together on occasion to pursue their collective interests as local public entities, they have proved unbending in their desire to retain autonomy and control over resources when confronted with efforts to coordinate local government responses at the subregional or regional level. As democratically elected and therefore accountable public organizations, this is an understandable reaction, however detrimental it may prove to regional corporatist aspirations.

Functional interest groups in the regions are constrained as well. The territorial representatives of capital and labor confront a basic fact – their members have few if any explicitly defined interests in this area. As King points out with reference to business, "[The] problem . . . is less one of controlling demanding members than one of resurrecting any interest at all from the bulk of the membership in their representational activities."[2] Regional business associations and trade unions in Britain and Germany operate in splendid isolation from member firms and workers where issues of regional regeneration are concerned, which leaves them considerable room for maneuver. The looseness of relations between members and association also condemns the latter to inefficacy, however. Large industrial employers, either private or nationalized, conducted rationalization policies in each of the regions while the territorial representatives of business stood by as supporters or ineffectual bystanders. Individual trade unions in their collective bargaining activities gave little if any consideration to the spatial ramifications of their settlements. In other words, capital and labor pursue territorial interests vigorously only when constituent members perceive no overriding functional interests. The inattentiveness of members limits the abilities of the producer associations to enlist their sustained participation in cooperative initiatives. Thus, although these organizations have made significant contributions to regional initiatives, they chafe against organizational limitations that hamper their ability to aggregate interests and to control members effectively.[3]

The internal constraints on subnational "peak" associations, when combined with the statutory independence of local authorities, produce very poor soil in which to plant regionwide corporatism, quite apart from the intentions of central government officials. As a result, stable corporatist arrangements that bring together monopolistic regional representatives and government actors at the subnational level are extremely unlikely to occur. Routinized relationships that result from the mix of cooperative and inclusive strategies are in fact less formal and less structured, corresponding to variants of corporate pluralism that lie closer to but not at the corporatist pole of the continuum. The dormancy of corporatism at the regional level suggests that it should be removed from the continuum of patterned interactions, leaving us with pluralism and corporate pluralism of varying strengths. Such a reassessment leads to the following revised predictive framework (see Figure 6.2), which reflects empirical realities much more accurately and therefore does a better job of relating predicted to actual patterns of interaction between national and subnational actors.

The robustness of this framework is underlined by developments in the regions which have taken place since 1986. In the North East, cooperation among subnational actors, which takes the organizational form of the NDC, has received the open financial and moral support of

---

[2] King, "Corporatism and the Local Economy," 205.
[3] I delve into this issue in greater detail in my article, "The Decentralization of Penury."

| | Central actors | |
	Inclusive	Exclusionary
Cooperative	strong corp. pluralism *4 strong corp. pluralism*	weak corp. pluralism *1 weak corp. pluralism* *1 pluralism*
Non-cooperative	weak corp. pluralism *3 weak corp. pluralism* *1 pluralism*	pluralism *3 pluralism*

Local/regional actors

Note: Framework predicts 84.6 percent of the cases correctly.

Figure 6.2. *Revised framework: predicted and actual outcomes*

the government, in effect placing the region in the upper left box of strong corporate pluralism. In the West Midlands, Whitehall continues to pursue inclusive approaches vis-à-vis the region, yet the modest resurgence of the regional economy since 1986 has led to the breakdown of cooperative strategies. The West Midlands Regional Economic Consortium no longer represents the vehicle of choice for subnational actors intent on pursuing local economic development goals, and even contributors to WMIDA are beginning to question whether the organization is needed any longer in the context of relative prosperity. In sum, good economic times and the urban emphasis encouraged by government policy have led to the atrophy of regional cooperation in the West Midlands. The result is a much weakened form of corporate pluralism. Developments in the two German Länder since 1986 have been characterized by continuities that have persisted into the postunification period. In the context of continuing retrenchment in the field of federal regional policy, strong corporate pluralist networks continue to result from the approaches of state governments in Düsseldorf and Saarbrücken.

The remaining outliers in Figure 6.2 point up several important nuances to the politics of regional decline. First, the West Midlands during the 1970s, where pluralism instead of the expected outcome of weak corporate pluralism emerged, underlines the crucial role of central government in helping subnational actors to overcome the competitive strains of organizational pluralism. In the absence of an inclusive approach by Whitehall, actors in this region were unable to transcend the fragmented structure of interest representation. Since no similar mix of central-peripheral strategies occurred in Germany, we are unable to determine whether this role of central government is of general significance, or relevant only in a unitary polity. Second, the case of the Saarland prior to 1970 highlights the strong possibility that the impacts of central inclusiveness in Britain and Germany are not strictly comparable. Instead of producing weak corporate pluralism, the inclusive stance adopted by the federal government had no effect on prevailing pluralist relations within the Land. This reinforces the likelihood, discussed briefly in the conclusion of Chapter 5, that intraregional relations in Germany are decoupled from the direct effects of central government strategies. In other words, national and subnational strategies have different impacts, depending on the political-institutional context in which they unfold. The ultimate source of decoupling remains obscured, however, at least in terms of the dimensions depicted in these tables. Since these outliers suggest variations in the patterns of interaction that might originate in cross-national differences in institutions, we need to move beyond the issue of predicted and actual outcomes to consider the causes and consequences of these patterns, particularly as these relate to the debate over problem versus political logic. It is to these questions that the discussion now turns.

The territorial imperative and regional crisis: political logic interprets problem logic

Politics in crisis regions unfolds in a way that can best be described as political logic interpreting problem logic. A pervasive governmental logic, which flows from the organization of the policy-making process and the territorial distribution of power, combines with the intermittent and, in the case of Britain, sharply constrained impact of a partisan logic to shape otherwise similar responses at the national and subnational levels to the problems thrown up by declining regional economies. As such, the compound influence of the two political logics not only places a discernible imprint on regional responses, but ensures that significant variations in the territorial imperative emerge along cross-national lines.

Elements of problem logic
The national and regional case comparisons attest to the strong effects of a common problem logic At the national level, the broad similarities between British and German regional assistance programs, detailed in Table 3.3, suggest that regional economic disparities present central

governments with uniform challenges that elicit comparable policy approaches. Incentives based on the principle of spatial bias and directed at firms and local authorities define the policy approaches of both national governments. Central bureaucrats tend to view regional disparities not simply as economic problems, but as administrative problems too. National policymakers perceive the need to acquire information, to limit inter- and intraregional competition for resources and development potential, and to manage the overall number of demands placed on the policy-making apparatus. These imperatives render the tasks of implementation and administration broadly comparable – namely, to reach out beyond the walls of the national bureaucracy on occasion and establish relations with policy clienteles in the regions. The ripple effects of a common problem logic at the center extend into the provinces. British and German regional policies generate territorial clienteles that closely resemble one another. Specifically, the principle of spatial bias produces competitive tendencies by dividing the periphery into haves and have-nots. This inherent characteristic of regional economic policy sets declining region against prosperous region, and designated declining region against "aspiring" declining region.

A reasonably strong problem logic originates in the regions too. The anatomy of regional decline reveals that spatially circumscribed economic crises affect comparably situated actors in similar ways. Indeed, problem logic at the regional level appears to subsume a wide range of industrial crises; there is no evidence that intranational variations in industrial structure modify significantly the content of the crisis and the definition of interests by subnational actors. The characteristics of an industrial problem region lead local and regional actors in Britain and Germany to a common act of objectives: infrastructure improvement, particularly transport, communications, and industrial sites; the attraction of new industry; the subsidization of existing industrial sectors; and the upgrading and retraining of the regional labor force. In short, subnational actors in both countries tend to define the solution to their problems in terms of removing locational disadvantages so as to improve the capacity of the regional to compete in the marketplace for mobile industry.

Although intranational variations in the type of problem region have not generated observable differences in the basic interpretation of decline, certain parallel similarities between the regional case sets suggest that these variations are not without impact. Subnational actors in the Saarland and the North East must contend with a much higher level of resource dependence than NRW and the West Midlands, and as a result have had to rely overwhelmingly on central government assistance. Extreme resource dependence left actors in both regions exposed to organizational disruptions caused by changes in their respective government's regional policies. By way of contrast, subnational actors in NRW and the West Midlands have attempted to escape the confines of national policies by building on their store of indigenous resources. The constant chafing of NRW officials against the constraints imposed by the GRW parallel the rejection by West Midlands groups of conventional regional policy. While actors in these regions have not spurned government aid, their principal objectives aim to encourage central government to facilitate the indigenous economic potential of their areas. These similarities across the pairs of regional cases can be traced to the timing of decline. Both the North East and the Saarland saw their economic glory days fade at the turn of the century, whereas the other two regions passed from growth to decline much more recently. This had two effects. First, the more recent disappearance of economic growth left the West Midlands and NRW considerably better endowed with resources – capital, entrepreneurial know-how, skilled labor – which facilitated the formulation of independent objectives. Second, the process of consensus building occurred at different times, with the West Midlands and NRW experiencing intraregional debate at a much later stage. For long periods, there was doubt among regional actors as to whether a problem even existed, and this encouraged go-it-alone strategies. The still-vivid memories of growth also prompted them to formulate policy objectives designed to tap what they believed were the lingering strengths of the regional economy. This aspect of problem logic confirms the close association between organizational objectives and the perceptions of resource requirements stressed by the modified power-dependence framework.

Most significant, the strategic calculations of subnational groups reveal the robust influence of a problem logic as well. In both sets of cases, subnational actors were forced to cope constantly with disruptions engendered by the fundamental objective of attracting mobile industry to the region. Intraregional competition for new employment opportunities, reflected in the efforts of each locality to beggar its neighbor, threatened to result in suboptimal outcomes for all localities. These competitive tendencies, which placed great strains on the pursuit of cooperative strategies, emerged from the standard definition of the problem and standard policy solutions, both national and subnational. The ubiquity of subnational competition severely undercuts Eisinger's assertion that federalism is responsible for the fierce competition among state and local governments for private investment.[4] Inter- and intrare-

[4] Eisinger, *The Entrepreneurial State*, 55.

gional competition is not dependent on the territorial distribution of power, but is an inevitable product of the problem matrix produced by regional economic decline.

Thus, national policymakers and subnational actors interpret regional decline in broadly similar ways, and confront comparable political and administrative challenges arising from the crisis. Nevertheless, there is more to the territorial imperative than the objective dictates of a problem logic. Above all, the federal-unitary distinction makes its impact felt in the way in which inter- and intraregional competition is channeled and in the resulting consequences for subnational groups. Political logics interpret problem logic.

Governmental logic and the territorial imperative

The dominant influence of a governmental logic upon responses in Britain and Germany flows directly from the vertical and horizontal resource asymmetries created by their respective constitutional orders. In both countries, the territorial distribution of power creates differences in the interests and capabilities of actors, which affect the implementation of national regional policy, the hierarchy of actors in the regions, the strategies adopted by national and subnational actors, and ultimately the dominant patterns of interaction that emerge.

The policy process at the center. National policymakers in both countries seek regularly to interact with policy clienteles on the periphery. However, their capabilities in determining relations with these clienteles vary substantially. Due to the structural weakness of English regional actors, government officials have not been forced to create a structured, multilateral system of access to the policy-making process. In fact, this option has been consciously avoided by Whitehall officials, whose actions suggest a distinct preference for bilateral relations with provincial actors. As a result, the option of pursuing inclusive or exclusionary strategies is readily available to British policymakers, who since the 1930s have shifted in and out of an inclusive stance as their need to acquire information, to manage clientele demands, and – increasingly since 1979 – to address electoral calculations has changed. The physical presence of central government in the regions endows Whitehall ministries with the ability to implement inclusive or exclusionary approaches on the ground. Conversely, the German policy process represents an extreme form of institutionalized inclusiveness, at least since the GRW took effect in 1970. Lacking the authority and instruments to control the disruptive actions of the Länder, the federal government ceded a coparticipant role to the states as compensation for the measure of coordination and control placed upon them. Thus, federal bureaucrats in Germany have been forced to adopt an inclusive approach, and are loath to change this for fear of the consequences: an expensive and inefficient bidding war of all against all in the German periphery. The inflexibility of approach forced upon federal officials is coupled with an inability to influence directly intraregional relations. Bonn lacks an independent field administration reaching down past the level of the Länder, a fact that lies at the source of the decoupling phenomenon.

These differences have had far-reaching and variable consequences for subnational actors in each country. The multilateral bargaining arena created by the PA in Germany encourages the formation of coalitions among the various Länder and the federal government, each of which is represented at the bargaining table. Länder officials attempted to wield influence inside the PA by employing a variety of bargaining strategies, and were assisted in their efforts by a decision-making process that regularly rewarded logrolling until the 1980s. Both regions benefited repeatedly in these circumstances. For example, the *Stahlstandortsprogramm* in 1978 resulted from the strong support of Länder with significant concentrations of steel manufacturing industry, most notably North Rhine–Westphalia, the Saarland, Rhineland–Palatinate, and Bavaria. Furthermore, the basic structure of interests in the PA favored the retention of the status quo, which redounded consistently to the advantage of the Saarland and its *Sonderstatus*.

In Britain, by contrast, regional policy is conducted on a centralized basis, such that decisions about the gains and losses of assisted areas are insulated from the combined pressures of regional interests. Representatives from British problem regions do not sit down collectively with the government to divide up the spoils or spread around the misery. Although a loose development-areas lobby exists in Parliament, it confines itself to general pronouncements about the need to maintain a government commitment to the areas in question. Periodic attempts have been made in British regions to extend cooperation beyond regional boundaries, but these have met with neither government encouragement nor tangible success. Nothing approaching the horse-trading that goes on in Germany's PA takes place. The implications for subnational interests are many. For example, NRW's ability to transcend its lingering but inaccurate reputation as a prosperous region – the legacy of a strong problem logic outlined in the previous section – at a much earlier date than the West Midlands was due in large part to the coalitional opportunities afforded by the regional policy-making process in the Federal Republic. Indeed, the difficult task of forging a regionwide consensus on the seriousness of the Land's crisis may have been eased by the presence of external allies, a situation which stands in sharp contrast to the lonely squabbles which hamstrung the West Midlands during the 1970s.

Complex, multilateral bargaining at the German federal level generates additional advantages for state governments. The policy process, a closed affair between state and federal officials, provides insulation and cover for the former to act upon their already strong predilection to prioritize among their localities according to economic, political, or other criteria (see below). Land officials are able to deflect local and subregional demands by blaming an intransigent Bund or an impenetrable joint policy-making process. As referee, initiator, and lightning rod, the federal government is only too glad to play the role of scapegoat for the Länder, since this facilitates PA decision making. Regional associations in Britain that attempt similar pass-the-buck approaches have met invariably with failure. British local interests view the regional policy process, which lacks transparent selection criteria and decision-making procedures, as perennially open to influence. Thus, any effort on the part of regionwide associations to act as a gatekeeper of first resort is doomed. In short, a narrowing of options at the subnational level occurs in Britain, again as a result of the structure of the national policy-making process.

It should be pointed out that differences in problem definition at the center offset to some extent the advantages conferred on the Land governments by the GRW. Since the late 1960s, regional policy has incorporated two distinct types of problem region – the underdeveloped rural periphery and the monostructural industrial regions. NRW and the Saarland, both blessed with high concentrations of the latter, have been forced to wage a constant battle in the PA to assert the claims of the industrial problem regions. Thus, the coalition possibilities created by the PA turn out to be double-edged. Trade-offs and alliances between and among the eleven states make progress possible, but they can also produce an intractable losing position for participants if the Länder resort to an unalloyed defense of their respective modal problem areas. In Britain, industrial regions are the sole focus of policy, which limits the range of competitors for government largesse. Indeed, bilateral relationships are often valued precisely because of their unshared nature, as the case of the North East demonstrates. However, government cutbacks combined with a more partisan approach to the periphery since 1979 have destroyed the value of restricted bilateral relations for most of the depressed areas, above all the North East.

In sum, national regional policies in each country, though they are based on similar principles and generate similar stresses and strains at the regional level, play very different roles in structuring the relations between center and provinces. As will be discussed in greater detail below, the flexible strategies available to government officials in Britain allow them to provide or withhold organizational and financial resources from actors on the periphery seeking to replace noncooperative with cooperative approaches. In Germany, the federal government lacks such flexibility; indeed, the *Gemeinschaftsaufgabe* provides state governments with a measure of insulation from subregional interests that enables them to manage their environment with greater room for maneuver than regional aspirants in Britain are capable of mustering. In this manner, the tendency of intra-Land relations to become decoupled from federal influence is enhanced. The constancy of the federal approach since 1970, to which it is in fact condemned, has left the field open for state governments to make and unmake patterns of interaction on their subperipheries. The source of these cross-national variations can be traced to the specific ways these policies are implemented, which in turn are the product of clear differences in the territorial distribution of power.

The hierarchy of subnational actors. The impact of a governmental logic on the politics of regional decline is revealed more dramatically in the different mix of actors and the unequal distribution of resources at the subnational level in Britain and Germany. A basic distinguishing characteristic of the German Länder shapes group interactions in such way as to set them apart from the British cases – the presence of an elected government at the subnational level. In the British regions, there is no indigenous middle-tier authority. To be sure, regional Whitehall departments perform many of the tasks and objectives assumed by the German state governments. However, one cannot describe British regional civil servants as the functional equivalent of German state officials. Though they can and do act on behalf of their provinces, their core allegiance is to Whitehall headquarters and their ministers. Moreover, they are not in a position to present a coherent face to subnational actors, given that individual Whitehall ministries determine the organization of their own field administration. These cross-national differences at the regional level have far-reaching consequences. In short, the king of the regional hill in Germany is state government, while in Britain, there are no kings, only suspicious, parochial barons entrenched in the localities. Although this is hardly an unanticipated result, it generates counterintuitive consequences for the strategies adopted by subnational actors and for the resulting patterns of interaction. Specifically, the widespread competitive tendencies generated by decline and by national regional policies are the target of repeated efforts by British subnational actors to control them, whereas they remain largely unchecked within the German states.

In Britain, the absence of a middle-tier of government creates an institutional vacuum at the regional level.[5] Consequently, provided that a degree of consensus over the nature of the crisis has been achieved, regional and local actors usually perceive an overpowering need to mobilize indigenous resources through a grass-roots institutional structure capable of speaking with a single voice for the region. The object is, succinctly stated, to replace chaotic, multiple links between center and region with a limited number of channels, preferably one. Subnational responses to decline in Britain generally aim at regionwide cooperative strategies.[6] Cooperative strategies, however, bring these actors face to face with the distributional conflicts generated by decline and national regional policies. The absence of state governments in Britain means that there is no single actor in the region possessing both a compelling interest and the means to carry out cooperative approaches. This leaves the regional hierarchy open to actors that do not necessarily take a first order interest in the economic region per se. Trade unions and business associations have proved notoriously reluctant to mobilize consistently; indeed, their active role in both regions after 1979 owes more to the actions and omissions of the Thatcher government than to intraregional factors. Above all, local authorities occupy a key position within the regional hierarchy. As the only representative public authorities below the level of central government, British local authorities possess the land, financial resources, democratic credentials, and planning powers necessary to the realization of regionwide cooperation and the subsequent pursuit of joint objectives. Local authorities, particularly those willing to free ride or to pursue purely local objectives, represent the barons whom any aspiring regional integrator must convince.

The solution to this conundrum has been to encourage an inclusive

[5] This vacuum is often more than just governmental, as the history of the North East reveals. By the early 1930s, a process that was to achieve full expression in the post-1945 period was already underway: the nationalization of the British provinces. A broad spectrum of indigenous organizations that had once defined regional life in the North East – banks, trade unions, employer associations, political parties – was either replaced by ones with a national focus (banks, producer groups) or were injected with a national focus by centrally located "parent bodies" (political parties). Regional organizations and regional characteristics did not so much cease to exist as become integrated into a national system of institutions, largely uncoordinated, whose functions were at a minimum interdependent. Thus, the deregionalization of institutional life in the North East was actually far more comprehensive than suggested above. See House, *The North East,* and McCord, *North East England.*

[6] This finds both resonance and dissonance in the standard literature on center-local relations. Samuels, for example, argues that centralization does not necessarily inhibit translocal cooperation; indeed, "it may in fact stimulate it." Samuels, *The Politics of Regional Policy,* 81. These tendencies at the regional level in Britain contrast with the fragmentation at the local level identified by Webman in his study of urban policy-making in Birmingham. See Webman, *Reviving the Industrial City,* Chapter 5.

stance by central government. Subnational actors interested in region-wide cooperation have repeatedly sought the financial and moral assistance of Whitehall to forge unity and to check rampant parochialism. On occasions when they succeeded, corporate pluralism resulted. In only one case, the North East after 1979, was a region able to organize itself in the face of an exclusionary central government. Even here, the support of the regional civil service opened the Whitehall door, albeit a servants' entrance, to groups seeking to put together a regional development agency. In short, British groups have sought, with government cooperation, to generate corporate pluralist relations to serve their perceived coalitional needs. Indeed, subnational actors in both regions consciously drew lessons from periods of pluralist fragmentation. Pluralist relations in the West Midlands prior to the 1980s supported a strategy of divide and conquer by government officials. The lack of consensus among regional actors until the late 1970s produced incoherent policy objectives that offered no effective response to continued central government neglect. In the North East, pluralist relations in the 1930s and the weakening of corporate pluralism in the 1970s were associated with an inability to carry the region's case to central government. As a seasoned observer of North East affairs commented, "The sheer proliferation of economic initiatives, plus the resulting increase in representations to departmental offices in Whitehall, has enabled the government to ignore them all much more easily, as opposed to earlier periods, during which a limited number of reasonably well organized groups were working the halls."[7]

What we shall call the British vacuum syndrome – a strong, shared desire to fill an institutional vacuum in the region is undercut by parochialism, which in turn prompts actors to ask central government to square the circle – leads to a number of severe constraints on responses in the regions. British subnational actors who pursue and achieve cooperation are forever walking on eggs, and this is reflected in their efforts to treat inherently divisive issues in a depoliticized environment. Political parties are kept well away from the process, both as participants in cooperative initiatives within the region and as channels of access to central political authorities.[8] This can be traced directly to coalition-building requirements. Since many local and regional actors have latent

---

[7] Professor of geography, Durham University, Durham, 18 October 1985. Interview with the author.

[8] It is important to distinguish party organizations as participants from MPs as participants. The latter have been very active in the British regions, particularly the North East, in their *national* capacity as representatives of individual constituencies. For example, see D. Wood, "The Conservative Member of Parliament as Lobbyist for Constituency Economic Interests," *Political Studies* 35(September 1987): 393–409.

or manifest associations with the Labour and Conservative parties, broad-based cooperation rules out potentially divisive political tilts. In fact, when groups have failed to maintain such a profile, cooperative arrangements have invariably been called into question by members; the decline of the North East RDOs in the 1970s provides the most telling example of the risks and consequences associated with dabbling in party politics.

The imperatives of apolitical unity impose severe constraints on the objectives of British regional coalitions too. First, the capacity to prioritize among subregions and localities and the ability to adapt policy objectives rapidly to changing national contexts are denied to British groups because of the strains they place on consensus and organizational stability. Regional umbrella associations are exposed to the claims of localities and subregions, pushing them to adopt a fair-shares approach within the region. Second, since regional issues do not represent major lines of division in national party politics, and since party politicization is destabilizing to group cooperation, links to Parliament have been supplemented, indeed replaced, whenever possible by relationships with the civil service. In the traditional literature, groups eschew party connections because they have better ways to influence government, usually through the bureaucracy.[9] British subnational actors pursuing cooperative strategies have no choice – they simply cannot afford to make use of the party option. The main thrust of British group cooperation proceeds neither through the ballot box nor Parliament, but through the bureaucracy. This too reinforces apoliticism.

Finally, the fact that subnational actors must employ central government to solve their intraregional conflicts means that these actors possess little leverage in their relations with government officials. Under conditions of severe resource asymmetries, government officials have many opportunities to modify the objectives and demands of subnational actors. Through control of information flows or a simple exchange – participation and possibly influence in return for demand moderation – they bring about adjustments on the part of groups that extend beyond strategies and tactics to the core of interest formulation itself. In fact, where cooperation-minded groups succeeded in gaining government support, the definition of economic objectives and the selection of policy options for the region was usually ceded to the Whitehall bureaucracy. During periods of strong corporate pluralist relations (the 1930s and 1940s in the North East, the 1980s in the West Midlands), groups explicitly adjusted their demands and objectives to the palette of options presented

[9] See earlier reference to Finer, *Anonymous Empire*, note 60, in Chapter 2, and Jordan and Richardson, *Government and Pressure Groups*, 237.

by government officials. Periods of weak corporate pluralism or pluralism (the 1970s in the North East, the pre-1979 period in the West Midlands) were characterized by a proliferation of demands that extended to the institutional division of power in the country. Nevertheless, those regional bodies that maintained close contacts with the bureaucracy, especially the planning councils, peddled a set of objectives much narrower in scope than their less government-bound regional competitors. Even the one episode of "corporate pluralism without the state" – the North East in the 1980s – exhibited the trademark narrowing of demands by subnational actors as they adjusted to their dimmed prospects in London.

German associational patterns depart in significant ways from the British, and these differences can be traced to the presence of elected governments at the regional level. The salience of this institutional characteristic is underscored by cross-national differences in the content of territorial reform proposals. In Germany, subnational reformers have focused not on political structures but on policy. In the main, conflicts have centered around the GRW as an unwarranted constraint on the states, the inadequacy of the amounts delivered, and allocation formulas. Although lone proposals for institutional reform have surfaced on occasion, they pale in comparison to the British scene, where regional actors consistently expressed demands to alter conventional linkages to national decision-making centers and to reform the rudimentary intraregional machinery for planning and consultation.

The presence of middle-tier governments in Germany ensures that each region contains an actor in possession of the interests and resources commensurate with a regional approach to decline. As a result, there is no widespread urge to manufacture a regional focus since a powerful defender of the region already exists. Though actors in the subregions and localities often disagree with state government priorities, the latter, when the dust settles, acts in the name of the region. The institutionalized voice for the region reinforces the predilection of subregional and local actors for noncooperative approaches. In other words, the parochialism that flows out of a problem logic permeates the German crisis regions too, but it goes unchecked in the absence of drives toward cooperation characteristic of British subnational actors. Instead, most local and subregional actors in Germany define their goals in terms of capturing the attention of state government. So where the objective of British groups is regional cohesion leading to corporate pluralism when central government obliges, the objective of German subregional and local actors is pluralist pressure politics.

The upshot is that the German state governments are in a position to decouple intraregional relations from national influence, a point of direct contrast with the British cases. Land officials, facing no pressure to assemble regionwide coalitions to achieve intraregional objectives or to press their case in Bonn, need not rely on federal government assistance to fashion intraregional relations of any particular type. Moreover, Bonn is unable to reverse decoupling because, under German horizontal federalism, it lacks the bureaucratic wherewithal. As a result, the state governments enjoy considerable freedom to organize, reorganize, and disorganize their subperipheries as political and economic needs dictate. The evidence for this assessment is overwhelming – pressure politics from below is prevalent in the German Länder, yet it is usually fragmented and takes place at the local or occasionally the subregional level. Witness the Ruhr Valley in NRW, which is the locus of highly organized and integrated activity by local and subregional actors. Even here, however, the hand of state government is visible. Most of the Ruhr's associational activities – the Kommunalverband Ruhrgebiet, the IHK *Aktionsgemeinschaften*, and the Ruhr Conference proceedings – were or are the products of Düsseldorf intervention. In general, local and subregional actors in both Länder are encompassed by informal networks organized by state government and the parties-in-power. These networks are transient, as state officials define and redefine the participants and basis of interactions in line with changing state and federal policy objectives. In short, the Land governments can pursue either cooperative or noncooperative approaches directed at their subregions.

Three basic consequences, which add up to an absence of the constraints that plague British subnational organizations, follow from the general state of affairs in the German Länder. In the first place, regional economic problems are overtly political issues, the stuff of party politics. Since state governments are the objects of party competition and the Landtage provided a permanent forum for partisan debate, state politics is rife with proposals and counterproposals from the major parties. Moreover, unlike Britain, the activation of parties at the regional level opens up important avenues of access to central government, since partisan links to Bonn can be employed without risking the disruption of fragile cooperative arrangements that are the norm in the British regions. State governments are thus able to ply both party and bureaucratic channels to their best advantage.

Second, regional problems can be treated as distributive issues within the Land. The capacity of state officials to act on behalf of the region, though checked by law and by the prospect of periodic elections, is not subject to the threat of defection (and therefore withdrawal of support resources) that accompanies the activities of British regional interests. State governments are thus able to discriminate among subregions, channeling resources to priority areas defined by policy, such as the need to favor growth points, or by partisan calculations of advantage. Examples of the latter would certainly include the consistently strong support for the Ruhr delivered by the SPD-led governments in NRW. Indeed, the natural tendency of parties to favor their territorial support coalitions – that is, to prioritize – is enhanced by the presence of state institutions that provide them with the necessary resources and political insulation. As outlined in the previous section, the political insulation of the Länder has been enhanced since 1970 with the passage of the GRW legislation.

Finally, the situation in the German Länder generates for the entire range of subnational actors a substantially lower level of resource dependence on central government than one finds in Great Britain. This is certainly the least surprising finding, but it is nonetheless significant. The presence of regional governments with independent powers to tax and spend decouples the states from the federal government in more ways than those suggested above. First of all, the Länder were positioned to pursue programs to reverse decline that did not rely overwhelmingly on central permission and support. This became particularly important after 1980, when the central government began to retreat from long-standing policy commitments to the declining regions. Second, decoupling allowed the Saarland and NRW to cope more effectively with the potentially negative effects of government regional policies. In short, German state actors were often able to devise objectives independently of the federal government, within overarching political and legal constraints of course. Again, the relevant point of comparison is Britain, not the abstract case. Even in the Saarland, where indigenous policy responses were slow to emerge, the capacity for policy and priority adjustment at the regional level is greater than in the British regions because of the presence of indigenous government institutions with independent bases of power and support.

With regard to regional policy, subnational actors in Germany were not as concerned about the impact of assisted-area boundaries on intraregional relations as their counterparts in Britain, who were well aware of the fact that broad-banded assisted areas fostered regionwide cooperation. When expansive assisted areas were not employed by government, organizations in the British regions responded critically. Behind their arguments lay deep concern over the strains that narrow banding would generate within the coalition. Quite simply, it was difficult to make compatible partners out of haves and have-nots. If Whitehall proved willing to promote a rationalization of clientele interests in the regions, as it did almost continuously in the North East, these complaints were taken into account. Where the scheduling decisions by central government did not match its inclusive intentions, as in the 1984 decision to schedule only a portion of the West Midlands, regionwide cooperative efforts were hampered. Contrast this with the situation in Germany. Under the terms of the GRW, the basic units are the *Schwerpunkte,* usually no larger than a city or township. The designation principle is narrow-banded, and therefore encourages the proliferation of parochial demands, as neighboring local authorities and IHKs band together to lobby for SPO status. However, this has not been a matter of concern for state policymakers – they are shielded from these demands – and therefore they have not pressed federal officials to adjust the *Schwerpunkt* principle accordingly. In this manner, the impact of national policy on intraregional relations is far more attenuated in Germany.

Similar differences between the two sets of regional cases emerge where the impact of sectional centralism is concerned. Historically, regional policy in Britain has been designed and implemented without regard for coordination with related policies. The resulting high level of sectional centralism narrowed the range of alternatives available to subnational groups, which attempted unsuccessfully to link regional policies to rationalization measures in automobiles, coal, and steel. These problems were compounded by the patchwork quilt of Whitehall field administration; despite the Herculean efforts of various regional departments to improve interministerial coordination in their regions, certain bureaucratic linkages – particularly to the nationalized industries – were not possible and others were marked by turf fights. Furthermore, the rise of a competing spatial policy in the late 1970s, namely, urban policy, encouraged additional fracturing at the regional level, as local authorities increasingly abandoned a regional approach.[10] Any sectional centralism transmitted from the federal to the state level in Germany is limited by the extent to which state governments, which serve as the principal arm of implementation for federal policy, can compensate by inserting their own measure of coordination.

To summarize, British regional actors, by virtue of the institutional context in which they operate, are more often than not compelled to pursue regionwide cooperative strategies despite the costs and constraints these entail. Their German counterparts, on the other hand, operate in a setting dominated by powerful Land institutions and active political parties. As such, there are no pressures on local and subregional actors to mobilize on a regional basis. This leaves the state governments considerable freedom to shape their intraregional environment. To be sure, in regional distributive matters as in other issue areas, German state governments are responsible to the entire electorate, however

---

[10] Thus, a fractured center does in fact increase the choices available to local officials, but the price is *regional* fractionalization. Samuels, *The Politics of Regional Policy,* 247.

spatially and functionally segregated it might be, and pressures to respond are strong. They do not encounter, however, the severe constraints that crop up repeatedly in the British cases. This leads to an interesting inversion of the strategic horizons of subnational actors in the two countries. At the regional level, they are broader in Germany. The situation, however, is reversed at the local level. Local and subregional actors in Britain are better able to stake a claim within regionwide initiatives that get off the ground, given their capacity to block these ventures. The range of options available to their counterparts in the German Länder is considerably narrower; these actors must hope to draw the attention of their state government with electoral resources or abject poverty.

The constrained impact of partisan logic
British and German national policymakers followed a clear partisan calculus during the infant stages of regional policies. In Britain, Labour's determination to preserve its electoral strongholds in the North, Wales, and Scotland accounts for the party's tenacious attachment to a strong regional policy during the interwar period and in the crucial debates of the wartime coalition. Similarly, conflicts in the Federal Republic during the 1960s over regional policy reflected the differing constituencies of the major contenders; the SPD at both federal and state levels pushed for incorporation of industrial, urban problem regions, while the CDU and CSU continued to defend the rural peripheries. As regional policy in each country reached middle age, however, the electoral calculus receded into the background as other, less brazenly political considerations took on importance: the administrative principles of fairness and consistency (treating like cases alike); the management of burgeoning clientele demands; and the restraint of competitive bidding between and among different parts of the periphery. During the 1980s, as both cause and consequence of a deterioration of broad national consensuses about the value of regional economic policy, overtly electoral calculations began to influence the actions of national policymakers. In light of these parallel cycles, what is the role of partisan logic in shaping subnational responses to decline in Britain and Germany?[11]

Variable resource dependencies in the regions, derived principally from the constitutional order, exert a strong influence on the ability of a partisan logic to make its presence felt. In Britain, the party political avenue is fraught with risk for subnational actors pursuing cooperative approaches. In these circumstances, which materialized frequently in

[11] The evidence of and theory behind policy life cycles are discussed in B. Hogwood and B. G. Peters, "The Dynamics of Policy Change," *Policy Sciences* 14(June 1982): 225–45.

the North East and the West Midlands, party politics played a very subdued role, both intraregionally and between region and center. Barriers to activation from below often eliminated the use of party channels to pressure governments and to exercise influence. These tendencies were strengthened by the effects of structural factors at the national level. Above all, parliamentary party discipline in the Commons restricted the general utility of party linkages for regional interests. Thus, while parties continued to transmit a whole range of electoral preferences to the center, they proved ill-equipped to handle something as potentially divisive to party unity as regional economic claims. As a result, regional actors interacted with parties to achieve limited objectives, primarily publicity-related. This corroborates previous work on the British political system. As Webman discovered in his work on urban policy-making in Birmingham, "the political parties provide a means of communication and of pressure without generating the complex network of influence found in France or in the United States. . . . Parties, in short, reinforce the legal and financial patterns of central intervention in Britain."[12]

Within the British regions, parties played a much more visible role during periods when strong cooperative approaches were either nonexistent or had come under increasing pressure. In other words, when patterns of interaction were either pluralist or weakly corporate pluralist, there was a much higher incidence of partisan activity in subnational responses to decline. The reasons, of course, flow naturally from the analysis outlined above. When fragmentation at the regional level is the order of the day, the insertion of party politics into the fray carries with it far fewer risks. In the North East prior to 1934 and again during the devolution episode of the 1970s, a politicization of regional decline could occur without endangering hard-won regional unity. The same can be said for the West Midlands, although with decreasing accuracy, for the period leading up to 1979.

The powerful constraints on partisan logic originating from within the British regions do not, however, rule out a partisan logic orchestrated from above. That is, regions may still benefit from the distributive programs of a central government seeking to court spatially circumscribed political favor. The collapse of the consensus over regional policy after 1979 ushered in a period in which central government, within the limits set by the decision to maintain a tepid commitment to the reduction of regional economic disparities, began to formulate policy decisions with an eye toward the electoral utility of subdivisions of the national territory. The operation of the partisan cycle in regional policy provided

---

[12] Webman, *Reviving the Industrial City*, 51.

an opening for West Midlands interests, especially business groups, to pursue territorial objectives through Conservative party channels. The politicization of regional policy from above did not, however, wholly remove the constraints operating from below; the West Midlands Regional Economic Consortium, as the only actor committed to regionwide cooperation, maintained a nonpartisan stance, while cooperative efforts in the North East, which resulted in the formation of the NDC, eschewed any overt identification with the Labour Party. Thus, the constraints on partisan logic loosened but did not disappear with the Thatcherite accession.

In NRW and the Saarland, partisan logic is much more pervasive since subnational actors are free from the kinds of constraints imposed on their counterparts in the British regions. Direct political contacts between state and federal governments have been employed frequently to address pressing industrial problems with regional implications. To be sure, the inauguration of the GRW in the 1970s had the effect of diminishing the level of vertical partisan jockeying over regional economic issues, but it did not eliminate this dimension of conflict. Political symmetry between federal and state levels in Germany provides regional interests with more opportunities than their British counterparts. The centrality of NRW in the SPD's national electoral strategy accounts for the timing of the federal coal programs of the late 1960s, while GRW concessions to the Land in 1970 can be traced in part to the SPD-FDP connection. The importance of political symmetry for the Saarland is apparent as well, though the simple national electoral connection is less obvious in view of the Land's trifling contribution to Bundestag majorities. During the 1960s, conservative governments in Bonn generally looked with favor on Saar requests for extraordinary assistance, a function of political sympathies and Bundesrat arithmetic. Political connections in the 1970s also produced impressive results, though these ran between the SPD-FDP coalition in Bonn and their opposition-government counterparts in the Land. Party linkages are thus critical, but simple straightforward symmetry appears less decisive a factor. Rather, partisan logic appears to be a pervasive characteristic of political relations between center and periphery in Germany, a condition which made the return in 1986 to overtly partisan calculations by the Kohl government less dramatic than the parallel development in Britain, however much the feathers of Land officials in the PA were ruffled.

In summary, party politics has been a perennial feature of intra-Land relations over economic decline, in large part because of the electoral incentives created by an elected regional parliament and because no premium is placed on achieving strong, regionwide cooperative relations in order to influence the federal government. Patterns of interaction serve the changing needs of state officials as they seek to manage the administrative and political problems associated with a redistributive regional policy.

The territorial imperative and constitutional orders

We have examined whether and how various actors, separated by geography and interests yet bound by mutual needs, come together to define common objectives and common strategies. With the help of the power-dependence framework, we have identified a common motive, arising out of organizational resource dependencies, which underpins the interaction between national and regional actors. Not all aspects of the territorial imperative differ across national boundaries. Those that do ultimately relate back to the federal-unitary distinction, which highlights the pivotal importance of constitutional orders as institutions. Succinctly stated, constitutions matter. In the politics of regional crisis, the constitutional ordering of territorial political power distributes interests, resources, and capabilities across space. It also governs the relative weights of governmental and partisan logics in shaping patterns of interaction among actors at the national and subnational levels. Certain aspects of the territorial distribution of power exercise a direct impact on the objectives, interests, and cooperative propensities of actors; others act more as contextual constraints, influencing the set of incentives and disincentives confronting those actors. In this manner, political logic broadly conceived interprets problem logic. At this juncture, it is appropriate to review the findings in light of the specific claims of the new institutionalism.

First, the findings provide conclusive evidence of the capacity of constitutional orders to shape the identities, preferences, and values of organizational actors. The clearest example surfaces in the variable roles adopted by, and in certain cases forced upon, subnational party organizations. In Germany, political parties define territorial economic objectives and serve as horizontal and vertical bargainers for resources. Quite simply, they have been in the thick of things. In the British regions, parties more often than not behave as little more than bystanders. Thus, regional problems under federal conditions are approached as partisan distributive issues. In a unitary system, the need to sustain regional unity precludes the participation of party organizations as party political actors. Consequently, other groups assume the role of aggregating and expressing interests within the region. That parties should be displaced as the principal vehicle for the injection of interests into the political process is not new; that it should happen in an area quintessentially suited to political parties – the expression of *territorial* interests – is surprising. And although there is little evidence to suggest that this has made a substantial difference in the definition of economic objectives within the British regions – the uniformity of problem logic is overpowering – the fact that producer groups have taken the lead instead of political parties is nonetheless significant. For example, the crises of legitimacy encountered by regional umbrella associations in the North East and West Midlands during the 1980s owed a great deal to the visible role of business associations and trade unions, which lacked accountable, representative ties to regional inhabitants. Because of the participation of parties in German subnational responses, the issue of democratic accountability simply does not arise.

The impact of the federal-unitary distinction on identities and interests extends beyond the individual actors to the relevant scope of political action in the region. Strong incentives arise out of the structure of the British unitary state for subnational actors to mobilize on a regionwide basis. In other words, the targeted scope of political activity is defined by the invisible walls of the administrative region itself, although success is not always achieved. In Germany, the political region rarely if ever defines the horizons of actor objectives. Interests are cast more often than not in local or subregional terms, a tendency that is directly attributable to the presence of a government at the regional level. Thus, as a direct result of processes set in motion by institutional structures, British local and subregional organizations, unlike their German counterparts, are often motivated to define and represent their interests at a higher level of aggregation than that which flows naturally from their own specific organizational boundaries. In this manner, they face incentives created by the constitutional order to subordinate their self-interested behavior to the pursuit of collective goals.

Second, the constitutional order influences the distribution of resources and rules. The concentration of statutory and material resources in German regional governments equips them to manage and to ignore the parochialism of local and subregional actors to a much greater extent than regional aspirants in Britain can afford to do. Moreover, German state governments enjoy a greater capacity to modify central government policies to their advantage, and to pursue alternative objectives and strategies than their counterparts in the British regions. Even the weakest German case supports the point. Despite the dependence of Saar elites on federal financing and initiatives, a situation resembling the British North East, they were able to adjust to the cutbacks of the 1980s with considerably fewer problems. The availability of a secure institutional base in the region, coupled with statutory access to resources and powers, facilitated a shift into technology policies, state-run regional policies, and the like. The fact that the Land had to borrow to do this, or to concede participatory roles to local actors, does not diminish the point; British regional interests are by definition prohibited from behaving like governments, with a right to tax, spend, borrow, or grant access to the policy-making process. In key respects, the typical Land government plays the part of central government within its boundaries. As such, it is subject to many of the same forces. For example, NRW's promotion of a local delivery system for technology assistance in the 1980s, which flowed from a desire to limit its political responsibility for success and failure, mimicked the federal government's decentralization of penury (as well as Thatcher's) during the same period. Constrained as they are by federal law and joint policy-making arrangements, however, state governments enjoy an advantage over their national counterpart – the capacity to absolve themselves from responsibility by blaming a higher authority. Thus, these relatively resource-rich actors, who are the natural targets of demands from countless interests within their jurisdictions, are able in certain circumstances to act with more autonomy vis-à-vis their immediate organizational environments than is the federal government.

The evidence proves as well that there is nothing immutable about the distribution of resources and rules in the political system. Both are subject to periodic and occasionally dramatic change. In both countries, one can point to abrupt, consequential alterations to the rules of the game governing the interaction between center and provinces. Examples from Germany include the inauguration of the GRW in 1970, whereas in Britain one can point to the creation of the regional planning machinery in 1965 and the devolution initiatives of the late 1970s. These changes not only destabilized relationships and hierarchies among organizations at all levels of the polity, but created new actors, new interests, and new relationships. While radical alterations to the institutional landscape are difficult to predict in advance, their impact on the basic contours of the territorial imperative is undeniable.

Nowhere is this likely to be more true than in a unified Germany. In August of 1990, the Bonn government designated all of eastern Germany as an assisted area under the GRW. Consequently, the joint regional policy-making process will have to bear a substantially higher problem load, since unification has bequeathed to Germany regional crises of a scale never before encountered. The addition of five new Länder to the PA will inject a common block of needs and interests that does not fit the historical division between underdeveloped rural peripheries and declining *Montan* areas. In the future, PA bargaining will become more complex, less consensual, and will generate many more losers among the original eleven Bundesländer. As if matters were not complicated enough, Bonn faces renewed pressure from the EC to reduce the area coverage of domestic regional policies. With the eastern Länder enjoying a *Sonderstatus* for the foreseeable future, all reductions in coverage – and therefore conflicts – will be concentrated in the western Länder. The federal government has already taken steps to reduce the political fallout by undertaking to end those aspects of domestic regional policy that are no longer justifiable in a unified Germany. By 1994, Bonn will phase out the a priori assisted-area status of the zonal border areas, which make up 11 percent of the population area coverage, as well as regional assistance for Berlin. Nevertheless, the government of a unified Germany now finds itself caught between local and regional demands on the one hand and the regulatory stick of the Community on the other.

Finally, the constitutional order influences the way in which conflicts that invariably accompany regional decline are regulated. The widespread drive toward cooperative strategies in the British regions restricts the use of party political access to the center. The imprint of the British constitutional order on territorial conflict does not cease there, however. Whitehall's predilection for bilateral, ad hoc regulation of interregional conflicts also emerges as a direct result of the setting created by Britain's unitary system. Bilateral mechanisms that include some regions and exclude others necessarily limit the emergence of interregional coalitions, a fact that enables government officials to achieve a measure of insulation from subnational claimants, as the case of the West Midlands demonstrates. Although the decades of pluralism in the West Midlands had many contributing sources, certainly the reluctance of central government to organize interests there for much of the period was absolutely essential.

In contrast, the regulation of conflict in Germany is politicized, since parties face so few incentives not to treat regional decline as a partisan issue. Significant benefits are accessible through party channels to the federal government, and regional initiatives neither stand nor fall depending on how far removed they are from the party political fray. What is more, German interregional conflicts are aired and resolved in a highly institutionalized, multilateral process that accords the Länder a good deal of autonomy and influence. To be sure, the GRW, a classic product of German cooperative federalism, altered significantly the formerly unrestricted prerogatives of the Länder in regional policy-making. The fact that state concessions were transferred to a multilateral decision-making framework, and not to the federal government acting alone, is indicative of the limits to central coordination and control that exist in a federal system. Since all Länder are by law granted a participatory role in the policy process, the option to exclude and therefore possibly to weaken the demands of certain areas is not available to the federal government. In fact, this luxury belongs to the Länder; the presence of regional governments, enjoying legitimacy and authority to act on behalf of the states' interests, shifts the locus of competition and cooperation and questions of inclusion and exclusion down the ladder to the level of the subregion and the locality. State government officials, standing above the fray as gatekeepers between their clienteles on the subperiphery and national policy-making arenas, are adept at managing subregional cooperation and conflict to advance their broader objectives. What is anathema for regional actors in a unitary system – a proliferation of subregional and local approaches – is feasible and often welcomed in a federal system.

In conclusion, it should be stressed that there is nothing deterministic about the impact of constitutional orders as institutions. According to March and Olsen, "The constitution of a polity defines the major institutional spheres in terms of the appropriate times and places for different types of decisions, and in terms of appropriate participants, problems, solutions, and decision rules, *but political orders are never complete.*"[13] Certain members of a given class of actors whose interests, resources, and capabilities are shaped by constitutional factors will make more or less of their allotments owing to skill, luck, economic resources, or institutional assets like bureaucratic expertise that are largely unrelated to the constitutional distribution of power. Saarbrücken is not Düsseldorf, nor is the Northern Development Company the consortium. Those who work in the tradition of institutional analysis are also quick to remind the skeptical reader that institutions are not juxtaposed to, let alone set above, politics as the pursuit of conflicting ideologies. A classic example taken from this volume is the decade of Thatcherism in the North East and the West Midlands. After 1979, Margaret Thatcher's governments not only changed the institutional setting of territorial politics in Britain – the forced removal of the planning councils in 1979, the abolition of the Metropolitan County Councils in 1986, the eliminations of RDGs in 1988 – but her governments infused governmental institutions with a new content in such a way as to alter the palette of options and the prevailing interests of groups in the regions.[14] It will be interesting to see whether this situation persists under the kinder, gentler stewardship of John Major. Institutions are not to be confused with apolitical agglomerations of mortar and brick. For all the reasons mentioned above, institutions are inherently political.

On the basis of a strong test of the federal-unitary distinction, this study has revealed the far-reaching impact of constitutional orders.

---

[13] March and Olsen, *Rediscovering Institutions*, 167. Emphasis added.
[14] See J. Anderson, "When Market and Territory Collide," *West European Politics* 13(April 1990): 234–57.

Given the limits of paired or even double-paired comparisons, however, the findings are by no means definitive. In other words, the Federal Republic of Germany is not a prototypical federal system, but is simply one variant of the federal genus; the same can be said for unitary Britain. To refine the collection of statements that specify the variable impact of constitutional orders as institutions, we would need to examine politics in crisis regions within other federal and unitary contexts. That is, the territorial distribution of power varies within the unitary and federal categories, and therefore the territorial imperative is certainly subject to nuances and constraints that are not necessarily present in the two cases selected for this study. This should lead not only to the adoption of different strategies by national and subnational actors, but also to problem and political logics of differing magnitudes and interrelationships. A few remarks on the probable contours of the territorial imperative in other countries will drive this point home.

For example, the Austrian political system has been described as a pale imitation of German federalism. That is, the basic structure of intergovernmental relations is quite similar, but the distribution of power and competence is not as evenly balanced, which leads to an ascendant position for the federal government across a much wider range of constitutional and substantive policy areas. As such, Austrian horizontal federalism should produce subnational responses to decline that are similar but not necessarily equivalent to the German patterns. In particular, political parties should play a key role in regulating conflict and organizing responses, although the extent to which they contributed to a *competitive* partisan logic of response within the Länder was probably held in check between 1945 and 1966, when the Red-Black coalition and the *Proporz* system regulated politics at the national level. Furthermore, relations among subregional and local actors should be characterized by unchecked parochialism and competition. However, considering the much weaker resource base of the Austrian Länder, responses should depart in two predictable ways from those found in the Saarland and NRW. First and foremost, decoupling should be less prevalent. In other words, Land governments should be less able to play the role of gatekeeper between federal impulses and their subregional clienteles. Thus, they will probably enjoy less insulation from subregional interests, have less control over their intraregional policy networks, and be less capable of compensating for the effects of sectional centralism emanating from Vienna. Second, state governments that confront the problems of regional decline will probably be forced to resort more frequently to strong corporate pluralist relations with local and subregional actors. The experiences of Styria and Upper Austria, two

Länder buffeted by the decline of steel in the 1970s and 1980s, provide supporting evidence for this prediction.[15]

We can consider another example of federalism, the American case. The presence of strong state governments should ensure that the principal focus of subnational responses will be at the local or subregional level, as in Germany, and likewise that partisan logic will be strong since political parties will insert themselves into the fray. However, the complete absence of party discipline at the federal and state levels, combined with a far more powerful and independent national legislature, should lead to very different patterns of access and bargaining for subnational actors at the national level. Above all, the cozy interactions of subnational interests, elected representatives, and federal bureaucrats ought to promote fruitful marriages of a partisan logic and a governmental logic.[16] Thereafter, the points of probable departure from the German model multiply. In the first place, American vertical federalism will translate into a nonexistent gatekeeping capacity for state governments. Since Washington possesses its own means of implementing federal policy, local and subregional interests in crisis regions are not forced to work through state governments to press their demands and achieve their objectives. This has several consequences. In the first place, it upsets the regional hierarchy; when in Washington, state government officials are as likely to find themselves as primus inter pares among a host of city and county lobbyists from their state as they are to find themselves leading a coherent, well-disciplined regional lobby. Second, it exposes the region to the full effects of sectional centralism; the American literature on distributive policies, which documents the welter of federal programs, each with its own method of distributing resources and each with its own coherent clientele, supports this prediction.[17]

The opportunities to test and refine the findings that apply to unitary constitutional orders are potentially even more interesting. Within the last two decades, French and Italian national governments have undertaken sweeping albeit incomplete reforms of the territorial distribution of power in their countries, transforming these polities in the process from unitary to, if not federal, then far more decentralized forms of intergovernmental relations.[18] Evidence from the French case suggests

[15] Katzenstein refers to the reproduction of Austria's national system of social and economic partnership at the Land level. P. Katzenstein, *Corporatism and Change* (Ithaca: Cornell University Press, 1984), 216.
[16] See D. Arnold, *Congress and the Bureaucracy* (New Haven: Yale University Press, 1979) and M. Rich, "Distributive Politics and the Allocation of Federal Grants," *American Political Science Review* 83(March 1989): 193–213, for excellent illustrative examples.
[17] Eisinger, *The Entrepreneurial State*, 122; Rich, "Distributive Politics," 197.
[18] On the background and content of the 1981 reforms in France and the region-

that the politics of regional decline prior to the 1981 reforms took on many characteristics of British patterns, in particular nonpartisan, regionwide cooperative approaches at the subnational level.[19] Still, there is good reason to suspect that French patterns of interaction were not carbon copies of those discovered in the North East or in post–1979 West Midlands. The importance of local power bases in French national politics – the *cumul des mandats* – may have encouraged many local authorities to use direct, personalistic ties to the national government to stake their local economic claims, which would tend to undercut efforts to sustain regionwide cooperative coalitions. Second, the prefectural system, which granted specific and general powers of coordination over central government programs to a single regional civil servant, presented to subnational actors a much more coherent territorial face of government than exists in Britain. Although they limited the potential impact of sectional centralism at the subnational level, the prefectures may have encouraged noncooperative, parochial strategies among local and subregional actors in the French regions, much in the way that elected regional governments do in federal systems. Whether a regional vacuum is filled by an indigenous elected government or a powerful, coherent agent of the center is likely to generate far-reaching consequences for subnational actors, of course.

As both France and Italy have regionalized their constitutional orders in recent years, patterns of interaction in declining industrial regions have become subject to very different incentives and constraints. The formation of democratically accountable councils and regional governments created new actors with new capabilities and new interests, which should lead eventually to the intraregional parochialism and partisanship characteristic of the German Länder. Indeed, fragmentary evidence suggests that this is already occurring.[20] Given their weaker resource base, however, these new entities at the regional level are probably not capable of playing a determining role in structuring the relationships between local and subregional actors. As a case in point, the Italian regions, although they enjoy many financial and economic powers, lack an administrative arm to implement these policies and must rely instead on local governments. This pattern of intergovernmental relations at

alization of Italy which took place during the 1970s, see: C. Grémion, "Decentralization in France," 229–36, and Y. Mény, "The Socialist Decentralization," 237–47, in *The Mitterand Experiment*, ed. G. Ross, S. Hoffmann, and S. Malzacher (New York: Oxford University Press, 1987); Y. Mény, "France," *West European Politics* 10(October 1987): 52–69; and R. Leonardi, R. Nannetti, and R. Putnam, "Italy," *West European Politics* 10(October 1987): 88–107.
[19] Tarrow, *Between Center and Periphery*; Mény, "France," 65.
[20] Leonardi et al., "Italy," 105.

the subnational level, a mesoversion of Bund–Länder relations in Germany, may lead to stronger forms of multilateral, institutionalized policy concertation at the intraregional level than anything discovered in the Saarland or NRW.

Most of these hypotheses must remain open to empirical verification. It is clear, however, that the modified power-dependence framework, coupled with a specific focus on the impact of constitutional orders, has produced a set of testable hypotheses about the territorial imperative that is capable of traveling. With this in mind, it is appropriate to return to an issue raised in the introductory chapter of this volume – namely, the ultimate significance of the regional variant of mesopolitics. What insights do these subnational explorations provide for the study of British and German politics, or for the larger field of comparative political economy? Are national patterns reproduced at the regional level? Or have we discovered a heretofore uncharted political arena, replete with actors, issues, and logics of interaction that are in some sense sui generis?

Mesopolitics: reassessing national policy styles and comparative political economy

As the monographic and comparative literature on the political economy of Western Europe burgeoned in the 1970s, scholars seeking to identify national policy "styles" were able to draw on new sources of raw data.[21] Although they were careful to acknowledge the common elements of problem solving and policy-making in advanced industrial democracies as well as the diversity of approaches extant within any given political system – uncomfortable facts which, taken seriously, would appear to limit the conceptual utility of the endeavor – researchers argued that policy-making unfolds according to a national style that reflects the organization of state and society and prevailing elite values and attitudes. Britain and Germany, this literature argues, possess their own methods of organizing the policy process, which in turn produce distinctive outcomes in otherwise similar policy areas. The present study of politics at the meso cum regional level neither wholly confirms nor wholly disconfirms the national policy style normally attributed to each of these countries. Rather, the findings expose core elements of each style as incomplete or perhaps exaggerated, and therefore in need of modification.

One of the dominant characteristics of British policy-making is said to be the strong emphasis placed by government officials on consultation

---

[21] For example, see J. Richardson, ed., *Policy Styles in Western Europe* (London: George Allen & Unwin, 1982).

with affected groups. According to the conventional wisdom, there is "a natural tendency for the political system in Britain to encourage the formation of stable policy communities, one of the primary purposes of which is to achieve a negotiated and stable policy environment."[22] A premium is placed by government on ordered and structured consultation with groups, with an eye to achieving consensus. Certain groups will win, others may lose, but all those affected by the actions of government will be heard before a final decision is reached.

Many aspects of regional economic policy-making resonate with this characterization of the British policy style. Major changes in government programs, like the initial decision to enact the special-areas legislation in the 1930s, the decision to set up the regional planning machinery in the 1960s, and the dramatic cutbacks in regional policy in the 1980s, were preceded by thorough, open consultation with public and private groups from all parts of the country. In other words, British government officials adhered to the precepts of the dominant policy-making style as they contemplated dramatic changes in existing programs. However, as the evidence from the British regions suggests, where the day-to-day administration of ongoing policy is concerned, a focus on consultation can obscure uncharacteristic and important dynamics.

In short, the conventional wisdom tends to ignore the capacity of British government officials to structure the system of access and consultation so as to exclude not just certain actors, but entire aggregations of geographically circumscribed interests in order to further the aims of government policy. The best examples of this phenomenon are derived from the West Midlands case. Prior to 1979, government officials not only denied subnational actors access to the regional policy process, but intentionally encouraged parochialism in the region. This left the field open for intraregional conflicts to fester, which in turn stabilized pluralistic fragmentation. Why is this particularly significant? Much ink has been spilled to support the assertion that untrammeled pluralism – a negative consequence of Britain's open, consultative policy style – produces a weak, penetrated, overloaded government. The West Midlands example, however, demonstrates that British state officials, facing redistributive claims they cannot or will not meet, can actually encourage pluralist fragmentation in order to enhance their autonomy vis-à-vis the group environment. In other words, the pluralism which results from the denial of access can be every bit as effective a means of managing group demands as corporatism or corporate pluralism.[23]

---

[22] Jordan and Richardson, *Government and Pressure Groups*, 181.
[23] On the subject of pluralism and overload, see S. Beer, *Britain Against Itself* (London: Faber & Faber, 1982), M. Olson, *The Rise and Decline of Nations*, and S. Brittan, *The Role and Limits of Government* (London: Temple Smith,

The policy-making style attributed to Germany is nicely summed up in Dyson's phrase, "the search for a rationalist consensus."[24] Like Britain, a premium is placed on consultation, negotiation, and compromise, but of a quite different nature. A decentralized state makes policy in cooperation with a centralized society, which results in a process that disperses responsibility widely.[25] Strong, well-organized groups capable of aggregating interests are welcomed by government officials into an incrementalist, consensualist policy-making process. Whereas Britain's system of consultation is typically marked by an arm's length relationship between state and society and by plenty of conflict among societal actors, Germany's consultative style, particularly where economic and industrial policies are concerned, is characterized by concertation, a lack of overtly partisan conflict, and a rational consensus about ends and means. Analyses of German policy-making at the sectoral and regional levels often suggest that this generic policy style – the politics of democratic corporatism – is not only reproduced at the mesolevel, but driven by many of the same factors, especially federal policy frameworks and producer groups, that lend their mark to the national policy style.[26]

The findings taken from the Saar and NRW regional cases point out that in this particular economic policy area, partisan conflict is in fact the order of the day. And although regional governments have been driven into the arms of local and subregional actors in the 1980s, they remain more than willing to prioritize among their subperipheries on the basis of marginal electoral utility – an entirely rational propensity, though hardly given to promoting consensus – and to include or exclude subregional actors as the need arises. The factors which strengthen decoupling amplify these tendencies. Such patterns do not necessarily contradict the assertions of those who have drawn lessons about German politics primarily from national and sectoral policy studies; rather, they fill in gaps that others have sought to describe either through extrapolation or by means of generalizations drawn from examples of successful sectoral adjustment.[27] In this regard, additional work needs to be done on the politics of regional adjustment in Germany to explore among

1983). An illuminating exploration of the theoretical relationship between pluralism and state autonomy can be found in E. Nordlinger, *On the Autonomy of the Democratic State*, Chapter 6.

[24] K. Dyson, "West Germany," in *Policy Styles,* ed. Richardson, 17–46.

[25] Katzenstein, *Policy and Politics in West Germany*, Chapter 1.

[26] Allen, "Corporatism and Regional Economic Policies"; P. Katzenstein, "Stability and Change in the Emerging Third Republic," in *Industry and Politics in West Germany*, ed. P. Katzenstein (Ithaca: Cornell University Press, 1989), 307–54.

[27] Where sectoral industrial adjustment is concerned, nothing breeds success like success; in other words, sectoral growth may provide the resources and side payments that permit experimentation and ultimately successful adaptation.

other things the growing tendencies toward decentralization,[28] unification with the German Democratic Republic, and the regional problems
generated by Allied troop withdrawals and base closures.

What of the broader issue of mesopolitics? To return to a theme
introduced in the opening chapter of this volume, many scholars see in
the mesolevel a sheltered laboratory "where margins of manoeuvre and
alliance possibilities are greater. . . . In the shady zone of the mesolevel,
negotiations and compromises may take place unobtrusively because
nobody fears so much to lose face and nobody cares too much about
what happens in other regions or sectors."[29] Recent developments at
the national and supranational levels have cast the potential of the
mesolevel into even sharper relief. Western democracies are in the midst
of a decentralization of penury that ranges far beyond regional assistance
programs. Discouraged by decades of middling policy achievements,
fiscal pressures, and the failures of Keynesianism, governments are
drastically overhauling social and economic programs by combining deep
expenditure cuts with a devolution of tasks to subnational actors both
public and private. National policymakers are shedding the political
burdens of responsibility with rhetorical flourishes about the values of
local democracy, initiative, and autonomy, rediscovering out of sheer
desperation the regional and local levels of the polity. On top of these
developments, the European integration process has resulted in a flow-
ering of regionalist sentiment and political activity across the Community. Expectant parents in the European Commission, the regions, and
academe eagerly await the birth of a *Europe des régions* that will replace
the moribund *Europe des patries*.

However attractive these scenarios may appear, we have seen that
politics at the mesolevel, at least insofar as territory is concerned, is
severely constrained. The most telling evidence of the structural constraints on alliance possibilities at the regional level concerns the absence
of corporatism. The empirical findings raise serious doubts about the
relevance of the corporatist model at the regional level. This study is
not alone in this regard. Samuels, for example, expresses considerable
discomfort with the suitability of the concept for his study of Japanese
localities, on both theoretical and empirical grounds. Relationships between Tokyo and its localities are simply too diverse and fluid, and the
nature of their exchange relationships too narrow, to qualify as corporatist. "The bargain between the state and corporate unit in which
the state grants a monopoly of political representation to secure regime
stability . . . is nowhere in evidence in center-periphery relations in Ja-

---

[28] Katzenstein, "Stability and Change," 332.
[29] Schmitter and Lanzalalco, "Regions and the Organization," 227.

pan."[30] He warns of the conceptual dangers of stressing corporatist form over function.

Some of these criticisms do not stick, particularly the point about the precise nature of the exchange relationship forged between state and subnational groups. Even if national corporatist arrangements represent a compact to preserve regime stability at the macrolevel, it does not necessarily follow that the bargain's mirror image has to be reflected in subnational corporatist arrangements. Are bargains of such consequence even possible at lower levels of political and economic interaction? What does regime stability mean at the regional or local level? If it means preserving capitalism or sustaining the legitimacy of the state, then subnational corporatist arrangements are likely to be irrelevant, or even misguided. If, on the other hand, it applies to a specific policy area, and involves the concertation of demands and interests in keeping with the available policy resources, then such arrangements are theoretically possible. In short, it is not difficult to identify the *potential* function performed by corporatist bargains between subnational actors and government.

Samuels' most relevant criticisms relate to the interest group side of the exchange arrangement, and support the conclusions drawn by this volume. The notion that governments grant a representational monopoly to network participants is either trivial, or seriously overstates the nature of the arrangement. Local authorities and state governments already enjoy unparalleled representational monopolies that set them apart from private interest groups. This, however, does not translate into a corresponding ability on their part to confer representational monopolies on other regional and local actors, such as producer groups. Seekers of meso- and microcorporatism who look for the subnational state, whether local or regional, to behave like its national counterpart, and then express surprise when it does not (i.e., cannot), are guilty of ignoring the confined parameters of territorial politics.

Moreover, subnational interest groups are rarely in a position to receive state-conferred representative monopolies in view of their tenuous holds on their respective memberships. To be sure, producer groups at the subnational level differ in their ability to formulate and pursue territorial interests successfully. Trade unions in particular do not appear to be outfitted for the task. While subnational trade union organizations devote considerable attention to the regional economy, they do not participate consistently in organized efforts to deal with decline. A good part of their tentativeness is due to the way in which regional problems

---

[30] Samuels, *The Politics of Regional Policy*, 257.

and policies are framed as a problem of capital.[31] Yet it also reflects the limited flexibility of trade unions as organizations. The world of twentieth century industrial workers represents a vast improvement over the world of their nineteenth century ancestors, despite the resilience of inequalities. Trade unions have played pivotal roles in this transformation. However, they have shifted to different spheres of activity, including the representation of territorial economic interests, with checkered results. Business associations, in contrast, have emerged as relatively flexible organizations, able to engage in a wide range of activities such as position-taking, networking with other local and regional actors, and active participation in public and private policy initiatives at the regional and subregional level. Yet even the parapublic IHKs in Germany lack the strong control over membership required for the pursuit of corporatist-style bargaining.

On the basis of this volume's analysis, one can point to additional constraints on alliance possibilities and strategies at the mesolevel. Regardless of the approach – inclusive or exclusionary – adopted by central governments, their ability to set the agenda for the periphery remains strong. The objectives and instruments of regional policy, which emphasize massaging the market to induce shifts in the geographic distribution of economic activity, often define the realm of the possible for subnational actors. The state can set the agenda in a negative manner as well. In the 1980s, actors in all four regions converged on the goal of modernizing the indigenous industrial base in response to the withdrawal of national governments from regional policy during this period. The British government's encouragement of local economic development programs and Germany's shift to local technology policy are both consequences of the decentralization of penury. As the findings show, not all regions are well-positioned to make this transition. The optimism surrounding the regional level of politics is dimmed as well by the modest payoffs realized by subnational responses. By 1966, the North East had arrived at the percentage share of regional assistance that was to come its way for the next twenty years, which suggests a capacity to maintain the status quo, but not much more. The West Midlands' share of regional benefits is also scant when compared to the magnitude of its problems. State officials in the Saarland and NRW had their hands full simply holding the line during the 1980s. And when one considers the comparatively modest sums represented by total expenditure on national regional policy, rarely more than a minuscule percentage of national

---

[31] The TUC in the North East has begun to use instruments available to organized labor in regional regeneration attempts. For example, a single union agreement, negotiated by the TUC and three of its member unions, was instrumental in attracting the huge Nissan automobile plant to the region in the mid-1980s.

gross domestic product, then evidence of sustained regional influence takes on an even less impressive cast.

Furthermore, a quick glance at some of the figures and tables presented in this book reveals a simple fact: In none of the regional cases has the regional economy rebounded completely. Granted, those regions that achieved robust variants of corporate pluralism were generally able to confront the challenges posed by economic crisis and decline with greater effectiveness than those regions where such structures were either weak or absent. According to the participants, close cooperation among subnational actors is essential if they are to exploit existing opportunities to the fullest possible extent, however meager these may be. Yet the efficacy of regional responses in both countries has been gauged largely in terms of slowing down the rate of economic change sufficiently to mitigate the social, economic, and political hardships that accompany these sweeping transformations. Political pressure, exercised at the center or in the regions, can often create breathing space for policymakers, affected communities, and worried politicians. The experiences of the North East, the West Midlands, the Saarland, and NRW differ in the degree to which the rate of change, as opposed to its direction, was affected, but the principle remains constant. When measured against the abstract case, making the best of a bad situation may appear inadequate, yet subnational actors value these modest results enough to continue to expend considerable amounts of scarce local and regional resources. In the end, questions about the efficacy of responses are akin to asking whether regional policies work. And although regional policies on many occasions have prevented the total collapse of regional economies, nowhere have they been able to keep pace with market-driven processes of industrial change. Efficacy is measured in terms of the second derivative. Politics against markets in declining industrial regions is an expensive, rear-guard action. Again, the limited horizons at the mesolevel are painfully evident.

Thus, as mesolevel actors try to mobilize available resources and to press their claims upon the state, they face the challenge of overcoming divisions created by political space – the product of political and administrative structures and the differing interests these generate. Compounding the problems at the base are a series of roadblocks on the way to the top, like the organization of the state and the cleavage lines generated by interest groups and political parties. Alongside the effects of political and institutional constraints, a robust problem logic circumscribes the alternatives open to subnational actors. The principal political organizations that inhabit the regional level – state and local governments, business interest associations, trade unions, political parties – all operate within the parameters set by a market economy, a fact which they share with their national counterparts. However, the relative dearth and dispersion of financial and statutory resources at the regional level leave subnational actors more vulnerable to the dictates of market crisis and provide them with fewer political options to cope. In short, as one descends from the national to the regional to the local level, the relative weights of problem and political logics would appear to shift in favor of the former. If the regional level is indeed a laboratory in which organizations experiment with new political alliances and policy approaches, then it is a small laboratory, modestly equipped and somewhat understaffed, constantly under the threat of funding cutbacks, and covered by a leaky roof that exposes it to the vagaries of the weather and other natural disasters.

List of abbreviations

AK-Saar	Arbeitskammer des Saarlandes
APR	Aktionsprogramm Ruhrgebiet
BCIC	Birmingham Chamber of Industry and Commerce
BoT	Board of Trade
BSC	British Steel Corporation
CBI	Confederation of British Industry
CDU	Christian Democratic Union
CSU	Christian Socialist Union
DGB	Deutscher Gewerkschaftsbund
DIHT	Deutscher Industrie- und Handelstag
DoE	Department of the Environment
DTI	Department of Trade and Industry
EPR	Entwicklungsprogramm Ruhrgebiet
ERDF	European Regional Development Fund
FDP	Free Democratic Party
GDP	Gross Domestic Product
GRW	Gemeinschaftsaufgabe "Verbesserung der regionalen Wirtschaftsstruktur"
IDC	Industrial Development Certificate
IHK	Industrie- und Handelskammer
IHK-Saar	Industrie- und Handelskammer des Saarlandes
NCB	National Coal Board
NDC	Northern Development Company (Ltd.)
NEDA	North East Development Association
NEDB	North East Development Board
NEDC	North East Development Council
NEIDA	North East Industrial and Development Association
NEPC	Northern Economic Planning Council
NIG	Northern Industrial Group
NoEDC	North of England Development Council
NRCA	North Regional Councils' Association
NRPC	North Regional Planning Council
NRST	Northern Region Strategy Team
NRW	North Rhine–Westphalia
PA	Planungsausschuß

RDG	Regional Development Grant
RDO	Regional Development Organization
SA	Special Areas
SDA	Special Development Area
SFA	Selective Financial Assistance
SPD	Social Democratic Party of Germany
SPO	Schwerpunktort
TUC	Trades Union Congress
WMEPC	West Midlands Economic Planning Council
WMFCC	West Midlands Forum of County Councils
WMIDA	West Midlands Industrial Development Agency
WMPAC	West Midlands Planning Authorities Conference

Bibliography

Books and journal articles

Abelshauser, W. *Der Ruhrkohlenbergbau seit 1945*. Munich: Verlag C.H. Beck, 1984.

Adamsen, H. *Investitionshilfe für die Ruhr*. Wuppertal: Peter Hammer, 1981.

Albert, W. "Die Entwicklung der regionalen Wirtschaftspolitik in der Bundesrepublik Deutschland." In *Handbuch der regionalen Wirtschaftsförderung*, edited by H. H. Eberstein, 1–16. Köln: Verlag Dr. Otto Schmidt KG, 1971.

Aldridge, M. *The British New Towns: A Programme Without a Policy*. London: Routledge & Kegan Paul, 1979.

Allen, C. "Corporatism and regional economic policies in the Federal Republic of Germany: The 'meso' politics of industrial adjustment," *Publius* 19(Fall 1989): 147–64.

Allen, K., C. Hull, and D. Yuill. "Options in regional incentive policy." In *Balanced National Growth*, edited by K. Allen, 1–34. Lexington, Mass.: Lexington Books, 1978.

Almond, G. "Review article: Corporatism, pluralism, and professional memory," *World Politics* 35(January 1983): 245–60.

Almond, G., et al. "Symposium: The return to the state," *American Political Science Review* 82(September 1988): 853–901.

Anderson, J. "When market and territory collide: Thatcherism and the politics of regional decline," *West European Politics* 13(April 1990): 234–57.

"Skeptical reflections on a 'Europe of regions': Britain, Germany, and the European Regional Development Fund," *Journal of Public Policy* 10(October–December 1990): 417–47.

"Business associations and the decentralization of penury: Functional groups and territorial interests," *Governance* 4(January 1991): 67–93.

Anderson, P. *Lineages of the Absolutist State*. London: Verso, 1974.

Anton, T. *American Federalism and Public Policy: How the System Works*. Philadelphia: Temple University Press, 1989.

Armstrong, H. W. "The reform of the European community regional policy," *Journal of Common Market Studies* 23(June 1985): 319–44.

Armstrong, H. W. and J. Taylor. *Regional Economics and Policy*. New York: Philip Allan Publishers, 1985.

Arnold, D. *Congress and the Bureaucracy*. New Haven: Yale University Press, 1979.

Ashford, D. "Review article: Are Britain and France unitary?" *Comparative Politics* 9(July 1977): 483–99.

Bahry, D. *Outside Moscow*. New York: Columbia University Press, 1987.

Becker, P., and G. Ringel. *Regionale Strukturpolitik und Gewerbeflächenför-*

229

derung in Nordrhein-Westfalen. Cologne: Deutscher Gemeindeverlag, 1976.

Beckerman, W., ed. *The Labour Government's Economic Record, 1964–1970.* London: The Anchor Press, 1972.

Beer, S. *Modern British Politics.* London: W. W. Norton & Co., 1965.

Britain Against Itself. London: Faber & Faber, 1982.

Bentley, A. *The Process of Government.* Bloomington, Ind.: Principia Press, 1908.

Bentley, G., and J. Mawson. *The Economic Decline of the West Midlands and the Role of Regional Planning.* Birmingham: Joint Centre for Regional, Urban, and Local Government Studies, 1985.

Berger, S. "Introduction." In *Organizing Interests in Western Europe,* edited by S. Berger, 1–23. Cambridge: Cambridge University Press, 1981.

Blair, P. *Federalism and Judicial Review in West Germany.* Oxford: Clarendon Press, 1981.

Bochum, U. *Industrie und Region.* Frankfurt a.M.: Peter Lang, 1984.

Bogdanor, V. "Devolution and the constitution," *Parliamentary Affairs* 31(Summer 1978): 252–67.

Booth, A. "An administrative experiment in unemployment policy in the thirties," *Public Administration* 56(Summer 1978): 139–57.

"The Second World War and the origins of modern regional policy," *Economy and Society* 11(February 1982): 1–21.

Booth, S., and C. Moore. *Managing Competition.* Oxford: Clarendon Press, 1989.

Borthwick, R. L. "When the short cut may be a blind alley: The Standing Committee on Regional Affairs," *Parliamentary Affairs* 31(Spring 1978): 201–9.

Brittan, S. *The Role and Limits of Government.* London: Temple Smith, 1983.

Bulmer, S., and W. Paterson. *The Federal Republic of Germany and the European Community.* London: George Allen & Unwin, 1987.

Bulpitt, J. G. *Territory and Power in the United Kingdom.* Manchester: Manchester University Press, 1983.

Buswell, R. J. "The Northern Region." In *Regional Problems, Problem Regions, and Public Policy in the United Kingdom,* edited by P. J. Damesick and P. A. Wood, 167–90. Oxford: Clarendon Press, 1987.

Butler, D., and G. Butler. *British Political Facts 1900–1985.* London: Macmillan Company, 1986.

Cameron, D. "The expansion of the public economy: A comparative analysis," *American Political Science Review* 72(December 1978): 1243–61.

"Social democracy, corporatism, labor quiescence, and the representation of economic interests in advanced capitalist society." In *Order and Conflict in Contemporary Capitalism,* edited by J. Goldthorpe, 143–78. Oxford: Oxford University Press, 1984.

"Distributional coalitions and other sources of economic stagnation: On Olson's *Rise and Decline of Nations,*" *International Organization* 42(Autumn 1988): 561–603.

Carney J., R. Hudson, and J. Lewis. *Regions in Crisis.* London: Croom Helm, 1980.

Casper, U. "Background notes to regional incentives in the Federal Republic of Germany." In *Balanced National Growth,* edited by K. Allen, 97–130. Lexington, Mass.: Lexington Books, 1978.

Cawson, A. *Corporatism and Welfare*. London: Heinemann, 1982.
"Corporatism and local politics." In *The Political Economy of Corporatism*, edited by W. Grant, 126–47. London: Macmillan Company, 1985.
ed. *Organized Interests and the State: Studies in Meso-Corporatism*. Beverly Hills: Sage Publications, 1985.
Chapman, R. "Public policy studies: The North East of England." In *Public Policy Studies: The North East of England*, edited by R. Chapman, 1–19. Edinburgh: Edinburgh University Press, 1985.
Chubb, J. *Interest Groups and the Bureaucracy*. Stanford: Stanford University Press, 1983.
Coleman, W., and W. Grant. "Regional differentiation of business interest associations: A comparison of Canada and the United Kingdom," *Canadian Journal of Political Science* 18(March 1985): 3–29.
Commission of the European Communities. *European Regional Development Fund: Annual Reports*. Luxembourg: Office for Official Publications of the European Communities, 1976–1987.
The ERDF in Numbers, 1987. Luxembourg: Office for Official Publications of the European Communities, 1988.
Craig, F. W. S. *British Parliamentary Election Results, 1918–1949*. Chichester: Parliamentary Research Services, 1983.
British Parliamentary Election Results, 1950–1973. Chichester: Parliamentary Research Services, 1983.
British Parliamentary Election Results, 1974–1983. Chichester: Parliamentary Research Services, 1984.
Crouch, C. "Pluralism and the new corporatism: A rejoinder," *Political Studies* 31(September 1983): 452–60.
Cullingworth, J. B. *Town and Country Planning in Britain*. London: George Allen & Unwin, 1982.
Dahl, R. *Who Governs?* New Haven: Yale University Press, 1961.
Dilemmas of Pluralist Democracy. New Haven: Yale University Press, 1982.
"Polyarchy, pluralism, and scale," *Scandinavian Political Studies* 7(December 1984): 225–40.
Damesick, P. J. "The evolution of spatial economic policy." In *Regional Problems, Problem Regions, and Public Policy in the United Kingdom*, edited by P. J. Damesick and P. A. Wood, 42–63. Oxford: Clarendon Press, 1987.
Dennison, S. R. *The Location of Industry and the Depressed Areas*. London: Oxford University Press, 1939.
Dyson, K. "West Germany: The search for a rationalist consensus." In *Policy Styles in Western Europe*, edited by J. Richardson, 17–46. London: George Allen & Unwin, 1982.
"The cultural, ideological and structural context." In *Industrial crisis: A Comparative Study of the State and Industry*, edited by K. Dyson and S. Wilks, 26–66. New York: St. Martin's Press, 1983.
Dyson, K., and S. Wilks, eds. *Industrial Crisis: A Comparative Study of the State and Industry*. New York: St. Martin's Press, 1983.
Eberstein, H. H. "Grundlagen der Regionalpolitik und ihre wesentlichen Grundsätze." In *Handbuch der regionalen Wirtschaftsförderung*, edited by H. H. Eberstein, 1–46. Köln: Verlag Dr. Otto Schmidt KG, 1972.
Ehrenberg, H. *Zwischen Marx und Markt*. Frankfurt a.M.: Societäts Verlag, 1973.

Eisinger, P. *The Rise of the Entrepreneurial State: State and Local Development Policy in the United States*. Madison: The University of Wisconsin Press, 1988.

Esser, J., and W. Väth. "Overcoming the steel crisis in the Federal Republic of Germany 1974–1983." In *The Politics of Steel: Western Europe and the Steel Industry in the Crisis Years (1974–1984)*, edited by Y. Mény and V. Wright, 623–91. New York: Walter de Gruyter, 1987.

Evans, P., D. Rueschemeyer, and T. Skocpol. *Bringing the State Back In*. Cambridge: Cambridge University Press, 1985.

Ewringmann, D., et al. *Die Gemeinschaftsaufgabe "Verbesserung der regionalen Wirtschaftsstruktur" unter veränderten Rahmenbedingungen*. Berlin: Ducker & Humbolt, 1986.

Fabritius, G. *Politik und Wahlen: Wechselwirkungen zwischen Landtagswahlen und Bundespolitik*. Meisenheim am Glan: Verlag Anton Hain, 1978.

Finer, S. *Anonymous Empire*. London: Pall Mall Press, 1966.

Flynn, R. "Co-optation and strategic planning in the local state." In *Capital and Politics*, edited by R. King, 85–106. London: Routledge & Kegan Paul, 1983.

Fogarty, M. P. *Plan Your Own Industries: A Study of Local and Regional Development Organizations*. Oxford: Basil Blackwell, 1947.

Först, W. *Kleine Geschichte Nordrhein-Westfalens*. Düsseldorf: Droste Verlag GmbH., 1986.

Frey, F. "The problem of actor designation in political analysis," *Comparative Politics* 17(January 1985): 127–52.

Georgi, H., and V. Giersch. *Neue Betriebe an der Saar*. Merzig: Merziger Druckerei und Verlag GmbH., 1977.

Geppert, K., et al. *Vergleich von Präferenzsystem und -volumen im Land Berlin und in den übrigen Bundesländern*. Berlin: Deutsches Institut für Urbanistik, 1979.

Gourevitch, P. *Paris and the Provinces*. Berkeley: University of California Press, 1980.

Politics in Hard Times: Comparative Responses to International Economic Crises. Ithaca: Cornell University Press, 1986.

Gourevitch, P., et al. *Unions and Economic Crisis: Britain, West Germany, and Sweden*. London: George Allen & Unwin, 1984.

Grant, W. *The Political Economy of Industrial Policy*. London: Butterworths, 1982.

Business and Politics in Britain. London: Macmillan Education Ltd., 1987.

Grémion, C. "Decentralization in France: A historical perspective." In *The Mitterand Experiment*, edited by G. Ross, S. Hoffmann, and S. Malzacher, 229–36. New York: Oxford University Press, 1987.

Gunlicks, A. *Local Government in the German Federal System*. Durham: Duke University Press, 1986.

Guthrie, R., and I. McLean. "Another part of the periphery: Reactions to devolution in an English development area," *Parliamentary Affairs* 31(Spring 1978): 190–200.

Hall, P. *Governing the Economy: The Politics of State Intervention in Britain and France*. New York: Oxford University Press, 1986.

Hayward, J., and M. Watson, eds. *Planning, Politics, and Public Policy: The British, French, and Italian Experience*. Cambridge: Cambridge University Press, 1975.

Hechter, M. *Internal Colonialism: The Celtic Fringe in British National Development 1536–1966.* Berkeley: University of California Press, 1975.

Heim, C. "Limits to intervention: The Bank of England and industrial diversification in the depressed areas," *Economic History Review* 37(November 1984): 533–50.

Hennessy, P. *Whitehall.* London: Secker & Warburg, 1989.

Hernes, G., and A. Selvik. "Local corporatism." In *Organizing Interests in Western Europe*, edited by S. Berger, 103–19. Cambridge: Cambridge University Press, 1981.

Hesse, J. "Wirtschaft und Strukturpolitik in Nordrhein-Westfalen." In *Nordrhein-Westfalen: Eine politische Landeskunde*, edited by Landeszentrale für politische Bildung Nordrhein-Westfalen, 210–38. Köln: Verlag W. Kohlhammer, 1984.

Hogwood, B. "The regional dimension of industrial policy administration." In *Regional Government in England*, edited by B. Hogwood and M. Keating, 97–117. Oxford: Clarendon Press, 1982.

Hogwood, B. and P. D. Lindley. "Variations in regional boundaries." In *Regional Government in England*, edited by B. Hogwood and M. Keating, 21–49. Oxford: Clarendon Press, 1982.

Hogwood, B., and B. G. Peters. "The dynamics of policy change: Policy succession," *Policy Sciences* 14(June 1982): 225–45.

House, J. W. *The North East.* Newton Abbot: David & Charles (Publishers) Ltd., 1969.

    ed. *The UK Space: Resources, Environment, and the Future.* London: Weidenfield and Nicolson, 1982.

Hudson, R. "The paradoxes of state intervention: The impact of nationalized industry policies and regional policy on employment in the Northern region in the post-war period." In *Public Policy Studies: The North East of England*, edited by R. Chapman, 57–79. Edinburgh: Edinburgh University Press, 1985.

Ikenberry, G. J. "The irony of state strength: Comparative responses to the oil shocks in the 1970s," *International Organization* 40(Winter 1986): 105–37.

Jay, D. *Change and Fortune: A Political Record.* London: Hutchinson, 1980.

Johnson, N., and A. Cochrane. *Economic Policy-making by Local Authorities in Britain and Western Germany.* London: George Allen & Unwin, 1981.

Jones, B., and M. Keating. "The British Labour Party: Centralization and devolution." In *The Territorial Dimension in United Kingdom Politics*, edited by P. Madgwick and R. Rose, 177–201. London: Macmillan Press Ltd., 1982.

Labour and the British State. Oxford: Clarendon Press, 1985.

Jordan, A. G. "Iron triangles, woolly corporatism, and elastic nets: Images of the policy process," *Journal of Public Policy* 1(February 1981): 95–123.

    "Pluralistic corporatism and corporate pluralism," *Scandinavian Political Studies* 7(September 1984): 137–53.

Jordan, A. G., and J. J. Richardson. *Government and Pressure Groups in Britain.* Oxford: Clarendon Press, 1987.

Katzenstein, P., ed. *Between Power and Plenty.* Madison: University of Wisconsin Press, 1978.

Corporatism and Change. Ithaca: Cornell University Press, 1984.
Small States in World Markets: Industrial Policy in Europe. Ithaca: Cornell University Press, 1985.
Policy and Politics in West Germany: The Growth of a Semisovereign State. Philadelphia: Temple University Press, 1987.
"Stability and change in the emerging Third Republic." In *Industry and Politics in West Germany*, edited by P. Katzenstein, 307–54. Ithaca: Cornell University Press, 1989.
Katznelson, I. "Working class formation and the state: Nineteenth-century England in American perspective." In *Bringing the State Back In*, edited by P. Evans, D. Rueschemeyer, and T. Skocpol, 257–84. Cambridge: Cambridge University Press, 1985.
Keating, M. "The debate on regional reform." In *Regional Government in England,* edited by B. Hogwood and M. Keating, 235–53. Oxford: The Clarendon Press, 1982.
Keating, M., and D. Bleiman. *Labour and Scottish Nationalism.* London: Macmillan Press Ltd., 1979.
Keating, M., and M. Rhodes. "The status of regional government: An analysis of the West Midlands." In *Regional Government in England*, edited by B. Hogwood and M. Keating, 51–73. Oxford: Clarendon Press, 1982.
Keinemann, F. *Von Arnold zu Steinhoff und Meyers: Politische Bewegungen und Koalitionsbildungen in Nordrhein-Westfalen, 1950–1962.* Münster: Kommissionsverlag, 1973.
King, P. *Federalism and Federation.* London: Croom Helm Publishers, 1982.
King, R. "Corporatism and the local economy." In *The Political Economy of Corporatism*, edited by W. Grant, 202–28. London: Macmillan Publishers Ltd., 1985.
Kock, H. *Stabilitätspolitik im föderalistischen System der Bundesrepublik Deutschland.* Köln: Bund-Verlag, 1975.
Krasner, S. *Defending the National Interest.* Princeton: Princeton University Press, 1978.
"Review article: Approaches to the state," *Comparative Politics* 16(January 1984): 223–46.
Kühn, H. *Aufbau und Bewährung.* Hamburg: Hoffmann und Campe, 1981.
Kvavik, R. B. *Interest Groups in Norwegian Politics.* Oslo: Universitetsforlaget, 1976.
Landeszentrale für politische Bildung Nordrhein-Westfalen, ed. *Nordrhein-Westfalen: Eine politische Landeskunde.* Köln: Verlag W. Kohlhammer, 1984.
Lange, P., G. Ross, and M. Vannicelli. *Unions, Change, and Crisis: French and Italian Union Strategy and the Political Economy, 1945–80.* London: George Allen & Unwin, 1982.
LaPalombara, J. *Interest Groups in Italian Politics.* Princeton: Princeton University Press, 1964.
Politics Within Nations. Englewood Cliffs, N.J.: Prentice-Hall, 1974.
Latham, E. *The Group Basis of Politics.* Ithaca: Cornell University Press, 1952.
Latz, R. *Die saarländische Schwerindustrie und ihre Nachbarreviere, 1878–1938.* Saarbrücken: Saarbrücker Druckerei und Verlag, 1985.
Law, C. *British Regional Development Since World War I.* Newton Abbot: David & Charles (Publishers) Ltd., 1980.

Lehmbruch, G. *Parteienwettbewerb im Bundesstaat*. Stuttgart: Verlag W. Kohlhammer, 1976.

"Liberal corporatism and party government." In *Trends Toward Corporatist Intermediation*, edited by P. Schmitter and G. Lehmbruch, 147–84. Beverly Hills: Sage Publications, 1979.

"Concertation and the structure of corporatist networks." In *Order and Conflict in Contemporary Capitalism*, edited by J. Goldthorpe, 60–80. Oxford: Oxford University Press, 1984.

Leonardi, R., R. Nannetti, and R. Putnam. "Italy: Territorial politics in the postwar years," *West European Politics* 10(October 1987): 88–107.

Lindley, P. D. "The framework of regional planning 1964–1980." In *Regional Government in England*, edited by B. Hogwood and M. Keating, 169–90. Oxford: Clarendon Press, 1982.

Lipset, S., and S. Rokkan. "Cleavage structures, party systems, and voter alignments: An introduction." In *Party Systems and Voter Alignments*, edited by S. Lipset and S. Rokkan, 1–64. New York: The Free Press, 1967.

Littlechild, M. "Germany: The economic promotion agencies for North Rhine-Westphalia and for the Borken district." In *Regional Development Agencies in Europe*, edited by D. Yuill, 168–234. Aldershot, Hampshire: Gower Publishing Company Ltd., 1982.

Loebl, H. *Government Factories and the Origins of British Regional Policy, 1934–1948*. Aldershot, Hampshire: Gower Publishing Co. Ltd, 1988.

Lomas, G. M., and P. A. Wood. *Employment Location in Regional Economic Planning: A Case Study of the West Midlands*. London: Frank Cass and Co., 1970.

Lowi, T. *The End of Liberalism*. New York: W. W. Norton, 1969.

Maclennan, D., and J. Parr, eds. *Regional Policy: Past Experience and New Directions*. Oxford: Martin Robertson and Co. Ltd., 1979.

Macmillan, H. *At the End of the Day: 1961–1963*. London: Macmillan Press Ltd., 1973.

March, J., and J. Olsen. "The new institutionalism: Organizational factors in political life," *American Political Science Review* 78(September 1984): 734–49.

Rediscovering Institutions: The Organizational Basis of Politics. New York: The Free Press, 1989.

Markovits, A. *The Politics of the West German Trade Unions: Strategies of Class and Interest Representation in Growth and Crisis*. Cambridge: Cambridge University Press, 1986.

Martin, R. "Pluralism and the new corporatism," *Political Studies* 31(March 1983): 86–102.

Mawson, J. "Changing directions in regional policy and the implications for local government," *Local Government Studies* 7(March/April 1981): 69–74.

Mawson, J., M. Martins, and J. Gibney. "The development of the European Community regional policy." In *Regions in the European Community*, edited by M. Keating and B. Jones, 20–59. Oxford: Clarendon Press, 1985.

Mawson, J., and C. Skelcher. "Updating the West Midlands regional strategy: A review of inter-authority relationships," *Town Planning Review* 51(1980): 152–70.

Mayntz, R., and F. Scharpf. *Policy-making in the German Federal Bureaucracy.* Amsterdam: Elsevier, 1975.

McConnell, G. *Private Power and American Democracy.* New York: Alfred A. Knopf, 1966.

McCord, N. *North East England: An Economic and Social History.* London: B.T. Batsford Ltd., 1979.

McDonald, J. "Members of Parliament: A regional perspective?" In *Regional Government in England*, edited by B. Hogwood and M. Keating, 219–33. Oxford: Clarendon Press, 1982.

Mény, Y., ed. *Center-periphery Relations in Western Europe.* London: George Allen & Unwin, 1985.

"France: The construction and reconstruction of the center, 1945–1986," *West European Politics* 10(October 1987): 52–69.

"The Socialist decentralization." In *The Mitterand Experiment*, edited by G. Ross, S. Hoffmann, and S. Malzacher, 237–47. New York: Oxford University Press, 1987.

Meyers, F. *gez. Dr. Meyers: Summe eines Lebens.* Düsseldorf: Droste Verlag, 1982.

Miller, F. "The unemployment policy of the National Government 1931–1936," *Historical Journal* 19(March 1976): 453–76.

Moe, T. *The Organization of Interests: Incentives and the Internal Dynamics of Political Interest Groups.* Chicago: University of Chicago Press, 1980.

Morgan, K. *Labour in Power, 1945–1951.* Oxford: Clarendon Press, 1984.

Nedelman, B., and K. Meier. "Theories of contemporary corporatism: Static or dynamic?" *Comparative Political Studies* 10(April 1977): 39–60.

Nicol, B., and R. Wettman. "Background notes to restrictive regional policy measures in the European Community." In *Balanced National Growth*, edited by K. Allen, 157–230. Lexington: Lexington Books, 1978.

Nordlinger, E. *On the Autonomy of the Democratic State.* Cambridge, Mass.: Harvard University Press, 1981.

"Taking the state seriously." In *Understanding Political Development*, edited by M. Weiner and S. Huntington, 353–90. Boston: Little, Brown & Co., 1987.

Offe, C. "The attribution of public status to interest groups: Observations on the West German case." In *Organizing Interests in Western Europe*, edited by S. Berger, 123–58. Cambridge: Cambridge University Press, 1981.

Olsen, J. *Organized Democracy: Political Institutions in a Welfare State.* Oslo: Universitetsforlaget, 1983.

Olson, M. *The Logic of Collective Action: Public Goods and the Theory of Groups.* Cambridge, Mass.: Harvard University Press, 1971.

The Rise and Decline of Nations. New Haven: Yale University Press, 1982.

Paddison, R. *The Fragmented State: The Political Geography of Power.* Oxford: Basil Blackwell Publishers, Ltd., 1983.

Panitch, L. "The development of corporatism in liberal democracies." In *Trends Toward Corporatist Intermediation*, edited by P. Schmitter and G. Lehmbruch, 119–46. Beverly Hills: Sage Publications, 1979.

"Recent theorizations on corporatism: Reflections on a growth industry," *British Journal of Sociology* 31(June 1980): 159–87.

Parsons, D. W. *The Political Economy of British Regional Policy.* London: Croom Helm Publishers, 1986.

Petzina, D., and W. Euchner, eds. *Wirtschaftspolitik im britischen Besatzungs-gebiet 1945–1949*. Düsseldorf: Schwann Verlag, 1984.

Przeworski, A., and H. Teune. *The Logic of Comparative Social Inquiry*. New York: Wiley, 1970.

Punnett, R. M. "Regional partisanship and the legitimacy of British govern-ments 1868–1983," *Parliamentary Affairs* 37(Spring 1984): 141–59.

Reissert, B., and F. Schnabel. "Fallstudien zum Planungs- und Finanzierungs-verbund von Bund, Ländern, und Gemeinden." In *Politikverflechtung: Theorie und Empirie des kooperativen Föderalismus in der Bundesre-publik*, edited by F. Scharpf, B. Reissert, and F. Schnabel, 71–235. Kronberg/Ts.: Scriptor Verlag GmbH., 1976.

Rhein-Ruhr-Institut für Sozialforschung und Politikberatung e.V. (RISP). *Be-gleitforschung zum Aktionsprogramm Ruhr: Programmbericht 1983/84*. Duisburg: RISP, 1984.

Rhodes, R. A. W. *Control and Power in Central-local Relations*. Westmead: Gower Publishing Co., Ltd., 1981.

The National World of Local Government. London: George Allen & Unwin, 1986.

"Territorial politics in the United Kingdom," *West European Politics* 10(October 1987): 21–51.

Beyond Westminster and Whitehall: The Sub-central Governments of Britain. London: Unwin Hyman Ltd., 1988.

Rich, M. "Distributive politics and the allocation of federal grants," *American Political Science Review* 83(March 1989): 193–213.

Richardson, H. *Regional Growth Theory*. London: Macmillan Company, 1973.

Regional Economics. Urbana: University of Illinois Press, 1979.

Richardson, J., ed. *Policy Styles in Western Europe*. London: George Allen & Unwin, 1982.

Richardson, J., and G. F. Dudley. "Steel policy in the U.K.: The politics of industrial decline." In *The Politics of Steel: Western Europe and the Steel Industry in the Crisis Years (1974–1984)*, edited by Y. Mény and V. Wright, 308–68. New York: Walter de Gruyter, 1987.

Rigby, N. "Industrial promotion or demotion?" *Northern Economic Review* 3(May 1982): 27–30.

Risse, J. "Parteiorganisation im Bundesstaat: Gebietlich-föderale Organisa-tionsstrukturen der politischen Parteien in der Bundesrepublik Deutschland," *Der Staat* 2(1982): 239–57.

Ritter, G., and M. Niehuss. *Wahlen in der Bundesrepublik Deutschland*. Mu-nich: Verlag C. H. Beck, 1987.

Robinson, F., C. Wren, and J. Goddard. *Economic Development Policies: An Evaluative Study of the Newcastle Metropolitan Region*. Oxford: Clar-endon Press, 1987.

Rohe, K., and H. Kühn, eds. *Politik und Gesellschaft im Ruhrgebiet*. Königstein/Ts.: Hain Verlag, 1979.

Rokkan, S., and D. Urwin. *Economy, Territory, Identity: Politics of West Eu-ropean Peripheries*. London: Sage Publications, 1983.

Rowntree Research Unit. "Aspects of contradiction in regional policy: The case of North-East England." *Regional Studies* 8(August 1974): 133–44.

Salisbury, R. "Interest representation: The dominance of institutions," *Amer-ican Political Science Review* 78(March 1984): 64–76.

Samuels, R. *The Politics of Regional Policy in Japan: Localities Incorporated?* Princeton: Princeton University Press, 1983.

Sargent, J. "Corporatism and the European Community." In *The Political Economy of Corporatism*, edited by W. Grant, 229–53. London: Macmillan Company, 1985.

Schaaf, P. *Ruhrbergbau und Sozialdemokratie: Die Energiepolitik der Großen Koalition 1966–1969.* Marburg: Verlag Arbeiterbewegung und Gesellschaftswissenschaft GmbH., 1978.

Scharpf, F. "The joint decision trap: Lessons from German federalism and European integration." Discussion Paper IIM/LMP 85–1. Berlin: Wissenschaftszentrum Berlin, 1985.

Scharpf, F., B. Reissert, and F. Schnabel. *Politikverflechtung: Theorie und Empirie des kooperativen Föderalismus in der Bundesrepublik.* Kronberg/Ts.: Scriptor Verlag GmbH., 1976.

Schlieper, A. *150 Jahre Ruhrgebiet.* Düsseldorf: Schwann Verlag, 1986.

Schmidt, M. "Does corporatism matter? Economic crisis, politics, and rates of unemployment in capitalist democracies in the 1970s." In *Patterns of Corporatist Policy-making*, edited by G. Lehmbruch and P. Schmitter, 237–58. Beverly Hills: Sage Publications, 1982.

Schmitter, P. "Still the century of corporatism?" In *Trends Toward Corporatist Intermediation*, edited by P. Schmitter and G. Lehmbruch, 7–52. Beverly Hills: Sage Publications, 1979.

"Reflections on where the theory of neo-corporatism has gone and where the praxis of neo-corporatism may be going." In *Patterns of Corporatist Policy-making*, edited by G. Lehmbruch and P. Schmitter, 259–79. Beverly Hills: Sage Publications, 1982.

Schmitter, P. and L. Lanzalalco. "Regions and the organization of business interests." In *Regionalism, Business Interests, and Public Policy*, edited by W. Coleman and H. Jacek, 201–30. London: Sage Publications, 1989.

Schmitter, P. and G. Lehmbruch. *Trends Toward Corporatist Intermediation.* Beverly Hills: Sage Publications, 1979.

Schmitter, P. and W. Streeck. "The organization of business interests." Discussion Paper IIM/LMP 81–13. Berlin: Wissenschaftszentrum Berlin, 1981.

Selznick, P. *TVA and the Grassroots.* Berkeley: University of California Press, 1949.

Sharpe, L. J. "The Labour Party and the geography of inequality: A puzzle." In *The Politics of the Labour Party*, edited by D. Kavanagh, 135–70. London: George Allen & Unwin, 1982.

"Central coordination and the policy network," *Political Studies* 33(September 1985): 361–81.

Shonfield, A. *Modern Capitalism.* Oxford: Oxford University Press, 1966.

Slowe, P. *The Advance Factory in Regional Development.* Aldershot, Hampshire: Gower Publishing Co., Ltd., 1981.

Smith, B. *The Administration of Industrial Overspill.* Occasional Paper No. 22. Birmingham: University of Birmingham Centre for Urban and Regional Development Studies, 1972.

Decentralization: The Territorial Dimension of the State. London: George Allen & Unwin, 1985.

Smith, G. *Politics in Western Europe.* New York: Holmes & Meier, 1984.

Smith, T. D. *Dan Smith: An Autobiography*. Newcastle upon Tyne: Oriel Press, Ltd., 1970.

Spencer, K., et al. *Crisis in the Industrial Heartland: A Study of the West Midlands*. Oxford: Clarendon Press, 1986.

Stepan, A. *The State and Society: Peru in Comparative Perspective*. Princeton: Princeton University Press, 1978.

Stewart, M. "The role of central government in local economic development." In *National Interests and Local Government*, edited by K. Young, 105–32. Aldershot, Hampshire: Gower Publishing Co., Ltd., 1983.

Storer, C., and A. Townsend. *The Northern Economic Planning Council*. London: Regional Studies Association, 1971.

Sundquist, J. *Dispersing Population: What America Can Learn from Europe*. Washington, D.C.: The Brookings Institution, 1975.

Tarrow, S. *Between Center and Periphery: Grassroots Politicians in Italy and France*. New Haven: Yale University Press, 1977.

Tarrow, S., P. Katzenstein, and L. Graziano. *Territorial Politics in Industrial Nations*. New York: Praeger Publishers, 1978.

Tilly, C., ed. *The Formation of National States in Western Europe*. Princeton: Princeton University Press, 1975.

Truman, D. *The Governmental Process: Political Interests and Public Opinion*. New York: Alfred A. Knopf, 1951.

Vanhove, N., and L. Klaassen. *Regional Policy: A European Approach*. Aldershot, Hampshire: Gower Publishing Co. Ltd., 1987.

Von Alemann, U., ed. *Parteien und Wahlen in Nordrhein-Westfalen*. Köln: Verlag W. Kohlhammer, 1985.

Von Herz, D. *Die Politik des verspäteten Machtwechsels*. Meisenheim am Glam: Verlag Anton Hain, 1970.

Von Voss, R., und K. Friedrich, eds. *Das Nord-Süd-Gefälle: Gemeinsame Strategien für neue Strukturen*. Stuttgart: Verlag Bonn Aktuell GmbH., 1986.

Wallace, H. "Distributional politics: Dividing up the Community cake." In *Policy-making in the European Community*, edited by H. Wallace, W. Wallace, and C. Webb, 81–114. New York: Wiley, 1983.

Wallace, W. "Europe as a confederation," *Journal of Common Market Studies* 20(September/December 1982): 57–68.

Wallerstein, I. *The Modern World System: Capitalist Agriculture and the Origins of the European World Economy in the Sixteenth Century*. New York: Academic Press, 1974.

Weber, J. *Die Interessengruppen im politischen System der Bundesrepublik Deutschland*. Stuttgart: Verlag W. Kohlhammer GmbH., 1977.

Webman, J. *Reviving the Industrial City*. New Brunswick: Rutgers University Press, 1982.

Wheare, K. C. *Modern Constitutions*. London: Oxford University Press, 1964.

Wild, K. P. "Stellung und Aufgaben der Länder." In *Handbuch der regionalen Wirtschaftsförderung*, edited by H. H. Eberstein, 1–16. Köln: Verlag Dr. Otto Schmidt KG., 1978.

Wilks, S. *Industrial Policy and the Motor Industry*. Manchester: Manchester University Press, 1984.

Wilks, S., and M. Wright, eds. *Comparative Government-Industry Relations: Western Europe, the United States, and Japan*. Oxford: Clarendon Press, 1987.

Wilson, D. *Power and Party Bureaucracy in Britain: Regional Organization in the Conservative and Labour Parties.* London: Saxon House, Lexington Books, 1975.

Wood, D. "The Conservative Member of Parliament as lobbyist for constituency economic interests," *Political Studies* 35(September 1987): 393–409.

Worms, J. P. "Le Préfet et ses notables," *Sociologie du Travail* 3(July–September 1966): 249–75.

Yuill, D. "Regional incentives in Britain." In *Balanced National Growth*, edited by K. Allen, 35–54. Lexington, Mass.: Lexington Books, 1978.

Interest group publications

Arbeitskammer des Saarlandes. *Bericht an die Regierung des Saarlandes 1971.* Saarbrücken: AK-Saar, 1971.

Bericht an die Regierung des Saarlandes 1982. Saarbrücken: AK-Saar, 1982.

1986 Daten zur Lage der Arbeitnehmer im Saarland. Dillingen/Saar: Krüger Druck & Verlag, GmbH., 1986.

Birmingham Chamber of Commerce and Industry. *Evidence to the Hunt Committee on Intermediate Areas.* Birmingham: BCCI, 1968.

Birmingham Chamber of Industry and Commerce. *Reversing Structural Decline in the West Midlands: A Strategy for Action.* Birmingham: BCIC, 1983.

Regional Industrial Development: A Response to the White Paper. Birmingham: BCIC, 1984.

Confederation of British Industry (West Midlands). *A Five Point Plan for the West Midlands.* Birmingham: CBI, 1983.

Regional Industrial Development (Cmnd. 9111): The Response of the West Midlands Regional Council. Birmingham: CBI, 1984.

Reviving the Cities. Birmingham: CBI, 1986.

DGB-Landesbezirk Nordrhein-Westfalen. *Aktionsprogramm zur wirtschaftlichen und infrastrukturellen Förderung des Westmünsterlandes.* Düsseldorf: DGB, 1975.

Zur wirtschaftlichen Entwicklung des Hagener Raumes. Düsseldorf: DGB, 1977.

Vorausschauende Strukturpolitik für Ostwestfalen-Lippe. Düsseldorf: DGB, 1980.

Vorausschauende Strukturpolitik für den Kreis Düren. Düsseldorf: DGB, 1982.

Vorausschauende Strukturpolitik für Südwestfalen und die Kreise Mark, Olpe, Siegen. Düsseldorf: DGB, 1982.

Industrie- und Handelskammer des Saarlandes. *Saarwirtschaft 1973: Jahresbericht der IHK-Saar.* Saarbrücken: IHK-Saar, 1973.

North East Development Association. *Annual Reports.* Newcastle upon Tyne: NEDA, 1944–53.

Some Notes on the Organization and Activities. Newcastle upon Tyne: NEDA, 1949.

North East Development Board. *Annual Reports.* Newcastle upon Tyne: NEDB, 1935–9.

North East Development Council. *Annual Reports.* Newcastle upon Tyne: NEDC, 1961–73.

North East Industrial and Development Association. *Annual Reports.* Newcastle upon Tyne: NEIDA, 1953–61.

North of England Development Council. *Annual Reports*. Newcastle upon Tyne: NoEDC, 1973–86.
A Statement of Claim. Newcastle upon Tyne: NoEDC, 1976.
Northern Industrial Group. *Annual Reports*. Newcastle upon Tyne: NIG, 1943–53.
Northern Regional Council of the Labour Party. *Lets Pull Together for a Better North*. Newcastle upon Tyne: 1978.
Teesside Industrial Development Board. *Annual Report 1964–65*. Middlesbrough: TIDB, 1965.
Trades Union Congress. *The Organization, Structure, and Services of the TUC*. London: Congress House, 1981.
West Midlands Regional Economic Consortium. *Regional Industrial Development: Submission in Response to Cmnd. 9111*. Birmingham: 1984.

Local, state, and national government publications

Chef der Staatskanzlei. *Strukturprogramm Saar: Möglichkeiten einer aktiven Sanierung der Saarwirtschaft*. Saarbrücken: 1969.
Landesentwicklungsprogramm Saar, Teil 2: Wirtschaft 1990. Saarbrücken: 1984.
Joint Monitoring Steering Group. *A Developing Strategy for the West Midlands: The First Annual Report of the JMSG*. Birmingham: JMSG, 1975.
A Developing Strategy for the West Midlands: The Second Annual Report of the JMSG. Birmingham: JMSG, 1976.
A Developing Strategy for the West Midlands: Updating and Rolling Forward of the Regional Strategy to 1991. Birmingham: JMSG, 1979.
Landesregierung des Saarlandes. *Memorandum der Regierung des Saarlandes an die Bundesregierung vom 13. November 1957*. Saarbrücken: Malstatt-Burbacher Handelsdruckerei GmbH., 1957.
Das Saarland: 10 Jahre nach seiner Eingliederung in die Bundesrepublik Deutschland, Bilanz und Aufgabe. Saarbrücken: 1967.
Memorandum der Regierung des Saarlandes and die Regierung der BRD vom 28.3.1977. Saarbrücken: 1977.
Saar-Memorandum 1986. Saarbrücken: 1986.
Landesregierung NRW. *Politik für das Ruhrgebiet: Das Aktionsprogramm*. Düsseldorf: 1979.
Minister für Wirtschaft, Mittelstand, und Verkehr des Landes Nordrhein-Westfalen. *Denkschrift: Notwendige Maßnahmen zur Verbesserung der Landesstruktur in Nordrhein-Westfalen: Analyse und Vorschläge zur regionalen Strukturverbesserung*. Düsseldorf: 1964.
Energiebericht NRW. Düsseldorf: 1982.
Information der Landesregierung 554/8/85, 1985.
Newcastle upon Tyne City Council. *Proceedings of the Newcastle upon Tyne City Council*.
Northern Economic Planning Council. *Challenge of the Changing North*. London: HMSO, 1966.
Outline Strategy for the North. Newcastle upon Tyne: NEPC, 1969.
Northern Region Strategy Team. *Technical Report no. 2: Evaluation of the Impact of Regional Policy on Manufacturing Industry in the Northern Region*. Newcastle upon Tyne: NRST, 1975.

Strategic Plan for the Northern Region, Vols. 1–5. Newcastle upon Tyne: Hindson Print Group, Ltd., 1977.

Plenary Sessions of the Landtag of NRW.

Plenary Sessions of the Landtag of the Saarland.

Proceedings of the Economics Committee of the Landtag of NRW.

Proceedings of the Economics Committee of the Landtag of the Saarland.

Regierung der Bundesrepublik Deutschland. "Memorandum zur Beihilfenkontrolle der EG-Kommission im Bereich der nationalen Regionalförderung." Internal Document, 1986.

Schriftenreihe des Ministerpräsidenten des Landes Nordrhein-Westfalen. *Vorschläge zur Strukturverbesserung förderungsbedürftiger Gebiete in Nordrhein-Westfalen.* Düsseldorf: Ed. Lintz Kg. Verlag und Druckerei, 1960.

United Kingdom. Department of Economic Affairs. *The West Midlands: A Regional Study.* London: HMSO, 1965.

Department of Industry. *Industry Act 1972, Annual Report (HC 619).* London: HMSO, 1976.

Parliament. Expenditure Committee (Trade and Industry Subcommittee). *Regional Development Incentives: Minutes of Evidence, Session 1972/ 73; HC327.* London: HMSO, 1973.

Parliament. Select Committee on Estimates. *The Development Areas, 2nd Report HC 139.* London: HMSO, 1956.

Parliamentary Debates, Commons, 5th series (1909–).

Public Record Office.

Secretary of State for Industry, Trade, and Regional Development. *The North East: A Programme for Regional Development and Growth (Cmnd 2206).* London: HMSO, 1963.

Secretary of State for Scotland. *Central Scotland: A Programme for Development and Growth (CMBD 2188).* Edinburgh: HMSO, 1963.

Secretary of State for Trade and Industry. *Regional Industrial Development (Cmnd 9111).* London: HMSO, 1983.

Secretary of State for Trade and Industry. *Industrial Development Act 1982, Annual Report 1985.* London: HMSO. 1985.

West Midlands County Council. *Regional Industrial Development: Assisted Area Designation Criteria and Boundaries: Supplemental Response of the County Council of the West Midlands.* Birmingham: WMCC, 1984.

Regional Industrial Development: Response of the County Council of the West Midlands. Birmingham: WMCC, 1984.

Research Paper no. 3: Economic Development and Regional Aid in the West Midlands. Birmingham: WMCC, 1985.

West Midlands Economic Planning Council. *The West Midlands: Patterns of Growth.* London: HMSO, 1967.

The West Midlands: An Economic Appraisal. London: HMSO, 1971.

West Midlands Economic Planning Council and the West Midlands Planning Authorities Conference. *A Developing Strategy for the West Midlands: Updating and Rolling Forward of the Regional Strategy to 1991; the Regional Economy, Problems and Proposals.* Birmingham: WMEPC/ WMPAC, 1979.

West Midlands Forum of County Councils. *Background Report no. 4: Employment and Economic Regeneration.* Birmingham: WMFCC, 1985.

Regenerating the Region: A Strategy for the West Midlands. Birmingham: WMFCC, 1985.

West Midlands Planning Authorities Conference. *A Developing Strategy for the West Midlands: Report of WMPAC with Statement by the Secretary of State*. Birmingham: WMPAC, 1974.
Current Developments in the Economy of the West Midlands Region. Birmingham: WMPAC, 1975.
A Developing Strategy for the West Midlands: Updating and Rolling Forward of the Regional Strategy to 1991; Consultations. Birmingham: WMPAC, 1979.
West Midlands Regional Study. *A Developing Strategy for the West Midlands*. Birmingham: WMRS, 1971.

Unpublished material

Bauer, G. "Die CDU im Saarland." Ph.D. dissertation, Universität des Saarlandes, 1981.
Guthrie, R. "An inquiry into the effectiveness of the contribution to the region of Northern MPs as regional representatives in parliament, with special reference to the period February 1974 to December 1976." M.S. thesis, University of Newcastle upon Tyne, 1978.
Martins, M. R. "Regional planning in the West Midlands region: A political-organizational perspective." Ph.D. dissertation, University of Birmingham, 1983.
Painter, C. "Group interactions and lobbies in West Midlands economic planning, 1965–1972." Ph.D. dissertation, University of Aston (Birmingham), 1973.

Interview sources

United Kingdom
1. Senior local government official, Tyne and Wear County Council, Newcastle upon Tyne, 18 March 1986.
2. Former senior civil servant, Northern Regional Office of the Department of Trade and Industry, phone interview, 26 March 1986.
3. Senior civil servant, Northern Regional Office of the Department of the Environment, Newcastle upon Tyne, 3 March 1986.
4. Official with the Birmingham Chamber of Industry and Commerce, Birmingham, 27 February 1986.
5. Senior civil servant, Northern Regional Office of the Department of Trade and Industry, Newcastle upon Tyne, 20 January 1986.
6. Civil servant, West Midlands Regional Office of the Department of the Environment, Birmingham, 12 February 1986.
7. Official with the West Midlands Forum of County Councils, Birmingham, 13 February 1986; letter to author, 20 February 1986.
8. Staff economist, TUC, London, 28 June 1984.
9. Researcher, Center for Urban and Regional Development Studies, University of Newcastle upon Tyne, Newcastle upon Tyne, 27 March 1986.
10. Official with the West Midlands Office of the CBI, Birmingham, 26 February 1986.
11. Civil servant, West Midlands Office of the Department of Trade and Industry, Birmingham, 22 January 1986.
12. Civil servant, Northern Regional Office of the Department of Trade and Industry, Newcastle upon Tyne, 27 March 1986.

13. Civil servant, Plans and Regional Policy Section, Department of the Environment, London, 2 July 1984.
14. Researcher, Center for Urban and Regional Development Studies, University of Newcastle upon Tyne, Newcastle upon Tyne, 14 March 1986.
15. Official with the Northern Office of the CBI, Newcastle upon Tyne, 9 December 1985.
16. Official with the Northern Regional Office of the TUC, Newcastle upon Tyne, 3 March 1986 and 25 March 1986.
17. Group interview with senior officials with the Northern Development Company, Ltd., Newcastle upon Tyne, 12 July 1989.
18. Civil servant, Industry and Regions Division, HM Treasury, London, 4 July 1984.
19. Official with the Northern Regional Council of the Labour Party, Newcastle upon Tyne, 17 March 1986.
20. Civil servant, Northern Regional Office of the Department of the Environment, Newcastle upon Tyne, 21 February 1986.
21. Official with the West Midlands Regional Council of the TUC; Birmingham, 6 February 1986; letter to author, 15 November 1985.
22. Senior civil servant, West Midlands Office of the Department of the Environment, Birmingham, 12 February 1986.
23. Senior civil servant in Regional Industrial Development, Department of Industry, London, 12 November 1976 (interview conducted by J. LaPalombara, Yale University).
24. Former civil servant and chairman of the Northern Regional Economic Planning Board (1966–71), Edinburgh, 20 February 1986.
25. Civil servant, Northern Regional Office of the Department of Trade and Industry, Newcastle upon Tyne, 6 March 1986.
26. Civil servant, Regional Policy, Department of Trade and Industry, London, 21 June 1984.
27. Senior civil servant, Regional Industrial Finance, Department of Industry, London, 5 May 1977 (interview conducted by J. LaPalombara, Yale University).
28. Former chairperson of the Northern Regional Economic Planning Council, Newcastle upon Tyne, 5 February 1986.
29. Civil servant, Plans and Regional Policy, Department of the Environment, London, 9 July 1984.
30. Civil servant, Economics Division, Department of Trade and Industry, London, 27 June 1984.
31. Professor of geography, Durham University, Durham, 18 October 1985.
32. Senior civil servant, Department of Trade and Industry, London, 12 July 1984.
33. Official with the CBI, London, 13 July 1984.

Federal Republic of Germany
34. Official with the Association of NRW Chambers of Industry and Commerce, Düsseldorf, 3 November 1986.
35. Senior civil servant, NRW Ministry of Economics, Düsseldorf, 29 October 1986.
36. Official with the Economic Performance Monitoring Division, NRW Ministry of Economics, Düsseldorf, 30 October 1986.

37. Senior official, Kommunalverband Ruhrgebiet, Essen, 18 November 1986.
38. Senior official, Industrie- und Handelskammer des Saarlandes, Saar-brücken, 12 November 1986.
39. Senior official, Arbeitskammer des Saarlandes, Saarbrücken, 12 November 1986.
40. Official, Development Agency for NRW, Düsseldorf, 5 November 1986.
41. Official with DGB–Landesbezirk, NRW, Düsseldorf, 2 December 1986.
42. Senior civil servant, NRW Ministry of Economics, Düsseldorf, 31 October 1986.
43. Senior civil servant, Saar Staatskanzlei, Saarbrücken, 11 November 1986.
44. Senior civil servant, NRW Staatskanzlei, Düsseldorf, 27 November 1986.
45. Official, SPD Parliamentary *Fraktion* (NRW), Düsseldorf, 28 November 1986.
46. Group interview, members of the Structure Policy/Industrial Policy Division, Saar Ministry of Economics, Saarbrücken, 11 November 1986.
47. Senior official in the DIHT, Bonn, 4 December 1986.
48. Senior official, City of Gelsenkirchen (NRW), Gelsenkirchen, 8 December 1986.
49. Senior civil servant, NRW Ministry of Economics, Düsseldorf, 24 October 1986.
50. Civil servant with the Planungsausschuβ, Federal Economics Ministry, Bonn, 4 December 1986.
51. Civil servant, Federal Economics Ministry, Bonn, 30 November 1990.
52. Economic adviser to the Parliamentary *Fraktion* of the Social Democratic Party (SPD), Bonn, 30 November 1990.

Index

247